W9-ASB-769

CHICANO ETHNICITY

CHICANO ETHNICITY

Susan E. Keefe
Amado M. Padilla

UNIVERSITY OF NEW MEXICO PRESS
Albuquerque

379147 ᴌennessee Tech. Library
Cookeville. Tenn.

Library of Congress Cataloging-in-Publication Data

Keefe, Susan E. (Susan Emley)
  Chicano ethnicity.

  Bibliography: p.
  Includes index.
  1. Mexican Americans—Ethnic identity. 2. Mexican
Americans—Cultural assimilation. 3. Ethnicity—
United States. I. Padilla, Amado M. II. Title.
E184.M5K43 1987   305.8'6872'073   87-9217
ISBN 0-8263-0992-5
ISBN 0-8263-0993-3 (pbk.)

© 1987 by the University of New Mexico Press.
All rights reserved.
First edition.

Contents

Illustrations

Tables

Figures

Acknowledgments

IN ANY PROJECT OF THIS SIZE, the contributions of others are essential to its completion. The authors wish to acknowledge the support provided by the National Institute of Mental Health, the Center for Minority Group Mental Health Programs, and Grant number MH26099, which funded the project for four years. As principal investigator, Padilla was responsible for the continued guidance of the study as a whole during the research period. Keefe supervised the daily operation of the project and subsequent data analysis. Additional funds for computer analysis were provided by the Academic Senate of the University of California, Santa Barbara. Keefe also acknowledges the support of NIMH Small Grant number MH33425, a Summer Research Grant from Appalachian State University, and summer funding from the Spanish Speaking Mental Health Research Center at UCLA—all of which made possible further analysis and writing.

Special thanks is due Manuel L. Carlos and Esteban L. Olmedo for their work on the project. Carlos participated in early discussions of the model of Cultural Awareness and Ethnic Loyalty and in developing the questionnaire that evolved from this discussion. His insight into and appreciation of Mexican culture have contributed greatly to this study. Olmedo was responsible for the factor and cluster analysis of Cultural Awareness and Ethnic Loyalty data and the social sphere data. We are extremely grateful for his dedication to and skillful execution of this massive task.

Keefe acknowledges with special fondness, the countless hours of stimulating conversation she shared with M. Jean Gilbert, friend, fellow anthropologist, and office neighbor while the project was housed at the Social Process Research Institute, University of California, Santa Barbara. These discussions contributed significantly to the final choices in methodology as well as to the way in which the data were analyzed.

The authors were extremely fortunate in finding the two research assistants who joined the project in the third year and collected the Mexican American case-study data: Frank Cota-Robles Newton and Mariluise Prieto Bayard. Together, they did an admirable job in gaining rapport with the selected informants, in compiling the case-study material, and in writing the original, lengthy case studies.

Many field workers performed the difficult and emotionally demanding task of survey interviewing—in particular, David Gómez, Rosa León Ramírez, Gloria Reyes West, Jesús Raúl Jimenez, María Elena Rodríguez, Irma Hidalgo, Bertha Chacón, Hector Pulído, Anita Nava, Nellie Soto, Beatrice Flores, Marisela Hernández, David González, Leslie Yerington, Gail Anderson, Randi Gottlieb, Susan Salisbury, Carl Borden, Robin Gerhart, Ernie Graziano, and Susan Hendrick. The task of processing questionnaires was managed with the help of Felicia Saunders, Philip Green, and Terry Reufli. Robert Jansen collected the case-study data from the Anglo Americans in the third phase of the research. Alex Ramirez performed additional statistical analysis. Art Rex drafted the maps for the manuscript. Finally, the authors are grateful to Teresa Isaacs and Alina Alas for their efficient and reliable typing of the manuscript.

Personal support is always important in the completion of any project, and the authors would like to thank their families for their understanding and patience. Tom Keefe has never ceased to give his encouragement, and it is his total support that has made this work so rewarding for Susan. Megan Keefe has contributed in ways she will never remember just by giving her Mommy joy. Kathryn J. Lindholm, companion and colleague to Amado, remained loving when there was too much to do and too many places to be.

Introduction

CHICANOS ARE ONE OF THE LARGEST ethnic minority groups in the United States. As of 1985 they constituted 4.4 percent of the population, were 10.3 million strong, and their impact on the United States—especially in the Southwest—is well recognized. Until the mid-nineteenth century, the history of the American Southwest was largely shaped by Spanish and, subsequently, Mexican control; migration from Mexico continues to affect the contours of social, economic, and political life in the region. Moreover, migrant farm-labor organization, bilingual education, and the rise of the Chicano ethnic vote have become national issues during the last two decades.

While the special impact of the Mexican American population on the country is undeniable, less commonly agreed upon is the nature of sociocultural change within the Chicano population itself. Some argue that Chicanos, like most American ethnic groups, have become less and less distinctive culturally from other Americans and eventually will be integrated into the larger society, even though the process is slowed somewhat by the continuing influx of Mexican immigrants across the border. Others insist that ethnicity is not so simply dismissed, citing as evidence the rise of the Chicano movement with its focus on ethnic consciousness; the effort by many Chicanos to preserve, through their children, their language and cultural and historical roots; and the persistence of racial discrimination within the larger population.

In order to understand changing ethnicity, we must have a clear idea of the way in which ethnicity is constructed among individuals. One of the primary aims of our research was to develop a sophisti-

1

cated and empirically based conceptualization of what it means to be a Chicano. We wanted to determine fairly precise ways of measuring cultural knowledge and ethnic identification, which would describe the ethnic population and its internal variation as well as accurately plot changes over time, especially from generation to generation. In order to evaluate Mexican American ethnicity, then, we developed empirical measures of acculturation and ethnic identification. We call these two scales Cultural Awareness and Ethnic Loyalty, respectively. Each scale was constructed in a multidimensional fashion, and variation in survey scores within the Mexican American population demonstrates the inaccuracy of stereotypes emphasizing ethnic homogeneity. Nevertheless, certain general trends can be observed in the ethnic group as a whole. The most important trend is the obvious and gradual decline in awareness of Mexican culture from generation to generation, compared to the greater tenacity of ethnic identity.

The construction of quantitative measures enables us to isolate more accurately the aspects of acculturation and ethnic identification. We have found, for example, that certain indices commonly used to characterize ethnic loyalty (like language preference, attitudes toward Mexico and the U.S., and identification with a group label such as "Mexican" or "Chicano") are actually more tied to cultural awareness. Quantitative measures also provide a statistical means of demonstrating the distinctive though interrelated nature of acculturation and ethnic identification. Furthermore, in the statistical analysis the added significance of social assimilation emerges as a third related yet distinctive concept in Chicano ethnicity—which is supported by our case-study data, where the social context clearly contributes to the maintenance of cultural awareness and ethnic loyalty and to the emergence of self-consciousness about ethnicity. Finally, through the application of quantifiable measures, we have been able to construct a typology which best describes the intra-ethnic variation in cultural awareness and ethnic loyalty. Eleven case studies illustrate the five cluster types, and through them we gain a more complete understanding of the role of ethnicity in the lives of individuals.

In any study of ethnic groups, it is impossible to grasp the full meaning of ethnicity and the ethnic microsystem without a greater understanding of the ethnic majority group and the larger social system. In our research, therefore, we focused not only on the

Chicano communities chosen for study, but we also observed the Anglo American residents and the cities as whole communities. Extensive interviews with Anglo Americans and Mexican Americans helped to clarify the sociocultural similarities and differences between the two ethnic groups. Particular attention was given to kinship systems and general social organization, which also allowed us to explore interethnic social relations and the ways in which ethnic group boundaries are maintained.

Throughout the book, we are concerned with the use of empirical measures to say something meaningful about the workings of ethnic maintenance and sociocultural change among Chicanos and to find answers to important questions: Over time, do Mexican Americans remain culturally distinctive in the U.S.? Do they *perceive* themselves as different, regardless of any objective measures of difference? Do they remain socially set apart from other Americans? What kinds of variation in these patterns exist within the ethnic population? What factors contribute to the separation or assimilation of Chicanos in American life? Why does ethnic persistence and/or change occur?

We examine these issues with data gathered from three cities in southern California selected for their variation in history of settlement, economic base, and population size. Two of these, Santa Barbara and Oxnard, qualify as core cities in U.S. Census Bureau–designated "Standard Metropolitan Statistical Areas." The third, Santa Paula, is representative of the smaller agricultural towns that proliferate in the interior valleys of California. While our data were not gathered from the largest California metropolitan areas, we believe that our findings are generalizable to the broader Mexican American population, at least in California.

The relationship between ethnicity and urban life in general has not been adequately explored. While social scientists early in the twentieth century predicted that ethnicity would disappear with increasing urbanization, many urban sociologists in the second half of this century now contend that ethnicity arises *only* in cities (see, for example, Yancey, Erickson, and Juliani 1976). Anthropologists prefer to see ethnicity as a concept involving two or more groups in a contact situation. Thus, ethnicity can emerge not only when immigrants settle in cities, but also when colonizer meets tribe or when nomadic group meets settled population. We would argue that ethnicity is definitely *not* urban bound. What about the size of the city and its impact on the shape taken by ethnicity? Recent theoretical discussions of ethnicity make no mention of urbanism as the key to ethnicity, but they isolate differences between groups in contact with regard to social structure, culture, and identity as the bases for ethnicity (Despres 1975; Keefe 1986; Reminick 1983). The fact that we find the similarities between the Chicano populations in our three cities so great, and the differences due primarily to historical context rather than to size of population, leads us to generalize about the ethnic group rather than emphasize distinctions by city. In fact, the largest city we studied (Oxnard) emerged as possessing the most "traditional" group of Chicanos due to the kind of *barrio* which had developed there. This discovery counters the expectation of many social scientists that smaller towns tend to retain more traditionalism.

The study of ethnicity has not been discipline bound. Sociologists, psychologists, anthropologists, and historians, among others, have been intrigued by the work involved in defining and explaining the roots, content, and dynamics of changing ethnicity among various groups. However, scholars in these fields tend to approach the subject from different perspectives employing their own methodologies. Sociologists, for example, tend to be concerned with ethnic relations, and more often than not, they use survey techniques. Anthropologists, on the other hand, have always been more concerned with the cultural attitudes and behavior that define an ethnic group, and they are more likely to gather ethnographic data in a community setting.

As an anthropologist and a psychologist, we have the advantage of drawing from the diverse analytical and methodological perspectives of two disciplines. This factor has been particularly important in strengthening the research design of our study, in which the application of survey research and quantitative methodology is enhanced by the ethnographic study of families and communities to substantiate notions of ethnicity. Psychological studies of ethnicity often fall short in providing the context of attitudes and behavior that contribute to their interpretation. Anthropological studies frequently are weak in providing empirical measurement of the sociocultural experience when cross-cultural comparisons might be made more easily.

We have worked with the hope that our collaboration might contribute to a better understanding of the presence, extent, and context of ethnicity among Mexican Americans. As an interdisciplinary study of ethnicity, our work emerges as relatively unique in social science research. While social scientists often call for interdisciplinary research, it is rarely undertaken, and when it is, it tends to be criticized from purely disciplinary perspectives. Nevertheless, we believe that the combination of cross-disciplinary approaches, and in particular, the use of both quantitative and qualitative methods, is essential in the investigation of such complex topics as ethnicity.

Theoretical approaches to the study of ethnicity attract as much controversy as methodology. The topic of ethnicity, and Chicano ethnicity in particular, is a political as well as an academic issue. Research findings may be used to oppose or support government policies and to bring about changes in the delivery of public services to particular segments of the general population. As such, this research, perhaps more than most basic research, often provokes a passionate response. In fact, it is not unusual in ethnic studies to find the ethnicity of the researchers themselves questioned in the evaluation of their work. We know that the findings we report here will be favorably received by some students of ethnicity, while simultaneously displeasing others; we recognize that a study of this type cannot please everyone.

Given the complicated way in which ethnicity reveals itself and the political issues involved in labeling, it is no easy task to arrive at terminology appropriate to the ethnic group as a whole. We use the terms *Chicano* and *Mexican American* interchangeably in discussing the entire group of people of Mexican descent in the United States. Modified versions of these terms are used to discuss subsegments of the ethnic population (for example, *immigrant Mexicans*, *native-born Mexican Americans*). Where terms indicate self-identification, quotation marks enclose the term (for example, "Chicano"). The term *Anglo American* is used to refer to white Americans of European descent.

After close scrutiny of the empirical data we collected, we adopted a pluralist model in interpreting Chicano ethnicity. Pluralism refers to the cultural, social, and structural ways in which ethnic groups are maintained as distinct groups within a single political state. As pointed out in chapter 2, the pluralist model emphasizes ethnic differences within the larger population as the primary means of understanding the social process. In the Mexican American case, as we stress repeatedly, pluralism involves, at one level, the distinction between first-generation immigrants and native-born Mexican Americans, and, at a more inclusive level, the distinction between Anglos and Chicanos as a whole. While our analytical emphasis is on ethnicity, socioeconomic class is obviously an important variable and one which we incorporate throughout the book in analyzing the data. It does not emerge, however, as highly significant in the analysis of variation in ethnic attachment in chapter 8, where generational status and *barrio* residence are of greatest importance; and while socioeconomic status is significantly related to extended familism among Mexican Americans, as discussed in chapter 9, the relationship is contrary to that predicted by most researchers: the local extended family is larger and more integrated for Chicanos of higher social class. In other words, the availability of socioeconomic resources appears to facilitate in the development of *ethnically* preferred and local extended-family networks. In our analysis of the kinship data, generational distinctions, with their implicit incorporation of both socioeconomic and migrational status, again prove to be of key importance.

In taking a pluralist position, we vigorously reject the acculturation–assimilation model, which is often used to describe sociocultural change among Chicanos. Theoretical discussions of acculturation and assimilation in the literature tend to be fraught with muddled thinking. We have been very careful to distinguish between acculturation and assimilation which, we argue, refer to two different concepts: (1) acculturation is the loss of traditional cultural traits and the acceptance of new cultural traits (these can be two distinct processes), while (2) assimilation is the social, economic, and political integration of an ethnic minority group into mainstream society. Obviously, the two processes are related, with most social scientists agreeing that acculturation must to some extent precede assimilation. However, while some social scientists argue that the processes are directly correlated and inevitable, it is by no means clear that the relationship between acculturation and assimilation is linear, for as Gordon (1964) has pointed out, acculturation does not always ensure assimilation.

We found acculturation and assimilation occurring in our study, but the processes do not conform to the model typically used in assimilationist studies. Acculturation certainly takes place, but it is neither as rapid nor as thorough as implied by most interpretations of the model. Even the fourth-generation Mexican Americans in our study retain aspects of Mexican culture—significantly, their value of and involvement in large and local extended families. In fact, our study indicates the need for a multidimensional approach to acculturation because while certain Mexican traits such as knowledge of Mexican history and the Spanish language decline significantly from one generation to the next, other traits such as Catholicism tend to be maintained; in some instances, such as extended familism, Mexican traits are strengthened over time in the U.S. This approach deviates from the ideal continuum incorporated in most versions of the acculturation model. Furthermore, the acculturation model tends to envision only two cultures: the immigrant and traditional culture and the host culture. Our study, on the other hand, provides convincing evidence that the culture of Chicanos who have lived for generations in the U.S. is distinctive and, moreover, a third way of life possessing many unique features, rather than simply an amalgamation of Mexican and American cultures.

Assimilation also must be qualified as a process occurring in the Mexican American population. Certainly, there is considerable increase in social interaction with Anglo Americans between first- and second-generation Mexican Americans, and language ability undoubtedly has an important impact here, as does the socioeconomic mobility experienced by the native born. Yet, when distinctions are made concerning the quality of interaction with Anglos, it is apparent that such contact occurs primarily in the formal spheres of work, school, and public life, while more intimate social life within the home and family tends to be ethnically enclosed. This distinction clearly evolves from a cultural propensity to remain geographically rooted in a community, thus fostering the development of large local kin groups. In addition, it is apparent that Anglos must practice avoidance of informal interaction with Mexican Americans. We found considerable evidence that ethnic group boundaries are strongly entrenched and pervasive, with Anglos and Chicanos interacting mostly with friends, neighbors, and coworkers of their own ethnic group, despite the fact that they tend to live and work in ethnically mixed places. These findings reconfirm recent social science research in which a network model of social relations, rather than a "place-community" model, best describes contemporary urban social groups.

While social assimilation, in formal spheres at least, increases from the first to the second generation, it tends to level off thereafter. Economic assimilation proceeds similarly: dramatic mobility takes place for second-generation Chicanos who become integrated into the stable blue-collar labor force, while white-collar jobs continue to remain out of reach for the vast majority of those from succeeding generations. Without mobility into the upper-middle class, political assimilation is stymied. As with acculturation, then, we see no gradual, consistent course of sociocultural change, but an initial burst of Americanization followed by a long-term process of settling into an ethnic community of Chicanos, a unique creation of the contact experience that contributes further to the ethnically plural society of the United States.

Both internal and external factors cement the plural nature of Chicano–Anglo relations. Not only does discrimination exist at group and institutional levels; it occurs at the personal level in the development of social networks whose ethnic enclosure replicates that which exists in the larger society. The farm-labor economy, which attracts first-generation immigrants, contributes to the persistence of separate residential areas for those of Mexican descent. While most Mexican Americans do not live in *barrios*, they are symbolic of the differentness of the Mexican people, and apparently they also serve as a refuge for those Chicanos who strongly identify with their ethnic heritage. In both symbol and reality, then, the *barrio* represents the heart of the ethnic community. However, the ethnic community as a whole is better conceptualized as a network of local social relations based primarily on family ties that transcend geographic place. And it is the value and practice of extended kinship which emerges as a key cultural trait reinforcing ethnic social boundaries and the symbolic dualism of Chicano/own versus Anglo/other.

Ethnic identification and extended familism are the two most significant internal factors that we find associated with the persistence of ethnicity among Chicanos. The process of ethnic identification, a topic involving much research during the last two decades, generally is used to refer to self-identification among group members as well as to their attitude toward and affiliation with one ethnic group and culture as opposed to another ethnic group and culture. Thus, the distinction between acculturation and ethnic identification is between (1) the knowledge and practice of cultural traits, as opposed to (2) feelings about cultural groups. Hypothetically, one might be more knowledgeable about one ethnic group, yet at the same time prefer another group. In fact, we often found this to be the case; one of our five ethnic cluster types consists of individuals who are culturally very Mexican, but also appreciative of the American way of life. Although it did not appear to be a statistically significant cluster in our particular sample, the converse might be found as well; that is, individuals who are Americanized may also *feel* a strong attachment to their Mexican heritage and to Mexican people. For example, a study of Chicano college students would probably produce such a cluster. Significantly, we find that self-identification (that is, choice of a group name such as "Chicano" or "Mexican American") is more closely tied to cultural knowledge rather than to ethnic identity, which is linked instead to pride in cultural heritage, the preference for and tendency to have ethnically similar associates, the consumption of ethnic foods, and the perception of ethnic discrimination.

Among most of the people in our study, ethnic identification with Mexican culture and people proves to be an enduring quality, and one that is not linked to generation as strongly as is the acculturation process. Residence in a *barrio* (defined as a neighborhood which is more than 40 percent Mexican American) is the primary factor related to ethnic identification; yet this factor could be either something which contributes to or is the outcome of the identification process. Long-term research is needed to capture the dynamic process of ethnic attitudinal formation among individuals.

Voluntary social interaction—particularly the tendency to choose ethnic associates—is clearly related to both cultural knowledge and ethnic identification. On the other hand, as discussed in chapter 9, Mexican American kinship ties respond to other factors, primarily migration and subsequent geographic mobility. The fact that Chicanos do not Americanize their extended-family pattern over time demonstrates the multidimensional nature of sociocultural change in the ethnic group. The propensity for Mexican Americans to be geographically stable, and to build up large local kin networks incorporating other Mexican Americans, ensures that socially they will always be set apart despite any other aspect of acculturation, assimilation, or increasing identification with Anglo Americans. However, rather than being seen primarily as a security net for bad times, or as a potential liability in the process of becoming accepted within the American social system, the local extended family is valued among Mexican Americans on its own terms, as something essential which makes life meaningful. There is a marked contrast with the social organization of Anglo Americans, who are more transient and retain geographically dispersed extended-family ties, but who are integrated into cohesive friendship networks on the local level, as described in chapter 10.

Although pluralism captures the general condition of Mexican Americans in the larger society, there are important distinctions within the ethnic group that are structured primarily by generation and the variation between different cities and *barrios*. Mexican immigrants form the most distinctive ethnic enclave. Not only are they most culturally different, with strong ethnic loyalty and the least social interaction outside their ethnic group; they are also quite isolated, with a relatively small social network made up of both kin and friends—although this is enlarged upon by young immigrants and by those who have lived in the U.S. for more than twenty-five years. The native born are likely to lose certain Mexican traits and adopt many American traits; but they also take on new traits unique to Chicanos, while retaining their ethnic loyalty. For the most part, social interaction continues to be ethnically circumscribed and dominated by kin ties. The native born tend to be a fairly homogeneous category; certain aspects of Mexican culture, however—the Spanish language, for example—are increasingly lost from one generation to the next, while local kin networks are strengthened.

The three California cities in which we worked present different portraits of the Chicano experience. Oxnard has the most distinctive ethnically isolated *barrio*, and the three census tracts that we sampled present three unique neighborhood patterns of ethnicity which most resemble the variation we originally thought might exist among Chicanos, from the ethnically enclosed *barrio* to the mixed ethnic neighborhood, to the more mainstream neighborhood. Santa Paula and Santa Barbara present us with other patterns. In reality, the three census tracts in Santa Paula cover only two types of neighborhoods, the ethnically mixed and the more mainstream, while Santa Barbara tends to most homogeneous. All three census tracts sampled (including the named *barrio*) are representative of the geographically stable and native-born experience. In other words, the study of only one of these cities would have given an inaccurate picture of Mexican

Americans in southern California. By covering three cities, we are more assured of making valid generalizations about Mexican Americans as well as identifying the variation in the population, a variation which is, in part, the product of the different social, economic, and historical factors shaping each community.

Chapter 2 reviews three models of sociocultural change applied by social scientists to American ethnic groups: acculturation–assimilation, internal colonialism, and ethnic pluralism. The models are evaluated for their contribution to an understanding of the process of adaptation by people of Mexican descent to life in the United States. Chapter 3 describes the selection of the research sites, the three phases of data collection, and the characteristics of the samples of Mexican American and Anglo American people interviewed.

The next five chapters are concerned with the nature of Chicano ethnicity and its change over time. Chapter 4 describes the construction of our survey measures of acculturation (Cultural Awareness) and ethnic identification (Ethnic Loyalty), and the development of a five-cluster typology of orientation based on these measures. In chapters 5 through 7, we examine eleven case studies representing the five cluster types set forth in chapter 4. Chapter 8 is devoted to an analysis of factors associated with our measures of acculturation and ethnic identity and a related measure of social assimilation.

The final chapters investigate the social context of Mexican American ethnicity, particularly family life and the ethnic community. Chapter 9 examines the significance of the extended family among Chicanos and basic differences between Anglo Americans and Chicanos in family structure and organization. The relationship between extended familism and the processes of acculturation, assimilation, and urbanization is also explored. Case studies of Mexican American familism are presented for the five cluster types in chapter 10. Chapter 11 evaluates the non–kin ties (among friends, neighbors, and coworkers) which are typical of Mexican Americans and Anglo Americans and the character of ethnic social networks generally. The decided persistence of ethnic boundaries in personal lives and in social institutions, and the variation found between ethnic communities in the three cities, are also discussed. The final chapter of the book reconsiders the models of changing ethnicity in light of our research findings.

2

Models of Ethnic Change

ACCORDING TO SOCIAL SCIENTISTS in the first part of this century, ethnicity would eventually disappear in urban, industrial societies, including the United States. This assumption stemmed from early theoretical formulations by Durkheim, Tönnies, and Weber, among others, who associated urbanism with increasing individualism, growing alienation in a mass society, greater geographic and socioeconomic mobility, and the loss of community (*gemeinschaft*), all of which would contribute to the decline of meaningful ties to any particular group. Empirical studies accomplished in the second half of this century, however, find much evidence to the contrary. Ethnicity does not disappear in cities; it not only persists, but in many ways is reinforced, and some would say that it is created by the urban social system (see, for example, Yancey, Erickson, and Juliani 1976). It is for this reason, perhaps, that we find the term *ethnicity* used more and more frequently by contemporary social scientists.

However, there is little agreement on the meaning of the term. In a review of ethnic theory, Leo Despres (1975) identifies two general approaches to the concept of ethnicity: the objective and the subjective. From the objective point of view—the earliest model of the two—an ethnic group is distinctive from other groups on the basis of cultural traits and/or the relative accumulation of resources including wealth, social status, and political power. Thus, ethnic groups have commonly been defined on the basis of language, religion, or national origin; and, in general, competition for scarce resources has produced the stratification of ethnic groups within a society. The subjective definition of ethnicity, on the other hand, emphasizes self-

13

identification and identification forced by others—an approach which has contributed to the growing interest in the concept of ethnic identity or a "shared feeling of peoplehood" (Gordon 1964).

Yet another factor, the nature of the social context, is significant for the understanding of ethnicity. In fact, some researchers have been led to define ethnicity wholly in relative social terms. According to theories of situational ethnicity, ethnic-group membership and identity can and do change in reaction to situations of contact with other groups (Nagata 1974; Okamura 1981). For example, Cohen (1978) argues that an individual who is Irish Catholic may identify as Catholic when in a group of Protestants or Jews, but as an Irishman when with Italians who are also Catholic. While ethnicity may be best understood in these terms at the individual level, situational ethnicity does not contribute to an understanding of group be-havior. Crucial to such understanding is an accurate account of the process of interethnic relations: the historical nature of the contact between cultural groups, the development of domination by one group over others, the rise of prejudice and discrimination, and the growth of ethnic communities and ethnic-inclusive social relations. Only within this context can the significance of ethnicity be fully appreciated.

During the investigation of ethnicity among Chicanos, it was the purpose of our research to examine the process of sociocultural change with the intention of evaluating the accuracy of various models applied to Mexican Americans by social scientists. As we shall see, the controversy among social scientists concerning the most appropriate way in which to interpret the Chicano experience mir-rors the general controversy concerning the ethnicity of minority groups in the United States. It is helpful to review in some detail the nature of these models of ethnic change, and their problems and promise in contributing to an understanding of Mexican American ethnicity.

Models of Changing Ethnicity

As Cohen (1978) points out, ethnicity arises from a situation of contact between different cultural groups. With the passage of time, the status of each group as well as their cultural character can change.

Several models of changing ethnicity are discussed in the literature on American ethnic groups, including acculturation and assimilation, internal colonialism, and ethnic pluralism. All of these models have been used to explain the process of adaptation by people of Mexican descent to life in the United States.

Acculturation and assimilation are generally discussed together because acculturation is assumed to be a prerequisite for assimilation (see, for example, Gordon 1964; Teske and Nelson 1974). But it is important to recognize the difference between the two concepts. The term *acculturation* appeared in the 1920s in American anthropology when researchers turned from an interest in studying and reconstructing traditional American Indian cultures to an interest in culture contact principally between primitive and civilized cultures. The definition of acculturation put forth by Robert Redfield, Ralph Linton, and Melville Herskovits (1936) remains generally accepted today. They state:

> Acculturation comprehends those phenomena which result when groups of individuals having different cultures come into continuous first-hand contact, with subsequent changes in the original cultural patterns of either or both groups. (1936:149)

Later reviews of the concept by Broom et al. (1954) and by Teske and Nelson (1974) retain basically the same interpretation. Thus, acculturation is defined as one type of culture change—specifically, change occurring as the result of continuous contact between cultural groups. The process of change may affect one or both groups, and furthermore, it may affect any cultural trait: Redfield, Linton, and Herskovits (1936) mention "cultural patterns"; Broom et al. (1954) speak of "cultural segments" and the "body of custom"; and Teske and Nelson (1974) list "material traits, behavior patterns, norms, institutional changes," and "values." There is no specification within this broad definition of the types of changes expected, the degree of change, or the direction of change. In practice, however, the concept of acculturation has been applied in a narrower sense to mean change primarily within immigrant or minority ethnic groups whose culture becomes more and more like that of the dominant majority group. In the United States, this process has been called Americanization, Anglicization, and Anglo-conformity.

This process has been conceptualized in several ways, with each involving a different notion of biculturalism, or facility with two cultures (see figure 1). The single-continuum model of acculturation assumes the gradual replacement of traditional cultural traits with Anglo American traits. Thus, a bicultural person is one who has changed to some extent in all aspects of life; change is conceived as consistent across culture traits. Spindler's (1955) study of acculturation among the Menomini Indians most clearly presents this model in graphic form, depicting a single continuum of cultural change (unacculturated, bicultural, acculturated). Numerous other studies imply such a continuum (for example, Bruner 1956; Linton 1940). Graves (1967) and Matthiasson (1968) use the model in their work with Mexican Americans, as do many early researchers in Mexican American studies (for example, Humphrey 1943; Samora and Deane 1956).

A second model of acculturation is the two-culture matrix, where the two cultural systems are treated independently as separate axes forming a matrix. Each culture is conceived as a single continuum, and individuals may vary in their acceptance of and adherence to the two cultures. Thus, individuals who add traits from the new culture to their native traits are bicultural, while individuals who do not fully accept either culture are marginal. Stonequist (1937) developed his conception of the "marginal man" in the 1930s, and Poggie (1973) makes use of the concept in his presentation of the life of an "American-Mexican." The matrix model was presented in graphic form by McFee (1968), and it has been applied to Mexican Americans by Ruiz, Casas, and Padilla (1977).

A third model of acculturation, the multidimensional model, recognizes that the acceptance of new cultural traits and the loss of traditional cultural traits varies from trait to trait. Individuals may quickly discard some native traits and adopt certain traits from the new culture, but other native traits may be maintained and strengthened. In other words, each aspect of culture change must be measured independently. According to this model, a bicultural person would have retained some traditional traits and adopted some new traits, but unlike the case of the two-culture matrix, there is no assumption that a bicultural person is highly adept in both cultures. The concept of selective acculturation has been used to describe the common tendency for immigrants and ethnic minorities to adopt

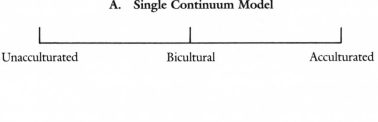

A. Single Continuum Model

Unacculturated   Bicultural   Acculturated

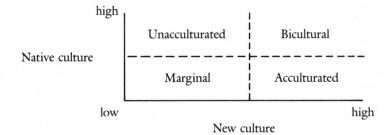

B. Two-Culture Matrix Model

high

Native culture

| Unacculturated | Bicultural |
| Marginal | Acculturated |

low   high

New culture

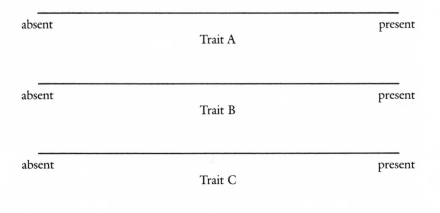

C. Multidimensional Model

absent   present

Trait A

absent   present

Trait B

absent   present

Trait C

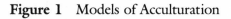

Figure 1   Models of Acculturation

certain strategic traits (especially those, such as learning English, which will improve their economic status), while retaining other traditional cultural values and patterns, including child-rearing practices, family organization, native foods, and music preferences (see, for example, Ambrecht and Pachon 1974; Collette and O'Malley 1974; Eaton 1952).

The advantage of the multidimensional model is that it can also take account of new cultural and social patterns created by migrants and ethnic minorities in the new society, a process that Watson (1977) refers to as "creolization." This process has long been of interest to researchers studying the Mexican American *barrio*, as in, for example, the investigation of the life and language of the *pachuco* (Barker 1947; McWilliams 1948). A multidimensional model has been suggested by Greeley (1974), Olmedo (1980), and Pierce, Clark, and Kaufman (1978); and it is the model used in our study of Mexican Americans.

While acculturation refers to the acceptance of cultural patterns and traits, assimilation refers to the social, economic, and political integration of an immigrant or ethnic minority group member into mainstream society. In order for assimilation to occur, the minority group member must have acculturated to some extent and must be accepted by the dominant group. Acculturation, however, does not ensure assimilation. On the contrary, Gordon (1964) argues that the experience in the U.S. of ethnic groups who are not of northern European descent has been acculturation without assimilation. Nevertheless, most researchers view the two processes as inevitably linked, and some even use the terms *acculturation* and *assimilation* interchangeably, visualizing one all-encompassing process.

It is important to recognize the distinct social, economic, and political aspects of assimilation. Social assimilation involves the integration of ethnic minorities into primary and secondary relations with members of the dominant group. Primary relations include intimate and informal interaction as family members (through intermarriage) and friends, and in private leisure activities in the home and in conjunction with family and friends. Secondary relations include the less intimate and more formal interaction which occurs at work, in school, at social agencies, in the political arena, and in places of mass entertainment. There is, of course, difficulty in carrying out a systematic distinction between primary and secondary relations; one hesitates, for example, to generalize about the relations between neighbors and between church or voluntary association members. Nonetheless, the distinction is important because in the process of assimilation, secondary relations between minority- and majority-group members occur first; and for non-Europeans in the U.S., at least, primary relations may never be achieved on a large scale.

Economic assimilation is fairly obvious as a process of integrating ethnic minorities into the social and economic institutions of mainstream society and as a guarantee of equal opportunity in competing for education, income, and occupational status. If there is a large gap in economic status between the minority group and the majority group, economic assimilation tends to be a long and perhaps endless process of achieving parity, and the process is most difficult for those ethnic minority groups of a different racial background than the majority group.

Political assimilation, or the elimination of any basis for ethnic political action, is closely connected to economic assimilation. Some researchers would argue that this is the last phase to occur in the assimilation process. For example, Glazer and Moynihan (1963) find that ethnics in New York City are, for the most part, indistinguishable except as political interest groups.

Investigators have detailed numerous factors that affect the rate of assimilation and the probability of full assimilation. These factors include characteristics of the ethnic minority group (such as the size and density of the population; the presence of separate ethnic institutions, including schools and churches; racial distinctiveness; the group's ethnocentrism and its desire to assimilate; and the economic background and skill level of group members) and characteristics of the mainstream society (including the nature of its power relations and the relative presence of inequality; and its historical experience with minority groups and the extent of prejudice and discrimination, racism and segregation that exists). Researchers who use the assimilation model acknowledge the difficulty of gaining equal status, but they assume that eventually ethnic minority groups will be absorbed into mainstream society (Park, Burgess, and MacKenzie 1925; Warner and Srole 1945; Wirth 1938). The massive study of *The Mexican American People* by Grebler, Moore, and Guzman (1970) follows, for the most part, an assimilationist model.

The assimilation model arose in the 1920s, as the U.S. experienced massive immigration from abroad. It was assumed that if the nation were to remain strong and undivided, these different ethnic groups would need to acculturate and become part of the main-stream society. However, except for white Protestants from northern and western Europe, as Gordon (1964) points out, true assimilation has not been achieved in the U.S. Studies of ethnic minorities tend to find only limited assimilation, even for those groups who have been in the U.S. for several generations. Reviews of Grebler, Moore, and Guzman's (1970) book by Alvarez (1971) and Ornelas and Gonzal-ez (1971) are highly critical of its assimilationist perspective in consideration of the apparent limitations experienced by Chicanos.

To account for the lack of assimilation by ethnic minorities, other models of ethnic social relations in the U.S. have been increasingly adopted by social scientists since the 1960s. The model of internal colonialism was developed by researchers working in third-world areas, where complete subordination of certain ethnic minority groups has occurred. Fanon (1968) and Memmi (1965) applied the concept to the native population of Algeria under French rule; Stavenhagen (1965) and González Casanova (1965) used the con-cept in analyzing the status of the Indian population in Mexico. As originally conceived, the model describes the exploitation of a group culturally different from the dominant group. Exploitation is for the benefit of the dominant group, and the situation is analogous to colonialism except that it occurs internally within the boundaries of the nation. The highly integrated dominant group has a strong political administration, while the internal colony, which constitutes a large population, serves as a cheap labor force. Because the colo-nized group can be identified culturally and the dominant group considers this culture inferior, a cultural division of labor is justified and easily enforced by the dominant group.

The internal-colony model has since been applied to non–third-world situations such as the Celtic fringe of Great Britain (Hechter 1975) and American ethnic groups, including Blacks (Blauner 1969) and Appalachians (Lewis, Johnson, and Askins 1978) as well as Chicanos (Acuña, 1981; Barrera, 1979). But there have been nu-merous criticisms of the blanket application of the model to these groups (Gonzalez 1974; Murguía 1975; Walls 1978). First of all, it does not take into account the socioeconomic mobility (however limited) experienced by minority groups in the U.S. While ethnic minority groups undeniably suffer from higher poverty levels, there is also a middle-class segment which must be considered. Furthermore, the elites within the minority group often "make it" by exploiting their own kind; in other words, domination may be the work of indigenous elites as well as external elites. Finally, the possibility of some individuals "passing" into the mainstream indicates that group membership may not be totally ascribed. While it may be accurate to apply the model of internal colonialism to limited areas such as ghettos or *barrios* (Barrera, Muñoz, and Ornelas 1972), its wholesale use with ethnic minorities in the U.S. seems untenable.

The model of pluralism was first used by Furnivall (1939, 1948) in the context of colonial tropical societies in the Far East, specifically, the Dutch Netherlands. M. G. Smith (1960) introduced the concept to a wider audience in his article "Social and Cultural Pluralism." In general, pluralism refers to the maintenance of separate institutions ("set forms of activity, grouping, rules, ideas, and values") by distinct social groups encompassed within a single political unit—in other words, vertical as opposed to horizontal stratification. The ethnic groups are in contact insofar as they live within the same political state, but there is little real interaction between them. While this case of extreme pluralism may be characteristic of certain colonial situations, its use as a general model is limited.

In a later revision of the concept, Smith (1969) made a useful distinction between cultural, social, and structural pluralism, one which broadens the potential application of the concept. Cultural pluralism involves the maintenance of a separate culture. Social pluralism refers to the maintenance of separate social relations, such as those with family, friends, and coworkers. With structural pluralism, ethnic minority groups achieve economic, social and political rewards within their own institutions when they are excluded from mainstream institutions. According to Smith (1969), cultural and social pluralism may be maintained independently, but structural pluralism presupposes social and cultural pluralism. Smith has been criticized by Léons and Léons (1977) and by others for failing to recognize the modifying influences of acculturation and socioeconomic mobility in plural societies. They argue that while acculturation may do away with cultural pluralism, social and structural pluralism may continue to persist (that is, acculturation without assimilation). Furthermore, they feel that Smith does not emphasize strongly enough the phenomenon of horizontal stratification, or class, which also shapes plural societies. Ethnic minority groups are not single-status groups, but are divided by class along the lines of Gordon's (1964) concept of ethclass. It would seem, however, that Smith's basic formulation could incorporate these changes and still remain viable.

More disturbing is the criticism that the model of pluralism is a functionalist one, that it does not incorporate processes of change and the potential for violence between groups (Cross 1968; Léons and Léons 1977; Newman 1973). The plural society, it is argued, is conceived as a state of peaceful coexistence; violence may occur, but it is viewed as basically destructive to the plural system. Critics contend that, on the contrary, all societies, including plural ones, incorporate both change and stasis. Interestingly, Kuper (1971) finds that pluralism offers an important alternative to Durkheimian, functionalist, and assimilationist models of ethnic relations, which assume that increasing contact between interdependent segments results in harmonious relations and the eventual withering of ethnic inequality due to the distribution of economic and political power along cultural lines. Kuper (1971) also suggests that pluralism differs from Marxist theory, which emphasizes class struggle and the common problem of inequality shared by all ethnic minority groups. This hypothesis tends to ignore the existence of class divisions within ethnic minority groups as well as the fact that there is little solidarity between workers of different ethnic groups. According to the plural model, ethnic segments are more significant than class segments in determining the process of change. Revolutionary change in plural society is more likely to occur on the basis of ethnicity rather than class inequalities, but the potential for evolutionary change exists where there is progressive incorporation of ethnic groups as equals in society. This view is echoed by Dotson and Dotson (1968), who suggest that pluralism is a phase in the evolutionary history of modern societies.

Conclusion

Despite any limitations in the plural model, it seems to best represent the current state of U.S. ethnic relations. When combined with historical and processual approaches, plural theory contributes to an understanding of the status of American ethnic minority groups and the reasons underlying their continued inequality. The need to distinguish between cultural, social, and structural aspects of pluralism is certainly apparent in our study. Mexican Americans experience acculturation, but it is selective. Socially, Mexican Americans remain within ethnically enclosed primary groups, although they may interact more often with Anglo Americans in secondary relations. And despite some generational mobility, Chicanos continue to predominate in working-class occupations, with limited opportunities for social status or political impact in the larger society. Discrimination, social segregation, and subordination contribute to the persistence of Chicanos' unequal status.

Yet, in addition to these factors that undoubtedly shape ethnic-group interrelations, there is another process of equal importance: ethnic identification. Members of ethnic minority groups may be proud of their cultural heritage, and feel positive bonds to their people. Unlike situations of internal colonialism, pluralism may actually foster the growth and maintenance of positive ethnic-group identities. This is not to say that ethnic identification is solely a product of the inequality characteristic of plural society. Although some researchers argue that ethnic identity is correlated with a continuum of acculturation and assimilation (Burma 1954; Grebler, Moore, and Guzman 1970; Rose 1964), we find that no such simple relationship exists and that ethnic identity responds, to some extent, to the ingrained "primordial attachments" referred to by Geertz (1963). It remains true, as Gordon (1964) pointed out two decades ago, that ethnic-group members are not positive that they want to assimilate. Recent investigations of symbolic ethnicity demonstrate the extent to which ethnic groups may endeavor to "create" an identity as a means of maintaining their ethnicity in a complex society (Gans 1979; Spicer 1980).

This book is concerned, then, with establishing a general theoretical framework for interpreting Mexican American ethnicity and sociocultural change. At the same time, we document carefully the multidimensional nature of Mexican American ethnicity and the need to recognize the heterogeneity of the Mexican American population. In comparing the relative presence of different cultural traits in the population, it is apparent that some traits are held fast from generation to generation, while others are neglected; still others are created as new traits. Acculturation is far from a simple, singular process. Moreover, there are many segments of the Mexican American population that are characterized by different combinations of traits. We have found the most important distinction to be between first-generation immigrants from Mexico and native-born Mexican Americans. But it is the interethnic contrasts between Mexican Americans and Anglo Americans that override the many implications of this intraethnic variation, and serve to demonstrate the significance of ethnicity in its broad sense as the key to understanding the condition and future of people of Mexican descent in American society.

3

Strategies for Research

FROM THE BEGINNING, the aim of our research was to gain a general overview of Mexican American ethnicity. The methods used to obtain the data reflect our concern for generalization, but at the same time, there was an attempt to obtain comparative data across the range of variability within the Chicano population. Above all, we recognized the need for data on Anglo Americans as well as on Mexican Americans, which would enable us to evaluate the significance of ethnicity. With these things in mind, we devised the research design and collected the data over a three-year period.

Selection of the Research Sites

Mexican Americans in the United States are primarily concentrated in five southwestern states: California, Arizona, Colorado, New Mexico, and Texas. California possesses slightly more than half the Mexican American population in the Southwest (*Hispanic Almanac* 1984). In California, as in the other four states, Chicanos are overwhelmingly urban dwellers. Over three-quarters of the Mexican Americans in California live in cities with a population of ten thousand or more. Over 90 percent reside in thirteen state metropolitan areas designated by the U.S. Bureau of the Census, and the majority of these are residents of the large urban areas along the coast of southern California. While the highest concentration of Mexican Americans in southern California is in Los Angeles, most Mexican Americans live in other towns up and down the coast. Very little is

25

known about the Chicanos in these smaller southern California urban areas, and it is in communities of this type that we chose to do our research.

Because of our desire to cover a broad cross-section of the Mexican American population, we decided not to limit the research to one city. Taking into consideration the time and monetary limits for our research, we chose to study three cities in close proximity to one another: Santa Barbara, Santa Paula, and Oxnard (see figure 2). These cities offer variation in population size, ethnic density, and economic bases. Santa Barbara has a population of over 74,000, 27 percent of which is Mexican American, and an economy based on tourism, retail trade, and light manufacturing. Oxnard, whose Mexican American population makes up 41 percent of the 108,000 residents, has a mixed agricultural–industrial economy. Santa Paula, with a primarily agricultural economy, is the smallest of the three cities; Mexican Americans make up 48 percent of its population of 20,500.

Data Collection

The collection of data proceeded over a period of twenty-eight months, and was divided into three phases. The first phase involved interviewing a large stratified random sample of Mexican Americans and Anglo Americans in the three cities, using a brief questionnaire on ethnicity and family. The second phase consisted of reinterviewing a subsample of respondents from the first survey, employing a much more comprehensive survey instrument covering the same topics. In the third and final phase, a small selected subsample from the second survey was reinterviewed to provide case-study material. Each of these phases is described in detail in the following sections.

Phase One: The Large Survey

In order to acquire as large a sample as possible during the given time period, the questionnaire was designed to be administered quickly and immediately upon contacting the respondent. Data gathered in this first survey were expected to give preliminary indications of ethnic differences in family structure, social support, cultural

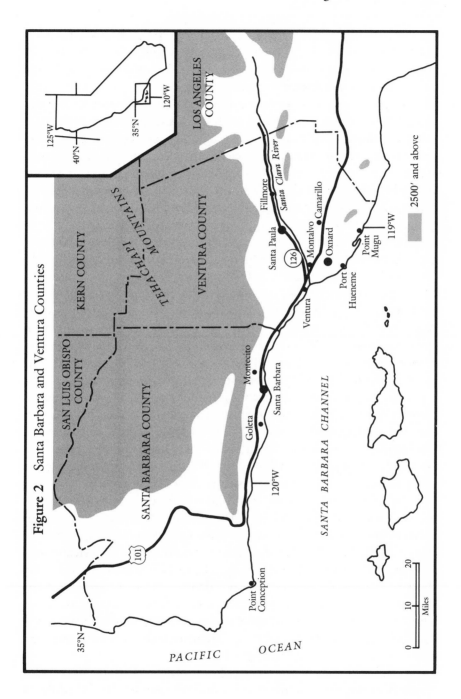

Figure 2   Santa Barbara and Ventura Counties

and socioeconomic background, as well as to provide some direction for the development of the more intensive interview schedule for phase two. The interview schedule had 123 variables in a format convenient for computer data processing.

Sampling was designed to gather an equal number of respondents in each of the three cities, with the Mexican American respondents stratified by cultural background and socioeconomic status. In order to obtain the stratified Mexican American sample, three census tracts in each city were selected to fit as closely as possible the following ideal types: (1) high ethnic density and low socioeconomic status, (2) mid ethnic density and mixed socioeconomic status, and (3) low ethnic density and high socioeconomic status.

Having chosen the census tracts, the sample was selected by using a city directory listing residents by address. A total of 860 Chicano households was contacted in this manner; 77 percent of these (or 666 Mexican Americans) consented to the interview and 23 percent declined. In all three towns, Mexican Americans living in the *barrio* were most willing to accept the interview. For the non–Spanish-surname sample, 776 households were contacted: 55 percent (or 425 respondents) accepted the interview, and 45 percent declined. The greater willingness of Mexican Americans to be interviewed, compared to Anglos, has been found in other studies as well (Freeman 1969; Weaver 1973). The non–Spanish-surname sample is 82 percent white Anglo American, 12 percent Black, and 6 percent other (including Asian American and Native American); in the interests of ethnic specificity, only the 340 white Anglo Americans were used in the analysis of data and for the subsequent subsampling.

The interviewers for the first phase were university students or former students who had recently graduated. Most of the interviewers were women. Bilingual Mexican American interviewers gathered the Mexican American sample, and Anglo American interviewers gathered the Anglo sample. The interviewers were trained in the procedures for securing respondents, administering the questionnaire, and interacting with the respondents during the interview. The interviewers were advised to be friendly but to follow the questions and the format verbatim. Throughout the survey, training and supervision continued in the field.

All of the respondents were first contacted in person at the selected address taken from the random sample. In an effort to reduce the number of refusals, it was decided not to schedule interviews by telephone, thinking that face-to-face interaction would elicit a more positive response. But once face-to-face contact had been established, the respondent might be reached by telephone to confirm an appointment. For the most part, however, respondents were interviewed at the first meeting.

Two procedures were followed to ensure a fairly large number of male respondents. First, interviewers were instructed to ask at the door for the head of the household, which was generally assumed to mean an adult male if one resided in the household. If the male head was not at home or there was none in the household, the interviewer was instructed to ask for the spouse or female head. Even with this procedure, however, it was rare to find males at home during week-days. Therefore, as a second method of contacting males, interviews were also conducted on Saturdays, a procedure which was somewhat more successful among Anglos than among Mexican Americans.

An average of thirty minutes was required to administer the interview schedule, and nearly all of the interviews were completed in one session. At the end of the interview, respondents were asked if they would agree to another interview later on; 98 percent of the Mexican Americans and 97 percent of the Anglos consented. In order to further ensure the follow-up interview, respondents were asked to provide the name and address of a relative or friend in town who would know their whereabouts if they moved. When the inter-view phase was completed, all respondents were sent letters of appre-ciation.

Our success in gathering a stratified sample of Mexican Ameri-cans is evident in table 1. The respondents interviewed in the census tracts, which were designated as high ethnic density/low socio-economic status in each town, are most likely to be first generation, Spanish speaking, and of low socioeconomic status. The low ethnic density/high socioeconomic status census tracts, in contrast, pro-duced more respondents who are third generation, English speak-ing, and of high socioeconomic status. The mid–ethnic density tracts in Santa Barbara and Oxnard produced a mixed range of cultural types and respondents who are somewhere between the *barrio* and the Anglo-dominated census tracts in educational achievement, but who are more like the *barrio* census tracts in occupational status. The percentage of farm-workers in our tract samples correspond to census data, except for a lower percentage in our samples for tracts 4 (36 percent vs. 46 percent) and 49 (24 percent vs. 35 percent). With

Table 1 Selected Characteristics of the First Mexican American Sample by Census Tract in Santa Barbara, Santa Paula, and Oxnard

Characteristic	Santa Barbara			Santa Paula			Oxnard		
	High Tract 8 (N = 86)	Mid Tract 11 (N = 69)	Low Tract 13.02 (N = 66)	High Tract 4 (N = 84)	Mid Tract 6 (N = 75)	Low Tract 7 (N = 69)	High Tract 49 (N = 72)	Mid Tract 37 (N = 73)	Low Tract 41 (N = 72)
Generation by percentage									
First	46%	42%	26%	54%	49%	23%	73%	47%	16%
Second	37%	36%	47%	33%	30%	47%	20%	38%	58%
Third	17%	22%	27%	13%	21%	30%	7%	15%	26%
Spanish language questionnaire	48%	37%	17%	69%	67%	23%	85%	45%	18%
Median years of education	9.3	10.4	11.8	6.3	6.6	11.5	5.6	8.1	11.8
Male white-collar occupation	15%	7%	33%	11%	3%	23%	3%	12%	22%
Male farm workers	4%	0	2%	36%	33%	9%	24%	6%	4%

Source: First Mexican American survey.

regard to occupation, again, the percentage of male white-collar workers is much the same in our data and in the census data for six of the tracts; in tracts 11, 37, and 41, our sample has a lower percentage. The median years of education varies to a greater extent between the two sets of data: the median years is roughly the same in our sample and in the census data for tracts 8, 11, 13.02, and 7; our sample has a lower median in tracts 4, 6, 49, and 37 (averaging .8 years lower); and our sample has a higher median in tract 41, (.9 years higher). Despite these socioeconomic differences between our sample and the census data, the fact that the Mexican Americans in both sets of data are overwhelmingly blue collar and have not graduated from high school lead us to believe that, in general, our data is representative in socioeconomic terms of the Mexican American population sampled.

A comparison of the characteristics of our sample with census data on Mexican Americans in the three cities, in urban California, and in the urban Southwest reveals some of the same differences. The Mexican Americans in our sample are somewhat less educated (9.1 years of school vs. 9.9 years) and fewer have white collar occupations (14 percent vs. 23 percent). Nevertheless, in general, our sample is representative of the majority of Chicanos who tend to be blue collar and lack a high school education. Any disparity with regard to generational proportions is probably due to the age distribution within the generations and the concomitantly small number of third-generation adults. While we believe our sample is fairly representative of urban Mexican Americans in California and the Southwest, we also caution against making any broad generalizations about Mexican Americans as a group without analysis across generations and socioeconomic levels. In other studies as well as our own (Dworkin 1965; Grebler, Moore, and Guzman 1970), significant intragroup differences in attitudes and behavior have been detected. It is our belief that generalizations which fail to take into consideration the potential intragroup variation only serve to promote cultural stereotypes, and prove to be of little intrinsic value.

Phase Two: The Subsample Survey

The purpose of the second survey was to gather more in-depth data on family and ethnicity among Mexican Americans and Anglos.

Respondents from the first sample who had consented to further interviews were recontacted three to seven months after their initial interview. We hoped to gather a good deal of qualitative as well as quantitative data in this phase, and the questionnaire was designed accordingly; it was lengthy and had numerous open-ended questions, and the interviewers were encouraged to jot down relevant information offered by the respondent that went beyond the questions asked. The data from this survey form the core of our findings.

Interviewers for the second phase were also primarily recently graduated university students. Anglo American interviewers were used with the Anglo sample; all of them were from Santa Barbara, and they drove to do the interviewing in the other towns. Bilingual Mexican Americans gathered most of the Mexican American sample; however, two bilingual Anglo Americans also did some interviewing. Several of the Mexican American interviewers were residents of Santa Paula and Oxnard, and completed most of the Mexican American sample in those two cities. The interviewers were trained in much the same way as the interviewers for the first phase. A few of the interviewers participated in both surveys.

As with the first survey, all respondents were, at first, contacted in person. After making face-to-face contact, telephone calls were permitted to set and confirm subsequent interview appointments. Generally, two interviews of one to two hours were required to complete the questionnaire. The respondent sometimes wished to complete the interview in a single three-hour session. However, a single session usually proved to be tiring for both the interviewer and the respondent, and other means of handling the interview schedule were preferred. On more rare occasions, respondents required three or four interviews to complete the questionnaire; this was likely to happen if the respondent worked odd hours or had several small children at home, with only small chunks of time to devote to an interview. Once begun, a questionnaire was always completed by the same interviewer. Typically, respondents requiring more than one interview completed the questionnaire within a one-week period. In only three instances were interviews begun but not completed.

Interviewers were told to ask by name for the respondent who had completed the first survey questionnaire. If the respondent was not at home, interviewers asked when the respondent could be contacted at home, and another call was made at that time. To ensure success in reaching original respondents, interviews were conducted during the day, Tuesday through Saturday, as well as in the evening if the respondent worked. A total of 85 percent of the second sample of Mexican Americans and 91 percent of the second sample of Anglos consisted of interviews with respondents from the first survey. For the remaining second sample, the original respondents could not be contacted, but the spouses agreed to be interviewed. Primarily for this reason, the second survey has more female respondents. In any case, while some of the respondents in the second survey are different from the first survey, no new households were added.

The long interviews in the second survey allowed considerable rapport to develop between interviewers and respondents. In many cases, the interviewers were asked by the respondents to return for more informal conversations. For the most part, respondents were very friendly, helpful, and interested in the research. At the end of the interview, respondents were asked again if they would participate in follow-up interviews; 95 percent of the Mexican Americans and 97 percent of the Anglos agreed to do so. Following the interviewing phase, respondents were once again sent letters of appreciation.

Of the first Mexican American sample, 486 respondents were contacted for the second interview. Among those contacted, 75 percent (or 372 respondents) agreed to be reinterviewed. This was about the same rate of consent that was obtained in the first survey. For the white Anglo American sample, 200 respondents from the first survey were reached, 82 percent (or 163 respondents) of whom agreed to complete the second interview. Thus, in using this procedure, the rate of consent among Anglos increased dramatically, becoming greater than the consent rate among Chicanos for the second survey. The sample distribution by census tract remained generally the same; no Anglos were interviewed in tract 49, however, because nearly all non–Spanish-surname respondents interviewed in tract 49 during the first survey were Blacks. Both the Mexican American and the Anglo American samples in the second survey appear to be fairly representative of the first survey samples.

Phase Three: The Case Studies

In the third phase of the research, in-depth case studies were made of twenty-four Mexican Americans, with emphasis on extended family interaction and ethnic identity. A more limited study was conducted with twenty-two Anglo Americans. In all, the case studies served to flesh out and enrich the statistical profile that had been obtained by means of the questionnaires. This multifaceted approach contributed to our overall understanding of the dynamic interrelationship between family and ethnicity.

Individuals selected for intense case study consisted of a subsample of respondents from the second survey. In order to facilitate data gathering during this phase, the sample was limited to respondents residing in either Santa Barbara or Oxnard. The purpose in sampling the Mexican Americans was to cover a range of cultural and extended family types (see table 2).

Interviews during the third phase were structured, for the most part. Interview schedules largely consisting of open-ended items were designed to cover the following topics: the informant's life history, personal support network (including relatives, friends, neighbors, coworkers, and others seen regularly), integration into the larger society (that is, use of health and child-care facilities,

Table 2   Sampling for Case Studies

Mexican Americans					
6 Unacculturated		10 Bicultural		8 Acculturated	
4 Low Family Integration	2 High Family Integration	5 Low Family Integration	4 High Family Integration	3 Low Family Integration	4 High Family Integration
		1 No Local Family		1 No Local Family	

Anglo Americans					
8 No Local Family		9 Low Family Integration		5 High Family Integration	
3 White Collar	5 Blue Collar	2 White Collar	7 Blue Collar	1 White Collar	4 Blue Collar

insurance, banks, lawyers; participation in voting, military service, recreational pastimes, and the schools), and degree of participation in and identification with Mexican American and Anglo cultures. Spanish and English versions of the questionnaires were constructed. Each Mexican American informant was visited between seven and twelve times over the nine-month period, with contacts made every two to three weeks.

The interviews were conducted by two research assistants, both second-generation Mexican Americans. Both research assistants were advised to follow the interview schedule as closely as possible, but also to develop as intimate and informal a relationship with the informants as possible, following up leads in conversations as they occurred. The desire was to obtain certain consistent information from all informants, while at the same time acquiring a sense of the informant's life as a unique experience and as perceived by the informant. In other words, we hoped to combine structured interviewing and participant observation. Close ties were established with most of the informants, who came to regard the researchers as friends and confidants. The field-workers met with these informants on occasions other than those when interviews were scheduled. Sometimes, they had dinner together or celebrated a special event. With some informants, relations were not quite so close, but informality and friendliness were still attained. Primarily due to the good rapport between the field-workers and the informants, this phase of the research was successful and productive.

The interviews were conducted at the informants' homes and typically lasted between one and two hours. Informants were asked if the interviews could be tape recorded, and all but two informants consented. The field-workers took notes while they tape recorded the interviews. After each interview was completed, field notes were typed, covering both the answers to structured questions and any unsolicited comments made by the informant. Notes were also taken on events occurring while the field-worker was present and on conversations between the informant and other visitors arriving while the interview was in progress. Friends, relatives, and neighbors frequently visited when the field-worker was present. Of course, the informant's spouse and children also appeared during the interviews. Meeting other people who were significant in the lives of the informants added to our knowledge about their interaction with others, the support received from others, and the kinds of life problems being experienced. These other people often confirmed certain interpretations that the field-workers had formulated about the informant, and they sometimes contributed a different perspective on the informant's life.

Resources did not permit us to pursue an entirely comparative study of Anglo Americans during this phase of the research. However, a limited study was undertaken. Two interviews for the Anglo sample, conducted about one month apart, gathered comparative data on personal support networks. Sampling covered a range of family and socioeconomic types (see table 2).

Description of the Samples

A more detailed description of the general characteristics of the Anglos and Mexican Americans sampled is presented in this section. In addition to making interethnic comparisons, the Mexican American data is analyzed by generations to illustrate intraethnic differences.

The two ethnic-group samples are fairly similar in age, sex, and marital status. The Mexican Americans and the Anglo Americans average forty-two and forty-three years of age, respectively. The majority (over 60 percent) of both groups of respondents is female and married.

In general, the Anglo households are smaller ($M=3.2$ vs. 4.5) and much less uniform in makeup than those of the Mexican Americans. Mexican American respondents are not only more likely to have children and to have larger numbers ($M=3.9$ vs. 2.8); they are also more likely to have children living at home. In fact, six out of ten of the Mexican American households are made up of nuclear families in which the father, mother, and children are present. Among Anglos, nuclear households predominate, but almost half of these have no children present. In addition, there is a large number of single-person Anglo households (20 percent vs. 6 percent). Extended family households make up only a small proportion (11 percent or less) of the households in either ethnic group.

Socioeconomic data indicate significant differences between the Anglos and Mexican Americans. Among the 86 percent of Mexican

American heads of household who have blue-collar jobs, the majority are employed in semiskilled and unskilled occupations. The median years of education for the Mexican American respondents is nine years; 69 percent have not completed high school. The majority of Anglos, on the other hand, are white-collar workers (55 percent) with one or more years of college (50 percent).

Residential stability is much more characteristic of the Mexican Americans than the Anglos. The average Mexican American has lived in town for about twenty-four years, compared to fifteen years for the average Anglo. Many of the Mexican Americans are natives of the city in which they were interviewed; 22 percent of the Mexican Americans are city natives, in contrast to only 4 percent of the Anglos.

To some extent, length of residence is associated with occupational status because blue-collar workers are generally more likely to remain longer in one area. It is possible that the difference in residential stability between the two ethnic groups might be due to their significantly different occupational patterns. However, in using partial correlation analysis, we find there is a greater tendency for Mexican Americans to live in town longer than Anglos, even when controlling for occupation ($r=23$; $p=.001$). Thus, we can conclude that transience is more characteristic of the Anglo Americans in our sample than the Mexican Americans.

It is important to set forth the variation within the Mexican American sample itself. As can be seen in table 3, the first-generation Mexicans (those born in Mexico) are most homogeneous. They generally have only an elementary school education, speak mainly Spanish, and identify as Catholic and as "Mexican." Second-generation respondents, who were born in the United States with one or both parents born in Mexico, are likely to have about ten years of schooling, to speak English and probably also Spanish, and to identify as Catholic and as either "Mexican" or "Mexican American." Lastly, third-generation respondents, who were born in the United States and whose parents were born in the United States, have an average of eleven years of education, speak mainly English, and tend to identify as something other than "Mexican" (that is, "Mexican American," "American of Mexican descent," or "Chicano"). It is only in the third generation that Protestants appear in any number, mostly as members of evangelical churches such as the Jehovah's

Table 3 Socioeconomic and Cultural Characteristics by Mexican American Generation

| Socioeconomic and Cultural Characteristics | *Mexican American Generations* | | | |
	First (N = 264) %	*Second* (N = 237) %	*Third* (N = 125) %	*Total* (N = 626) %
I. Language Ability				
Speaks primarily Spanish	83	16	7	43
Bilingual	14	42	30	27
Speaks primarily English	3	42	63	30
Total	100	100	100	100
II. Ethnic Self-Identification				
"Mexican"	91	36	22	58
"Mexican American"	7	46	49	29
"American of Mexican Descent"	1	9	17	7
"Chicano"	1	9	12	6
Total	100	100	100	100
III. Religious Affiliation				
Catholic	91	89	83	89
Protestant	8	9	16	10
Agnostic; Atheist	1	2	1	1
Total	100	100	100	100
IV. Education				
0–8 years	73	31	22	47
9–11 years	12	31	28	22
12 years	10	24	38	22
College	5	14	12	9
Total	100	100	100	100
V. Male Head of Household Occupation				
Professional/Managerial	6	13	15	10
Clerical/Sales	1	7	6	4
Skilled Worker	8	20	25	17
Semiskilled/Unskilled	85	60	54	69
Total	100	100	100	100

Source: First Mexican American Survey.

Witness and the Pentecostal churches. As such, they remain religiously distinct from the Anglo Americans sampled who tend to be Protestant (57 percent), mostly members of mainline churches, or to have no religious affiliation (25 percent).

The majority of all three Mexican American generations are blue-collar workers. Although most of the first-generation heads of household are in the lowest occupational categories of semiskilled and unskilled laborers, many in the second and third generations hold skilled-labor jobs or white-collar positions. In sum, the immigrants from Mexico differ both culturally and socioeconomically from the native-born and second- and third-generation Mexican Americans. Furthermore, although the second-generation respondents make important educational and occupational gains in comparison to the immigrants, there is very little difference between the attainments of the second- and third-generation respondents, and both of these segments are far outranked by the Anglos.

4

Cultural Awareness and Ethnic Loyalty

THE STUDY OF CULTURE CHANGE is a major concern in research with Mexican Americans as well as other American ethnic groups. The process has generally been conceived in terms of "acculturation." While the definition of acculturation (as discussed in chapter 2) includes culture change in both groups, most studies focus on change occurring in one group, the ethnic minority. It is assumed that there exists a unilineal continuum of change in minority group members' cultural orientation, and that the process of change replaces traditional cultural traits with Anglo traits. Other researchers examining acculturation argue that a unilineal continuum oversimplifies the process of change. Instead, cultural traits vary in their rate of change, with some disappearing quickly and others persisting or even intensifying. Rather than assume a constant rate of change in all aspects of culture, then, it appears necessary to adopt a multidimensional approach to the study of acculturation.

As a result of the apparent inability of the acculturation model to deal with variation in the process of culture change, researchers have increasingly turned to the study of ethnic identification. Here, the particular assemblage of cultural traits becomes less important than the attitudes of members toward the people and culture of in-group versus out-group as well as members' self-identification. With the concept of ethnic identity, it has been possible to explore the impact of such phenomena as voluntary versus forced ethnicity (Friedlander 1975; Valentine 1975), situational ethnicity (Nagata 1974), and multiple identities (Keyes 1976).

Although much research in the U.S. assumes a single continuum of change, in which the adoption of Anglo cultural traits and ethnic identification with Anglo Americans is a single process (see, for example, Graves 1967; Rose 1964; Rubel 1966), numerous studies indicate that acculturation and ethnic identification are, in fact, separate processes. Glazer and Moynihan's (1963) classic study of ethnic groups in New York City demonstrates that ethnic identity can remain unchanged or can be strengthened despite virtually complete acculturation. Like Glazer and Moynihan, Greeley (1974) points out the advantages of retaining ethnic affiliation, including political power and social mobility within the ethnic group. The confusion of the two processes of culture change, acculturation and ethnic identification, is apparent in the inapposite "debate" between Patterson (1979) and Kushner (1980) in the journal *American Anthropologist*. Patterson argues that ethnicity is disappearing in the U.S., citing the loss of cultural traditions and gradual Americanization of ethnic minority groups. Kushner counters that ethnic groups survive through the adoption of symbolic traits of difference and a separate group identification. In considering the distinction between the two processes, it is entirely possible for acculturation to proceed while ethnic identification is maintained.

Measurement of Culture Change

Given the cross-disciplinary interest in acculturation and ethnic identification, it is puzzling that there have been relatively few attempts to measure the two concepts empirically. Some researchers have simply settled on single items to indicate acculturation, such as language ability (Samora and Deane 1956; Tharp et al. 1968; Griffith 1983; Ortiz and Arce 1984), generation (Kitano 1976), intermarriage (Mittelbach and Moore 1968), and dress (Peters 1976), or have asked respondents for their self-identification (Garcia 1981) as a way of determining ethnic identity. Others have developed scales based only on a small number of items that are not clearly related to either acculturation or ethnic identification. For example, Olmedo, Martinez, and Martinez (1978) have developed an acculturation measure that consists of four concepts—"mother," "father," "male," and "female,"—rated along fifteen pairs of bipolar adjectives such as "hard–soft," "ugly–beautiful," and "happy–sad." In addition, the measure contains eighteen items covering background information concerning the respondent, his or her family, the head of household, and the language spoken at home. In spite of the fact that the measure dichotomizes Chicanos and Anglos, it is not certain what this acculturation scale measures.

A search of the literature indicates seven studies in which acculturation and/or ethnic identification are measured in a sophisticated and quantitative way; interestingly, three of these deal with Mexican Americans. Masuda, Matsumoto, and Meredith (1970; see also Matsumoto, Meredith, and Masuda 1970) constructed a fifty-item, Likert-scaled questionnaire for Japanese Americans, which was administered in Seattle and Honolulu. While the authors refer to it as an ethnic-identity questionnaire, it actually contains items on both acculturation and ethnic identity. No factoral or correlational analysis was attempted; therefore, little can be said about the relationship between items. From an item-by-item analysis comparing generations, the authors conclude that there is a "graded erosion" of Japanese traits over the three generations, but considerable retention of ethnicity even by third-generation (Sansei) individuals. A subsequent study of Japanese Americans in Sacramento by Connor (1977), using the questionnaire created by Masuda, Matsumoto, and Meredith (1970), is more explicit in distinguishing between the concepts of acculturation and ethnic identity; it also concludes that while acculturation occurs from generation to generation, the Sansei retain significant ethnic identification.

Dashefsky and Shapiro (1974) are more specifically concerned with ethnic identity in their study of American Jews in St. Paul. They constructed a Jewish Identification Scale, beginning with thirty-one Likert-scaled items measuring attitudes toward Jewish life and Jewish people. Factor analysis produced a seven-item scale that is strongly correlated with selected acculturation measures. The study indicates that Jewish ethnic identity declines somewhat from the father's generation to the son's generation, but the majority of sons interviewed maintain some Jewish identity.

Acculturation is the focus of a study of Cuban Americans in Miami by Szapocznik et al. (1978). In making the assumption that there are at least two distinct dimensions of acculturation (behavioral acculturation and value acculturation), Szapocznik et al. developed two scales, subjecting the items to factor analysis. The twenty-four-item self-reported behaviors scale loaded on a single factor. The value scale was much less successful. Twenty-two items were created, tapping the five value dimensions outlined by Kluckhohn and Strodtbeck (1961). Only one value dimension made up of ten items proved significant in the factor analysis, and this accounts for only 13.5 percent of the total factor variance compared to 48.1 percent accounted for by the behavioral factor. The behavioral factor is related to age and male sex. Both the behavior and value scales are related to years spent in the U.S. The scales are intercorrelated ($r=.57$, $p<.0001$), and Szapocznik et al. conclude that behavioral and value acculturation are "parallel processes."

Prompted by Szapocznik et al.'s work on Americanization, Garcia and Lega (1979) developed a complimentary scale testing the degree of Cubanness in two populations in Miami and New Jersey. Although they refer to it as a Cuban Ethnic Identity Questionnaire, it is more concerned with acculturation and the knowledge of Cuban cultural traits than with self-identity and attitudes. The eight-item Likert scale loads on a single factor that accounts for 89.5 percent of the common-factor variance. The factor is related to age upon arrival in the U.S., number of years spent in the U.S., and Cuban neighborhood density.

Like Szapocznik et al., Teske and Nelson (1973) also conceptualize value and behavioral components in their study of Mexican American identity. As constructed, the two scales (referred to as an Identity Index and Interaction or Behavior Index) appear to represent the dimensions of ethnic identity and acculturation. The Identity Index consists of sixteen Likert-scaled items, and the Interaction Index consists of nineteen Likert-scaled items. Because factor analysis was not employed, no conclusions can be drawn about the internal relationship of items. The two scales are significantly correlated ($r=.64$, $p<.0005$). Comparison with independent judges' scores of respondents' identification as Mexican American indicates significant correlation with both scales.

Clark, Kaufman, and Pierce (1976; see also Pierce, Clark, and Kiefer 1972 and Pierce, Clark, and Kaufman 1978) have undertaken the most comprehensive examination of acculturation and ethnic identity to date. Beginning with the concept of acculturation, Clark, Kaufman, and Pierce conceptualized three distinct components:

cognitive, attitudinal, and behavioral. A picture-cognitive scale was developed for Mexican American and Japanese American samples, which measured knowledge of Anglo American and traditional ethnic cultural items. The resulting Acculturative Balance Scale (ABS) produces a ratio of traditional (Mexican American items=8 and Japanese American items=7) to Anglo (11 items) cultural knowledge. In both ethnic groups, the ABS is highly related to generation, but unrelated to age and education. Attitudinal acculturation was to be measured with questions based on Kluckhohn and Strodtbeck's (1961) value orientations. Statistical analysis of the data yielded no consistent patterns, however, and the value orientation scale was omitted from subsequent analysis.

Clark, Kaufman, and Pierce's (1976) behavioral component was designed to measure ethnic behavior and attitudes. Ten variables were submitted to cluster analysis, and two dimensions emerged. The first dimension, Traditional Orientation, indicates the degree to which the individual behaves ethnically (in language, religious affiliation, and so on), while the second dimension, Anglo Face, reflects feelings toward own-group and an objective judgment of ethnic identification. Clark, Kaufman, and Pierce find that while ABS and Traditional Orientation are related to generation, Anglo Face is not. Construction of a typology of Six Ethnic Identity Types indicates that within each of the three generations sampled, there are two possible patterns of ethnic identification. For the first generation, the difference is primarily in Traditional Orientation; immigrants in general, who are less Americanized but positive about their American ethnicity, differ in their tendency either to retain their traditional culture or to discard it. For the second and third generations, Anglo Face is the salient dimension; the native born are generally more Americanized and less traditional, differing most in whether they choose to identify with their own ethnic group or with the dominant Anglo American group. The authors suggest several factors that might affect this selection process. While the sample is unfortunately quite small (twenty-seven Mexican Americans and twenty-two Japanese Americans), the items measuring each dimension are few in number, and there is no indication of the intercorrelation of the three scales. Clark, Kaufman, and Pierce's study is the first to demonstrate with empirical, quantitative measures the distinction between acculturation and ethnic identity.

Development of the Model

We began our research with the assumption that at least two processes of cultural orientation and change exist among Mexican Americans. We call these cultural awareness and ethnic loyalty. Cultural awareness refers to an individual's knowledge of cultural traits (for example, language, history, culture heroes) of the traditional and host cultures. Ethnic loyalty is the preference for one cultural orientation and ethnic group rather than another. These two concepts correspond in many ways to those of acculturation and ethnic identity, as described above and in chapter 2. We believed that the two concepts were obviously related because it is impossible to prefer the traits of one culture rather than those of another culture unless there exists, to some extent, an awareness of both cultural systems. However, a person might not necessarily choose to identify with the culture with which he/she is most familiar. The phenomenon of revitalization, for example, refers to the conscious re-creation of cultural traditions that have declined or disappeared (Wallace 1956). In other words, it should be possible to identify two relatively separate, though interrelated, processes of culture change.

Secondly, we assumed that culture change is multidimensional. That is, change may occur at different rates in different spheres of cultural activity. For example, an immigrant may learn to speak English after living only a few years in the U.S. and adopt American standards of behavior, but continue to identify as *mexicano* for all of his/her life. In order to more fully understand the complex process of culture change, it is necessary to tap several cultural and ethnic-loyalty spheres simultaneously.

During Phase Two of the study, we developed a questionnaire with items in five cultural spheres, each having features of awareness and loyalty. The five cultural spheres include: (1) language familiarity and usage, (2) cultural heritage, (3) ethnic pride and identity, (4) ethnic interaction, and (5) interethnic distance and perceived discrimination. Other spheres could be identified, but we chose to develop these five, which we felt were probably among the most important for culture change.

The section on language familiarity and usage asked questions about the respondent's knowledge of Spanish and English, and the respondent's preference in using one language or another in different situations. The section on cultural heritage contained questions on the respondent's knowledge of Mexican cultural symbols, historical events, and contemporary personalities; the respondent's cultural inheritance and contact with Mexico; and the respondent's perception of life in Mexico and preference for Mexican food. The section on ethnic pride and identity asked for the respondent's ethnic identification, preferred first name and children's first names, and perception of Mexican culture. The fourth section, ethnic interaction, contained questions concerning the ethnicity of the respondent's peers during childhood and adolescence and the respondent's present associates. The final section evaluated the respondent's perceived ethnic-group discrimination and perceived personal discrimination as well as the respondent's preference for the ethnicity of associates.

In addition to examining the respondent's personal characteristics, the questionnaire also covered the respondent's familial cultural context, since it was assumed that parents and spouse contribute to the respondent's cultural awareness. Each of the cultural spheres—except interethnic distance and perceived discrimination—contained questions about the cultural awareness and ethnic loyalty of parents and spouse. Thus, the respondent was asked about the parents' and spouse's knowledge of and preference for Spanish and English, contact with Mexico, legal and preferred first names, and ethnic identification.

As finally conceived, the questionnaire contained 185 items tapping the five cultural spheres. There were 108 items grouped as measuring 18 cultural awareness concepts, and 77 items grouped as measuring 15 ethnic loyalty concepts. Each item was scaled in the direction of Mexican cultural awareness and ethnic loyalty, so that a high score reflected awareness of or loyalty to the Mexican culture and people.

The questionnaire was administered to all of the Phase Two respondents. Among those respondents whose generational level could be specified with certainty, 144 are first-generation immigrants, 85 are second generation, and 27 and 20 are third and fourth generation, respectively. In addition, a mixed second-generation sample is identified. Respondents falling into this category have one parent who is first generation, while the second parent is second- or later-generation Mexican American. A total of 45 cases fall into this mixed second-generation grouping.

Data from the awareness and loyalty questionnaire were factor analyzed. The statistical techniques employed in the factor analysis are more thoroughly described in appendix 1. The results support empirically our theoretical model of cultural orientation and change. Two superfactors emerged, which we labeled "Cultural Awareness" and "Ethnic Loyalty". Cultural Awareness is composed of five lower-order factors: Respondent's Cultural Heritage (RCH), Language Preference (LP), Spouse's Cultural Heritage (SCH), Parent's Cultural Heritage (PCH), and Cultural Identification (CI). The Ethnic Loyalty factor is composed of two lower-order factors: Perceived Discrimination (PD) and Ethnic Pride and Affiliation (EPA). Another factor, Ethnic Social Orientation (ESO), was found to load on both the Cultural Awareness and Ethnic Loyalty factors. A list of the 136 questions contributing to the eight factors can be found in appendix 2.

As we had originally conceptualized, the Cultural Awareness factor reflects an individual's familiarity with the Mexican people and culture through their parents' and spouse's experience as well as his/her own past experience. In addition, it reflects certain preferences in language use, identification with group names (for example, "Mexican American," "Chicano"), and national orientation to Mexico versus the U.S.—all of which appear to develop from cultural background circumstances rather than resulting from emotionally laden choices.

The Ethnic Loyalty factor, on the other hand, reflects perceptions and preferences that arise from more individually shaped interpretations about cultural groups. This factor involves an individual's attitudes and feelings concerning Mexican culture, people of Mexican descent, and ethnic discrimination. Our data demonstrate that these attitudinal qualities are not necessarily associated with any of the aspects of the individual's cultural experience that are tapped by the Cultural Awareness factor. These qualities are, rather, the mental construct—the symbolic reality, if you will—which individuals *create* concerning their ethnicity.

The emergence of the unique patterning of the Ethnic Social Orientation factor gives an indication that a third process operates along with Cultural Awareness and Ethnic Loyalty in culture change. In referring to the tendency to interact with others of Mexican descent and to prefer ethnic foods, Ethnic Social Orientation taps

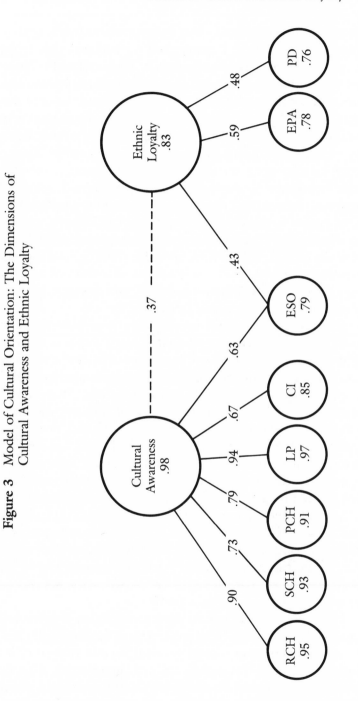

Figure 3 Model of Cultural Orientation: The Dimensions of Cultural Awareness and Ethnic Loyalty

aspects of social assimilation and correlates with both Cultural Awareness and Ethnic Loyalty; and yet it is uniquely shaped, suggesting that while social assimilation is interrelated with acculturation and ethnic identification, it is a distinctive process. Due to the emergence of this process and its uniqueness, we devote considerable attention to the social context of ethnicity in the following chapters.

The two superfactors—Cultural Awareness and Ethnic Loyalty—along with their associated lower-order factors, are depicted in figure 3. In addition, the correlation coefficients between the lower-order factors and Cultural Awareness and Ethnic Loyalty are shown along the connecting lines, while the reliability coefficients for each factor are located within the circles. As can be seen, the individual factors are highly reliable in terms of internal consistency with four of the scales (RCH, SCH, PCH, and LP), yielding coefficients equal to or greater than .90. The correlation between the Cultural Awareness and Ethnic Loyalty dimensions is .37, which suggests that the two dimensions are independent of each other.

To assess how the dimensions of Cultural Awareness and Ethnic Loyalty vary between generational levels of respondents, each of the eight scales was standardized to a mean of 50 and a standard deviation of 10. Then, the mean of the five scales associated with Cultural Awareness was obtained for each generational level. Similarly, the mean of the two scales constituting Ethnic Loyalty was obtained for each generational level. Since the Ethnic Social Orientation scale loaded on both Cultural Awareness and Ethnic Loyalty, it was not averaged into the composite scaled score for either of these two superfactors, but is pictured separately. The mean scale scores were then plotted by generational level, and are presented in figure 4.

As can be seen in figure 4, the largest decrease in Cultural Awareness (CA) occurs between the first and second generation, and thereafter continues to decrease steadily through the fourth generation. Interestingly, the second mixed generation shows a Cultural Awareness score that falls midway between the second and third generation, just as one might predict.

The more interesting data depicted in figure 4 pertain to Ethnic Loyalty (EL). As seen in figure 4, Ethnic Loyalty decreases slightly between the first and second generation, and thereafter it remains virtually constant through the fourth generation. This finding is extremely important because it demonstrates that culture change is

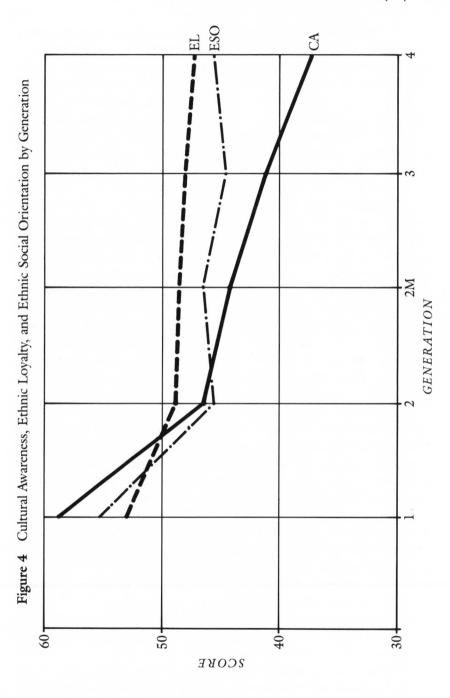

Figure 4   Cultural Awareness, Ethnic Loyalty, and Ethnic Social Orientation by Generation

not a simple unilinear dimension, as suggested by earlier investigators. In fact, the loss of Cultural Awareness on the part of our respondents is at least partially independent of Ethnic Loyalty, which explains why it is not uncommon to meet a third- or fourth-generation Mexican American who does not speak Spanish and knows relatively little about his/her cultural background, but retains pride in his/her Mexican heritage and enjoys associating with Mexican people. This phenomenon is not unique to Mexican Americans, for it is found among members of many ethnic communities throughout the world.

To understand more fully how awareness and loyalty interact with generational level, mean scores on each of the eight lower-order factor scales were obtained by generation. Notable and deserving of comment in the findings is the sharp continuous decrease by generational level for three of the five scales associated with the dimension of Cultural Awareness: Respondent's Cultural Heritage, Parent's Cultural Heritage, and Language Preference. Clearly, the attributes of culture measured by each of these three scales decrease with succeeding generations, and are lowest by the fourth generation. For the other two scales, (Spouse's Cultural Heritage and Cultural Identification), the loss in Cultural Awareness occurs only from the first to the second generation, and leveling out in subsequent generations.

More interesting still are the findings for the two subscales of the Ethnic Loyalty dimension: Perceived Discrimination and Ethnic Pride and Affiliation. Results on the two subscales show no decrease across generations. In other words, both first-generation Mexicans and fourth-generation Mexican Americans are likely to score high on personal and group perceived discrimination. Similarly, ethnic pride and affiliation among third- and fourth-generation individuals does not differ from that observed in immigrants, even though individuals among the later generations do not possess nearly the same degree of cultural knowledge as their immigrant counterparts.

The Ethnic Social Orientation scale shows a decrease between the first and second generations, followed by a leveling out in subsequent generations. An interesting feature here is that even third- and fourth-generation individuals continue to associate primarily with members of their own ethnic group.

To summarize, the results show that cultural change is an orderly process that occurs between immigrants and their later generational offspring. Factor analysis also indicates that Cultural Awareness is the more general component of culture change. Cultural Awareness reflects Cultural Heritage (of respondent, spouse, and parents) as well as Language Preference, Cultural Identification, and Ethnic Social Orientation. Ethnic Loyalty is derived from fewer items tapping Ethnic Pride and Affiliation, Perceived Discrimination, and some aspects of Ethnic Social Orientation. The two factors correspond to the concepts of acculturation and ethnic identity, which are separate but interrelated processes; this correspondence is demonstrated by the isolation of the two superfactors, which nonetheless remain somewhat intercorrelated. Further, the multidimensionality of cultural change is proven, as is the ability to show quantitative changes in cultural orientation across generations.

A description of the "ideal" types implied by our model is helpful in understanding the general concepts employed at the individual level. Individuals with a high degree of Cultural Awareness have a heritage deeply rooted in Mexican culture, which is also true of their parents and spouses. It is manifested by their knowledge of, their contact and identification with, and their preference for Mexico, Mexican culture, and the Spanish language. Concomitantly, the United States, American culture, and the English language figure less importantly in their lives. These individuals grew up interacting with others of Mexican descent, and their primary relations continue to be with Mexican people. Individuals of low Cultural Awareness, on the other hand, know little of Mexican culture or of the Spanish language, and culturally are more American. They have had little contact with Mexico, tend to prefer life in the U.S. to life in Mexico, and identify as American in some way. Their parents and spouses are also more American than Mexican in their cultural heritage and identification. Individuals revealing low Cultural Awareness are more likely to have interacted with Anglos as a child and to have some Anglos as friends and neighbors at the time our research.

Individuals with a high degree of Ethnic Loyalty are characterized by their sense of pride in Mexican culture, their preference for being with others of Mexican descent, and their heightened perception of discrimination against Mexican people in the U.S. They are also likely to have Mexican friends and neighbors and to frequent places where people of Mexican descent gather. In contrast, individuals with a low degree of Ethnic Loyalty reveal no significant pride in their Mexican heritage, nor do they show any preference for or great likelihood of moving among Mexican people. Furthermore, they perceive little or no discrimination against Mexicans in the U.S.

A Typology of Mexican American Ethnic Orientation

In order to construct a typology that would simultaneously take into account both Cultural Awareness and Ethnic Loyalty, a cluster analysis of cases was conducted. The basic statistical procedure involved the empirical classification of our respondents into more or less homogenous groups (or "clusters") according to the locus of their scores on a two-dimensional space defined by the Cultural Awareness and Ethnic Loyalty second-order factors.

The results of the cluster analysis reveal five well-defined and homogenous clusters (or types). Table 4 shows the number of cases in the clusters as well as the mean Cultural Awareness and Ethnic Loyalty scores for all of the cases in each cluster. Respondents in Type I are characterized by their high scores on both Cultural Awareness and Ethnic Loyalty. Type II individuals have high scores on

Table 4   Results of Cluster Analysis Based on Awareness and Loyalty Scores

| | Cluster Size | | Cultural Awareness[b] | Ethnic Loyalty[b] |
| | Total | N = 370[a] | | |
Cluster	N	%	Mean	Mean
Type I	94	25	59	59
Type II	50	14	59	47
Type III	129	35	46	51
Type IV	78	21	44	42
Type V	19	5	30	41

Source: Second Mexican American survey. Adapted from Padilla (1980).

[a]Eleven cases could not be clustered because of missing Cultural Awareness and/or Ethnic Loyalty scores.

[b]Based on a normalized mean of 50 and a standard deviation of 10.

Cultural Awareness, but only average scores on Ethnic Loyalty. Type III includes individuals with average scores on Cultural Awareness and Ethnic Loyalty and who make up a modal type. Type IV is characterized by individuals who have moderately low scores on both Cultural Awareness and Ethnic Loyalty. Finally, Type V individuals score very low on Cultural Awareness and moderately low on Ethnic Loyalty.

The five types offer some idea of the relationship between acculturation and ethnic identity as they are manifested in individuals. Respondents in Type I are clearly unacculturated and identify as Mexicans and with Mexican culture. They demonstrate high Mexican Cultural Awareness and Ethnic Loyalty and little affinity with Anglo culture. As we will soon see, many first-generation individuals fall into this category. However, first-generation status is not a necessary condition for inclusion. Type V individuals, who represent the other extreme in our typology, are highly Anglicized and possess very little knowledge of or identity with Mexican culture; and, notably, very few of our respondents (5 percent) fit into this category of high acculturation and low ethnic identity. Type III individuals, who constitute the largest group, represent a modal type with a moderate amount of Mexican Cultural Awareness and Ethnic Loyalty and some knowledge of Anglo culture. While they might be considered "bicultural" by some because of their ability to interact in both Mexican and Anglo cultural spheres, it is significant that they retain their ethnic identity and are conscious of their Mexican heritage.

Types II and IV are more difficult to interpret. Both of these clusters differ from their respective preceding cluster in the typology, primarily due to a lower Ethnic Loyalty score. Type II individuals are as unacculturated as those in Type I, but they identify only moderately with their ethnic group. Type IV individuals are only somewhat more acculturated than the modal Type III, but they identify much less with others of Mexican descent. In fact, their mean Ethnic Loyalty score is almost the same as that of the most acculturated individuals in Type V. Types II and IV illustrate the multilineal rather than unilineal nature of the process of culture change. There is no neat correlation between acculturation and ethnic identity, which seem to vary somewhat independently. If we go further in our interpretation of the cluster-analysis results in table 4, it appears that ethnic identity declines before the process of acculturation begins in earnest, but acculturation proceeds to an extreme low level of awareness of the traditional culture while ethnic identity appears to be more consciously maintained (see figure 3). The relationship between Cultural Awareness and Ethnic Loyalty will be examined more thoroughly in chapter 8; we simply summarize here by pointing out that the vast majority of our respondents (74 percent) are bicultural or unacculturated individuals who retain moderate or high ethnic identity.

Factors Related to Cluster Types

Generation is strongly related to all five cluster types. To interpret more fully this relationship, a descriptive breakdown by generation is provided in table 5. It is clear that Types I and II consist mostly of first-generation immigrants; Types III and IV are primarily native-born Mexican Americans; and Type V tends to be at least third

Table 5 Breakdown of Percentage of Cluster Types by Generation and Education

			Clusters		
Descriptive Variables	Type I (N = 94) %	Type II (N = 50) %	Type III (N = 129) %	Type IV (N = 78) %	Type V (N = 19) %
Generation					
First	79	86	18	16	0
Second	12	14	58	63	22
Third	9	0	24	21	78
Total	100	100	100	100	100
Education					
0–8 grades	74	74	30	26	5
9–11 grades	16	14	33	23	37
12 grades	10	8	23	37	42
College	0	4	14	14	16
Total	100	100	100	100	100

Source: Second Mexican American survey.

generation. Considering percentages across rows rather than down columns, 22 percent of the immigrants are classified as Type III or IV, and 13 percent of the third generation fall into Type I. In other words, generation is a significant predictor of cluster type, but it is not absolute. In large part, this is the result of the relatively low correlation of Ethnic Loyalty with generation (see chapter 8).

All but Type V are related to the indicators of socioeconomic status; Type I is more likely to be lower status, while Types III and IV are higher status. Interestingly, Type V is not highly correlated with the socioeconomic variables except for the factor of education. Table 5 indicates, in descriptive terms, the relationship between the clusters and education. Individuals in Types I and II tend to have less than nine years of education, reflecting their immigrant status and their education in Mexico. Types III and IV are much better educated and tend to have at least nine years of education, with one-third to one-half graduating from high school. No similar advancement is registered for Type V, however; only a few have extremely low educational levels, but also relatively few have had any college education. It would appear that the influence of an American education is most important in the initial drop in awareness, and is less important in any further decline.

As can be seen in table 6, the indicators of socioeconomic mobility show lower correlations than those of socioeconomic status with the cluster types. Only Type I is very significantly related to mobility, and the relationship is negative ($r = -.20$, $p < .001$). Similarly, no strong associations appear between cluster types and religion, urban background, age, or sex. However, *barrio* residence is positively correlated with the two unacculturated cluster types and negatively correlated with the two most acculturated types.

In sum, the following picture emerges of the five cluster types. Type I tends to be first generation, especially immigrants who arrived in the U.S. as adults or who have been in the U.S. less than fifteen years. Type I is also likely to be lower class (57 percent are laborers), less educated, less socioeconomically mobile; and they are likely to live in *barrios* (84 percent). Type II tends to have similar characteristics largely because of the corresponding predominance of immigrants. This type is also likely to be lower class (48 percent laborers), less educated, and *barrio* residents (73 percent).

The other three cluster types differ from these two types, primarily due to the predominance of native-born individuals. Type III is likely to be second generation, better educated, and higher in socioeconomic status (20 percent have heads of household in white-collar occupations). Type IV also tends to be second generation, but these individuals have experienced more socioeconomic mobility and have relatively higher levels of education and occupational status (30 percent white collar) than Type III. Type IV is somewhat more likely to be Protestant (18 percent) and tends to live outside the *barrio* (69 percent). Finally, Type V is likely to be third or later generation, to live outside the *barrio* (68 percent), and to have an urban background. Type V is somewhat more educated than the other cluster types, but this does not translate into higher occupa-

Table 6   Pearson Correlation Coefficients for Clusters

	Type I	Type II	Clusters Type III	Type IV	Type V
Descriptive Variables	*r*	*r*	*r*	*r*	*r*
Generation	−.33***	−.33***	.25***	.15**	.35***
Socioeconomic Status					
Respondent's education	−.40***	−.29***	.26***	.27***	.18***
Family income	−.15**	−.15**	.09	.13**	.06
Head of household occupation	−.30***	−.14**	.13**	.22***	.10*
Head of household SEI[a]	−.28***	−.13**	.13**	.19***	.11*
Socioeconomic Mobility					
SEI change, first job to present	−.19***	−.08	.08	.14**	.06
SEI change, father's job to son's	−.20***	−.06	.12*	.14*	−.02
Religion					
Catholic	.08	.04	.00	−.14**	.04
Protestant	−.06	−.02	−.04	.15**	−.03
Agnostic/atheist	−.07	−.05	.11*	.00	−.03
Barrio residence	.31***	.11**	−.05	−.29***	−.13**
Urban background	−.09*	−.08	.03	.07	.12**
Age	−.01	.07	.02	−.02	−.10*
Female sex	.00	.10*	−.07	.00	.01

Source: Second Mexican American survey.
[a]Duncan's Socioeconomic Index (SEI).
Significance levels: .05*, .01**, .001***.

tional status (26 percent white collar), higher income, or greater socioeconomic mobility.

How do these results compare with the previously described quantitative studies? First of all, our research further supports the assumption that acculturation and ethnic identification are concepts that can be measured and analyzed in a quantitative manner. Moreover, like Clark, Kaufman, and Pierce (1976), we find that acculturation and ethnic identity are distinct processes which are nonetheless interdependent. Individuals can be categorized into cluster types that range from unacculturated/high ethnic identity to acculturated/low ethnic identity. But as both Clark, Kaufman, and Pierce's (1976) study and our own demonstrate, these clusters do not form a unilineal continuum because of the uneven character of ethnic identity. Third, while our data indicate the same decline in awareness of the traditional culture as was found by the other studies reviewed, it is important to observe that acculturation is a very gradual process, and the vast majority of our diverse sample retains considerable ethnic-specific knowledge. The acculturation process is neither as rapid nor as complete as many researchers have presented it.

Lastly, our findings concerning the relationship of ethnic identity and acculturation differ from those of Clark, Kaufman, and Pierce (1976). Whereas these researchers find no difference in ethnic identity between their two most unacculturated types, it is between our two most unacculturated types (Clusters I and II) that we find the greatest difference in loyalty scores. Furthermore, our statistical analysis did not produce the types found in the Clark, Kaufman, and Pierce study, in which individuals were acculturated and yet chose to identify strongly with their traditional culture and ethnic group. Perhaps this is the result of differences in sample populations, the items used to measure acculturation and ethnic identity, or the type of data analysis employed. In any case, our study supports the possibility of this combination occurring, given the distinct nature of acculturation and ethnic identity. It simply does not appear to have been very common among our respondents.

The Case Studies

In order to understand better the complex dynamics of culture change and ethnic-group shift among our Chicano respondents, we turn our attention to case studies of eleven respondents who were interviewed extensively during Phase Three of our study. These eleven cases are representative of the five cluster types just described. Table 7 presents a summary of the major demographic characteristics of each of the respondents, along with an indication of their cluster type. The table serves as a useful guide to individuals' generation and education. Information about spouses is also presented because of the importance of the spouse in much of the material to be presented in the case descriptions.

The next three chapters are devoted entirely to an in-depth analysis of these eleven respondents. In chapter 5, we take up the Mexican Ethnics, which include Types 1 and 2; while chapter 6 discusses Cultural Blends, which correspond to our Type 3. Finally, in chapter 7, we consider the situation of "Americans . . . Set Apart," who comprise our Types 4 and 5.

Table 7   Descriptive Characteristics of Mexican American Case Studies

Name	Age	Generation	Years of Education	Spouse's Generation	Spouse's Education	Cluster Type
1. Carmen Muñoz	54	1	4	1	3	I
2. Dolores Guerrero	36	4	13	3	4	I
3. Hermila Gutierrez	34	1	8	2	12	II
4. Rosa Hernández	30	1	8	D	D	II
5. Magadalena Rivera	37	2	8	D	D	III
6. Anthony Reyes	36	2	18	A	16	III
7. Anna Fuentes	23	2	14	2	12	III
8. Celia Torres	35	2M	12	1	10	IV
9. Catarina Machado	52	2	10	2	12	IV
10. Kathy Marquez	31	2	9	3	9	V
11. Margaret Camacho	30	4–Mother A–Father	10	3	10	V

Note: D = Divorced; A = Anglo; M = Mixed Generation.

5

Mexican Ethnics

THE CASE STUDIES PRESENTED HERE are summaries of many hours of tape recordings made with our informants. They have been prepared to give the reader a flavor for the person's background and current life circumstances. Because the case studies presented are arranged by cluster type, we have tried to set down information that best illustrates the features exemplified by the various types that emerged from the statistical analysis. In many places, we use the informant's exact words to make a point or to highlight an important attitude or contradiction. By reading these case studies, the reader will derive an appreciation for the complexity involved in understanding how our informants interpret ethnicity, culture, intergroup relations, and adaptation to a different culture.

The uniqueness of this study of ethnicity, unlike other quantitative works, is that we made every effort to go beyond the mere survey questionnaire. We studied the historical record of each of our three community sites to understand the pattern of intergroup contact and relations. We also studied each community and its social institutions, as they currently exist, to understand how our informants fit into their respective communities. The immediate neighborhood surrounding an informant's place of residence was important. We were almost as interested in the informants' neighbors and friends as we were in the informants themselves. Our goal in doing in-depth interviews with informants was to collect as much qualitative data as possible, data that could subsequently be used to enrich our statistical profile of culture change in the Chicano communities studied.

In order not to bias our qualitative data, all interviewing was conducted *before* we analyzed our survey data. It was only sometime after we completed our interviews that we began in earnest our statistical analysis of the survey data. Once the analysis was complete, and we had derived the cluster typology discussed in chapter 4, we returned to our interviews to identify informants by type based on their scores on the Cultural Awareness and Ethnic Loyalty scales. Working in this fashion assured us that our interviews were as standardized across informants as is possible under such circumstances.

As we will show, what emerges from the interviews is the relative importance our informants give to ethnicity, culture, intergroup relations, and adaptation to Anglo norms. Some of what our case-study informants said is not surprising and conforms to our common-sense understanding of what people think and do when they confront contrasting cultural values and practices. At the same time, other things said by our informants are surprising and unexpected. The case studies reflect the individuality of our informants.

In this chapter, we present four case studies representing the first two cluster types described in chapter 4. Two cases per type are described to give some indication of both the similarities and differences between individuals in each category. All of these individuals are referred to by pseudonyms. As is evident from the case material in the following chapters, there is noticeable variation in ethnic orientation both within and between the five types. Nevertheless, the individual cases bear out the general patterns elicited from the cluster analysis, and serve to validate the statistical types derived from the analysis.

La Raza

Carmen Muñoz

Carmen Muñoz is a fifty-four-year-old housewife with seven children. She was born in Hermosillo in the state of Sonora, Mexico, where she received five years of schooling. She has been in the United States for twenty-two years, living mostly in Santa Barbara. She was married, for the second time, sixteen years ago. Her husband, Miguel, who is seven years her junior, is a cook at a large restaurant in town. Born in Michoacán, Mexico, he has been in the U.S. for nearly thirty years. Carmen's life has been filled with hardship and hard work, but she claims to enjoy her family and cherishes her youngest "baby," born to her late in her life. Although during the interview period, she appeared depressed because of her failing health, she was hospitable and friendly, as expressive in discussing her hardships and despairs as in discussing her joys. To Carmen, the struggle to keep body and soul together is the focus of life; ethnicity is of little conscious concern to her.

The Muñoz family lives in a two-bedroom home in a middle-class neighborhood with mostly Anglo residents. The house could use a coat of paint, but seems to be in good repair. Inside, the carpet is old, and the furniture is well worn but covered with attractive scarfs. Throughout the house are religious statues and pictures, mostly of Mexican saints such as the *Virgen de Guadalupe* and *San Martín de Porres*.

Both Carmen and Miguel identify as "*mexicano*," as do all of their children; and there does not appear to be any ambiguity in this identification. Although her English is good for a first-generation person, Carmen feels much more comfortable in her native Spanish. The interviews, therefore, were conducted in both languages, but primarily in Spanish. The children's language ability ranges from dominant Spanish, with very little English, to bilingual. Carmen prefers Spanish-speaking radio and television and Mexican music and food. She always had Mexican music playing on the radio or phonograph during the interviews, and often there would be *chorizo* and beans or *cocido* (Mexican stew) cooking on the stove. Carmen's knowledge of Mexican traditions and customs is naturally extensive, especially regarding Mexican national and religious holidays. In contrast, she knows relatively little about U.S. holidays and customs, even after having lived in California for twenty-two years.

While she professes to have little difficulty in relating to Anglos such as her nearby neighbors, Carmen has very distinct ideas about the differences between the two ethnic groups. A major difference she sees lies in the relationship between neighbors. People in the U.S., she believes, are more isolated and unfriendly. She states:

> In Mexico, our neighborhood was more or less like this one. But it was different because the neighbors there treat you more cordially, more friendly. Here, you shut your doors, you shut your

windows and here is where you live. This is your world. In Mexico, life is not the same. It is different, more friendly and charita-
ble. It is more—more—how can I put it? They visit you; they
greet you. Here, no. If you go out and a neighbor is working in
his yard and you are working in your yard, never does anyone
say "good afternoon, how are you?" The people here, when you
go to their door, they say "yes?" They don't say "Come in. What
can I offer you? How can I help you?" The people here are very
distinta [different].

During this same interview, Carmen goes on to relate an experience when she was kept on the porch waiting, while a neighbor tried
to locate by phone the household where both of their daughters were
playing. This, she says, occurred after she had sent over cookies and
fruit several times because her own daughter spends so much time at
the neighbor's house. It is difficult to know whether discrimination
plays a role in the relations between Carmen and her neighbors. The
neighborhood is not predominantly Mexican or Mexican American,
but a large number come from this background. In fact, Carmen says
she finds discriminatory behavior among persons of Mexican descent
as well. She jokes that if you lived alone in this country and happened
to die, no one would find you for days.

Another major difference that Carmen sees between Mexicans
("*La Raza*") and Anglos (whom she refers to as "*gringos*") is related
to daily habits and diet. Actually, her distinction is primarily between
people in Mexico and people in the United States, as she chided the
interviewer (a Mexican American woman) on some of these points.
She believes that "*comida mexicana*" (Mexican food) is distinct from
every other cuisine in the world. In addition, she maintains that the
strength Mexicans have is directly due to their diet.

In Mexico, people work hard—with their hands. They sweat
and breath hard. Here, no. Everyone is comfortable. If you eat
like a Mexican, you will feel better. People think that is has to
make you fat. Beans are not fattening, without grease, in *la olla*
(the kettle). They give you energy. Here they eat a hamburger or
a hot dog. But it is very good for you, Mexican food. Here, I
have some food cooking now, have some.

She goes on to talk of the various ways that she cooks Mexican food
and how it gives one energy. She scoffs at her husband's doctor, who

gives Miguel monthly vitamin shots. She states that "*Los mexicanos no necesitamos vitaminas. Las vitaminas de nosotros son de frijoles, claro!*" ("Mexicans don't need vitamins. Our vitamins come from beans, that's true!"). She jokes that the doctor's shots are "*pura agua!*" (pure water).

Lastly, Carmen believes that the Mexican people are generally stronger and can endure more than Anglos. She believes that the strongest families are Mexican families. In describing her days in San Diego, where she lived in crowded quarters, near her sister after first immigrating to the U.S., she says, "Mexicans are different. Americans would be unhappy, say that there wasn't enough room, and they wouldn't sleep on the floor!" She believes that Mexicans, on the whole, are more vigorous and alive than the more sedentary Americans.

In speaking of discrimination against Mexicans, Carmen agrees that it is prevalent in the schools, the social welfare offices, the police force, the immigration service, and the job market. She also agrees that persons of Mexican descent have to work harder to get ahead. However, she claims to never have experienced discrimination personally in any of these areas; this is understandable because her primary social network involves her own children and others of Mexican descent who speak Spanish. Also, she admits that she prefers parties, neighborhoods, and her family to include only persons of Mexican descent.

Carmen is unmistakably Mexican in her traditions, daily habits, and values. Although she has been unable to visit Mexico and her relatives and friends there since she emigrated twenty-two years ago, she has retained her Mexican citizenship and possesses a strong identification as "Mexican" rather than "American." She has taught her children Mexican customs and the Spanish language. Carmen is proud of her heritage and finds Mexican culture and Mexican people superior to what she has encountered in the U.S. All of this remains true despite the irony of immigrating more than twenty years ago.

Dolores Guerrero

Dolores Guerrero is a thirty-six-year-old woman who has been married over sixteen years and has three children. Although she was born in El Paso, Texas, she has lived most of her life in Oxnard. Her parents and grandparents were born in United States border towns, thus making her a fourth-generation Mexican American. She works as a part-time clerk in a local variety store. Her husband, Joe, is a blue-collar worker in an engineering firm. Joe is a third-generation Mexican American, born in California.

The lower-middle-income neighborhood where Dolores lives is in the better part of the *Colonia*. Its streets are lined with tract houses that have small patches of front and back yards, most of them well kept and fenced. The overwhelming majority of her neighbors are Mexican or Mexican American. Inside, her three-bedroom home is neat and straightened, but shows the wear of time and children.

Dolores and Joe have had chronic marital problems stemming in part from their different orientations to ethnicity. For example, while Dolores wants her children to learn Spanish as well as English, Joe does not. In Dolores's words, Joe says "when you're in the United States, you should talk right." Dolores and Joe also have difficulty in agreeing on, for example, where to go for a night out. They both enjoy dancing, but he is uncomfortable in the very Mexican places and she is uncomfortable in the "country-and-western *gabacho*-style places" that he likes to frequent. (*Gabacho* is a derogatory term for Anglo Americans.)

Joe, who does not like to be considered Mexican, often passes himself off as Indian. He tells of being a favored customer in a certain country-and-western bar, where the majority of the customers are Anglos and everyone considers him an Indian. When a Mexican entered once and racial slurs were made, he objected but was told that the remarks did not include Indians. He did not correct the misidentification. He tells his wife that if a person is more Anglo he has more of a chance to get ahead, and frequenting the Anglo bars offers more opportunities for what he calls "connections." Dolores and her neighbor, Helen, joke that they can't understand why he identifies as American, as he is darker skinned than both of them. Helen, who is also Dolores's *comadre*, claims that he is only fooling himself because most of his friends know he is Mexican. She says that people treat Mexicans the same, no matter what the person says he is.

In contrast to Joe, Dolores identifies as "Mexican." She does not identify as "Mexican American" because she perceives the term to mean that one is half Anglo. When asked by the interviewer if she felt more American or Mexican, she tried to explain her ethnic orientation:

I feel more Mexican. I don't know why. I just feel it. *Que hablo más inglés* sometimes but I still feel Mexican. I might act more *gabacho* style, but I feel Mexican. *¿Me entiendes?* My accent and my ways might be *gabacho* style but I only act that way. For example, I don't cook the real Mexican food. I barely know how to make tamales. I make spaghetti, you know. So, in a way, I'm living *gabacho* style.

Besides food, Dolores also feels that knowledge of the Spanish language is an important part of being Mexican, and it especially upsets her that her children do not know the language. She remembers a time when her boy was collecting for a fund raiser, and was told by a neighbor how shameful it was that he could not speak his own language. "*Me da vergüenza*" ("It shamed me"), she recalled. She also remembers being embarrassed at work when Spanish-speaking customers corrected her Spanish or when she could not understand their more correct usage. While she admonishes herself for not living up to her conception of a Mexican style of life, she appears to attribute the essence of being "Mexican" more to one's feelings or "*sentimientos.*"

Dolores's use of language is one of the distinctive aspects of her ethnic orientation. Although her primary language is English, the interview was conducted in a profuse mixture of both English and Spanish. "*Mi* doctor," "he was *muy enojado*," "style *de otro lado*," and "*me da* nervous" are typical examples of the many mixed phrases that she utilizes. Many of her conversations in English will include scattered Spanish sentences, and vice versa. English idioms are often adapted with slight variations; for example, "that cut the cake," "where there's a way, there's a will," and "I didn't go around the bush." In general, Dolores speaks neither language in a standard way, but she speaks both of them well enough to communicate with monolinguals in either language.

Dolores makes a sharp distinction between Mexicans and what she consistently calls "*gabachos.*" She views things as either *gabacho* style or Mexican style. According to her, *gabachos* do not get jealous; they are more simple; the men are not grouchy with girls; and they do not mind being sent from one place to another as Mexicans do. *Gabachos* have more patience and don't show their feelings as readily; "they're cold." "They're way different. *El modo de vivir*, the way they handle their problems. They take things more calm. Mexicans are more *corajudo* (angry)." She believes that Mexicans are more rowdy, more possessive of their wives; they show their feelings easily and often express jealousy by heading for the bars. However, she feels more comfortable in interacting with Mexicans or Mexican Americans, and hopes that her children will eventually marry within their ethnic group.

Despite Dolores's extended exposure to the Anglo world via the media, the educational system (she has attended junior college), and other carriers of culture, Dolores has never had any strong personal relationships with Anglos. Her friends have almost always been primarily Mexican and Mexican American, although in high school some of her friends were Black and Anglo. She recalls that the only time she dated an Anglo was a strange and uncomfortable experience. In her present social network, her coworkers are the only Anglos with whom she has frequent contacts. However, she does not socialize with them outside of work, and most of the other people in her personal network have not met them. In addition, she cannot recall the last time she visited an Anglo home, and remembers attending only one party where the host was Anglo. This affair was held in a bar by a friend of her husband whom she did not know. Because of factors like neighborhood composition and stability of interrelated social contacts, Dolores has maintained a social network consisting primarily of Mexicans and Mexican Americans, which contributes to her Mexican identity and her maintenance of many Mexican traits.

In any case, Dolores's knowledge of the Anglo cultural and social system is vastly superior to that of her friends and neighbors, and she often functions as a broker for them. Friends have asked her to call banks, insurance companies, and the immigration service for them and to handle paperwork that is giving them trouble. At tax time, she did the short tax form for many of her friends and neighbors. When one of her friend's children died, Dolores handled all of the funeral arrangements. Her access to information and her bilingual communication skills indicate how successfully she has acquired what is necessary to be able to function in Anglo society.

Dolores and her family have experienced many incidents of discrimination, both overt and subtle, in many areas and over many years. She remembers being called derogatory names in her elementary school in Texas, where the Mexican children were given separate classrooms with inferior desks and supplies. "We used to pick walnuts," she recalls, "and they would say that we used to stink like walnuts, so they kept Mexicans out of the *gabacho* part of school." When Dolores heard about a current interethnic conflict at the high school in Oxnard, she concluded that things had not changed much and there was still animosity between Mexican and Anglo students. She also perceived continuing institutional racism. A few years ago, her daughter's school bus struck a telephone pole. Most of the children on board were of Mexican descent. Several of the children suffered minor injuries, including her daughter whose neck was strained. The children were left at a nearby city bus stop and told to make their way home. Dolores feels that this would never have occurred if the passengers had been Anglo children. Later litigation resulted in small settlements for the parents, which she now interprets as a political compromise.

Dolores also reports several incidents at work that reflect what she feels is a widespread prejudice against Mexicans and Mexican Americans. When she first began work, she felt that her boss did not like Mexicans and had hired her only because he needed someone who was bilingual to help with Spanish-speaking customers. Recently, an Anglo truck driver had come into the store asking for an item that was unfamiliar to Dolores. Angered because she did not know what it was, he immediately began a crude tirade including references to her citizenship and her intelligence, calling her a "wetback" and other derogatory terms. He left when she threatened to call the police. The incident deeply upset her, and it remained a sensitive area for several weeks. "I have never, never in my life, been so humiliated," she said. "Never have I been cut down so low, like that."

Dolores perceives basic injustices in American society, in which essentially two ethnic groups, Anglos and Mexicans, are at odds, with the more powerful Anglos always succeeding. She has strong convictions about Anglo power:

> They have more privileges than we do. That's natural. You know very well if you go apply for a job, they're going to get it first. They have more privileges even if they know less. It's harder for a Mexican to make it. They can, but they have to be willing to

be stepped on. You can go to college and study, but the Anglos still get the job regardless.

While Dolores's roots as a fourth-generation, native-born American are in the United States and she has never visited Mexico beyond the border towns, Dolores does not feel American nor does she really know much about the day-to-day life of Anglo Americans. She identifies as "Mexican" and perceives a vast difference between Mexicans and "*gabachos*." Her intimate social life is spent almost exclusively with other Mexicans. Mexican culture has been diluted in Dolores's life, but she still values it more than Anglo American culture, and she certainly cannot be considered "Anglicized." Dolores is unacculturated in that sense, and it is apparent from her case that Mexican culture can change in the United States to something quite different which would not be more Anglo American. More will be said about this "third" emerging culture in chapter 11.

Changing Ethnics

Hermila Gutierrez

Hermila Gutierrez is a thirty-four-year-old housewife with four children. Born in Nuevo Laredo, Mexico, where she received eight years of schooling, she has been living in the United States, in Santa Barbara, for the fourteen years that she has been married. Recently, Hermila began a part-time job as a maid, and she now works one day a week. Her husband, Joseph, a second-generation Mexican American, was born in Los Angeles. He is employed as a mid-level civil servant, a job he has held for nearly twenty-two years. At forty-eight years of age, he is considerably older than Hermila. The Gutierrezes have had chronic marital problems, stemming in many ways from their intraethnic differences, and Hermila has sought professional help to cope with these problems (see Keefe 1982).

For the first thirteen years of their marriage, the Gutierrezes lived in an older, lower-middle-income neighborhood, where most of the residents are of Mexican descent. Recently, they purchased a home in a middle-income suburb, where almost all of their neighbors are Anglos. The furnishings in their home are sparse, and the decor offers no indication of the Gutierrezes' Mexican background. Hermila speaks only Spanish; she understands some English, but speaks only a few words. Having lived in Mexico over half her life, her knowledge of Mexican customs and traits is extensive, and she says that she feels Mexican, not American. In fact, one of the interesting things about Hermila's sense of ethnicity is her complete lack of awareness of its being measurable or having gradients. When asked if she thought that her parents were more "Mexican" than her, she responded:

> How can someone be more Mexican than another? We were all born in Mexico. I was born in Mexico, and that won't ever change. And I'm still a citizen there so I'm still a Mexican. Just because I live here doesn't mean that I am not Mexican. I have known people who try and say that they are American or that they are not Mexican. *Que tonterías* [what foolishness]! Just by living here doesn't change what you are.

When asked about what possible changes or situations she may have experienced that could have affected her feelings of being "Mexican" or "American," she answered patiently:

> I feel the same as I always have felt. I have felt some changes that have happened just because I have lived here [in the U.S.]. Obviously it is not the same as living in Mexico. It is natural to pick up American ways, but I feel like the same person basically. I feel the same as far as Mexicanness whether I am here or in Mexico. I feel Mexican in any situation. I am a citizen [of Mexico].

Some of the measures of her expression of her cultural background indicate a diversity in tastes and activities. She likes American foods in the same sense that an American might enjoy Mexican food. She is a devout Catholic and celebrates the Twelfth of December (the birthday of the *Virgen de Guadalupe*) with religious services, but usually she does not do anything for *Cinco de Mayo* or the Sixteenth of September (Mexico's Independence Day). In Mexico, her sister had a *Quinceañera* (Mexican coming-out party), but Hermila did not because she had already learned to drive and, as she said, she had already "presented" herself to the community. She said that her own daughter, Alicia, would not have one because it was not a custom here and she had never heard of anyone having a *Quinceañera* in the

United States. When Alicia was small, Hermila began celebrating the American holiday of Halloween, and she was introduced to Thanksgiving by her in-laws. Basically, however, Hermila has no concept of choice between two known cultures. She lives as a Mexican, sharing a few of the Anglo customs. She has no sense of what it would be like not to be Mexican, and she has no aspirations—indeed no conception—of becoming Anglicized.

Hermila is strongly attached to her cultural heritage. While attending a family day-care center, she overheard some Mexican mothers criticizing Mexico and some Mexican customs. She became very upset and silently left the room. When relating this story, she commented angrily that she thought they were unappreciative of Mexican culture and were rejecting a part of themselves. She misses her country and someday hopes to return to Mexico to live, but she does not dislike the United States, nor is she particularly unhappy about living in this country. Hermila has genuinely positive feelings toward *americanos* (her term for Anglos), but she does not advocate trying to become one or denying one's own heritage. She says that people of Mexican descent who identify as "American" have the right to do so if they desire, but she feels that they are attempting to deny their own blood.

Ethnicity, in general, is not a subject that had been discussed within her family prior to the study. When asked how her husband identified, she did not know and had to ask him. She reported later that he identified as "Mexican American," which she felt was correct for him. However, when her eight-year-old son, Joseph, came home from school and she asked him how he identified, she was surprised and embarrassed because he said "American." She explained to him that he was wrong because she had been born in Mexico, as had his grandparents, and he should call himself "Mexican American."

Hermila has little sense of ethnicity determining peoples' lives or their opportunities in general. She believes that the most important element in determining people's lives is their individual character, which develops in the family and is not a culture-bound process. Hermila does not think in terms of Mexicans being superior to Anglos, or vice versa:

> There are Mexican families, like there are families of other races, both good and bad, with and without troubles. If the question is

whether one race is better, maybe someone could say that this is true in things like economics. But I would say that what is important is how prepared a person is for his life—not his race.

When asked what she likes best about her life in the United States, she says she likes the way Americans act very controlled and well behaved; they have a "*bonito modo*," or a good way about themselves. One of the few differences she sees between Anglos and Mexicans is that Anglos do not yell as much when they are mad; they keep things inside, while Mexicans are more passionate and let things out when they are angry. Other than this difference, she feels that Anglos and Mexicans share similar life problems.

Hermila appears to be unaffected by discrimination. When presented with statements concerning discrimination in various situations such as jobs, housing, school, and public agencies, she did not agree that any of these situations involved discrimination. Afterward, she commented, "I don't see the need in answering these questions, for what reason? It exists but I just have not run into it."

When probed more personally about discrimination, she relates some of her feelings about it:

> There is not much discrimination these days. In Texas, there was much more. Here in California there is not as much. You can work anywhere. I have not seen discrimination either in work or in school. When people are discriminated against, it is because of the differences in customs and in language. They [Mexicans] are not saints either; they have their problems. But somehow, when a Mexican does anything, more attention is paid to it. It is some idea that they get into their heads, [the Anglos] that our customs are bad and that our dark complexions, a color like the night, is ugly.

While acknowledging its existence, she seems to consider the discrimination issue as an unpleasant part of life that she does her best to avoid. For Hermila, such avoidance is most successful if one lives an exemplary life and if one has a strong character.

As for her children's education, she has no complaints about how they have been treated. She was at a meeting once where another Mexican American woman maintained that her son was getting treated badly by his teacher and that teachers generally did not care enough. The woman added that it was the teacher's fault that her son was not doing as well as he should have. Hermila related this story very indignantly, maintaining that the teachers in this country work very hard and that it was most likely the lady's son who was at fault. Because her own children have always gotten along with their teachers, Hermila contends that children will be treated well in school if they are well behaved. Hermila espouses the merits of bilingual education. However, she also believes that Mexican and Mexican American people should never criticize these programs, but should be grateful that they exist at all:

> They don't owe it to us to teach our children in Spanish and English. The language of this country is English. They are doing a lot by having these programs at all. That lady, by insulting the teachers, was showing her ignorance and meanness. When I go to a meeting and I don't understand what is going on, I feel very ignorant, but it is my fault because I haven't learned the language as I should.

From Hermila's perspective, things like discrimination and prejudice will decrease if people work within the system and do their best.

Primarily because of her lack of facility with English, Hermila acknowledges that she has experienced minimal contact with Anglos and has never known any socially. She has little contact with her Anglo neighbors, and actually feels quite isolated in her new home. Her current employment as a maid for an Anglo couple is also marked by communication problems, which limit the extent to which she is affected by this contact. She tends to be very deferential to the couple and overly grateful for any consideration that they might show her. She is very worried that she will offend them through some social error. When they offered her a large rug they no longer needed, she could not explain that her house, which is fully carpeted, had no place for it either. Instead, she thanked them profusely, took it home, and later turned it over to the Salvation Army.

Ethnicity is of little conscious concern to Hermila. While she is confident of her Mexican identity and criticizes others who attempt to deny their Mexicanness, she is not enculturating her children with much sense of their heritage. Although her two oldest children are bilingual, their language of preference is English and they conduct most of their discourse in English. Her children's enculturation is probably affected a great deal by her husband, who is bilingual but prefers English and does not emphasize his Mexican heritage. Hermila likes the United States and has been favorably impressed by Anglo Americans, who she feels are no better in character but certainly no worse than any other ethnic group. Thus, while she is strongly attached to Mexican culture, she feels no similar strong sentiment toward Mexican people in general. She has no preference for interacting with Anglos or Mexicans, but her social contact with Anglos is restricted because of her limited language ability.

Rosa Hernández

Young and attractive Rosa Hernández grew up in the *vecindades* (slums) of Mexico City. At the age of twenty, she came to the United States to escape the personal and financial troubles she had experienced in Mexico, only to bring her problems with her. Since then, her life has become a tangle of many homes, journeys back and forth from Mexico, numerous unsatisfactory jobs, emotional problems, and over a dozen unsuccessful relationships with men, including a divorce. The pressure of these difficulties have led her to seek help from mental-health professionals many times during her life. However, her problems appear to have little to do with ethnicity, and are more the result of a breakdown in familial structure and support. For Rosa, the processes of acculturation and ethnic identification are of minimal concern when compared to her experience with loneliness and rejection.

Rosa is thirty years old, vivacious, quite friendly, and talkative. She has been living off and on for the past four years in the same apartment building in Port Hueneme, a town adjacent to the city of Oxnard. Dilapidated houses and apartments characterize her predominantly Mexican American lower-income neighborhood. Her two daughters live with her in her small two-bedroom apartment. When the interviews began, Rosa was living with her boyfriend and not working. After fighting with him and throwing him out, she started working as a waitress to supplement her food stamps.

Rosa expresses no confusion or concern about a sense of cultural identity. Born and raised in Mexico, she has always considered herself "*mexicana*." Educated through the eighth grade, she shows high awareness of Mexican history and modern culture; but because of her character and personal problems, she has an ambivalent, somewhat cynical sense of ethnic loyalty. In contrast, she has a uniformly positive attitude about the United States.

She has continued her adherence to basic Mexican cultural elements: she speaks Spanish most of the time, especially when expressing her feelings; she has a strong preference for Mexican food and music; she enjoys Spanish mass media (radio, television, movies, and magazines, for example), although at the moment she prefers English media because it helps her to improve her English. With regard to many other cultural traits, she is ambivalent. National holidays are of little importance to her: when in Mexico, she celebrates Mexican holidays; and when in the United States, she celebrates American ones, principally for the benefit of her daughters. Her attachment to Mexican religious customs has been negligible, even in childhood. Although her mother always had religious artifacts in the home, Rosa possesses only a crucifix. She received the basic holy sacraments, including baptism, communion, confirmation, and marriage in the church, and she had *padrinos* (godparents) for each ceremony, but she says that she never felt close to them and cannot remember who they were. For the communions of her own daughters, she had *compadres* only because she felt obligated to do so. She has not maintained contact with her *compadres*; she feels no obligation to them or any sense of close interpersonal bond, and in general, she feels that the custom of *compadrazgo* (godparenthood) is not significant.

In regard to the enculturation of her daughters, Rosa generally feels that they are and should be American. Both were born in Oxnard. They have Mexican names, but Rosa calls them by the American equivalents of those names. The two girls learned Spanish from Rosa, but they are more fluent and literate in English, and they speak to Rosa mainly in English. Rosa has not taught them Mexican history or customs, and she only celebrates American holidays with them. When asked, in general, if Mexican American children should be taught Mexican history in school, she had "no opinion."

Rosa's attitudes about Mexicans, Americans, and the problem of discrimination are tinged with cynicism. Yet, in some ways, she feels quite positive about Mexico and Mexicans. She believes that Mexican people are generally friendlier than Americans; and when asked about her cultural identity, she not only asserts that she is "*mexicana*," but she also strongly objects to Mexicans who come to the United States and try to change their cultural identity.

In certain ways, Rosa is indifferent to Mexican and American distinctions. Her current set of friends and acquaintances includes Mexicans and Anglos, and in the past she has had boyfriends of both ethnic groups. She has no ethnic preferences regarding such establishments as theaters, movies, or nightclubs; nor does she have a preference for either Mexican or Anglo parties. Although she has experienced it, discrimination has never been of much concern to her because she believes that discrimination exists "wherever you go." Rosa does not feel that American employers discriminate against Mexicans, nor does she believe that school teachers or public agencies give preferential treatment to Anglos; and she disagrees with the idea that local police discriminate against Mexicans. Because of her own immigration difficulties, however, Rosa does believe that most Mexican people are suspected of being illegal aliens by the Immigration and Naturalization Service. Regarding her personal experiences, she says that she has never been treated rudely or given poor service at any commercial establishment because she was Mexican, nor has she ever been denied a job because she was Mexican. But she was once turned down as a renter because she was a Mexican, and she believes she was once discriminated against by a Mexican American nurse who was rude to her and another Mexican lady. In general, though, Rosa feels that the question of a person having a better chance to get ahead in either the United States or Mexico is entirely an individual matter, and anyone anywhere can achieve success if she wants it and tries hard enough.

Her cynicism about Mexico is clearly evident in her strong disagreement with the idea that the Mexican government helps its people more than the American government assists its population. In conjunction with this, Rosa believes that a child growing up in the United States is "luckier" than one in Mexico. She also says that she would not like to live in a Mexican American community because "Mexicans are too nosy." When asked if Mexicans in her town had to work harder to get ahead than Anglos, she agreed, but she explained her response with the remark that "most Mexicans are dumb." And yet Rosa was ambivalent when asked about her ethnic preferences regarding her daughters' future marriage choices, saying that it was entirely up to her daughters, although she would prefer that they marry Mexicans; at the same time, she acknowledged that this would create many problems because Mexican men are too demanding.

To summarize, Rosa oscillates in her identification with and participation in Mexican and American cultures. She has positive and negative feelings about Mexico, and in some ways, she is cynical and ambivalent. She strongly identifies herself as Mexican, but she recognizes certain advantages in living in the United States, and she promotes the Americanization of her daughters. Rosa says that she has no ethnic preferences regarding restaurants, nightclubs, or parties, and yet she would not like to live in a Mexican neighborhood. Other inconsistencies are evident: her preference that her daughters marry Mexicans is qualified by her belief that such a marriage would create problems; her belief that Mexicans are "dumb" contrasts with her loyalty in maintaining a Mexican identity and her criticism of Mexicans who try to deny their origins; and her nominal participation in *compadrazgo* is contradicted by her lack of belief in that custom. While discussing ethnic preferences, attitudes, and her feelings about discrimination, Rosa conveys the strong impression that these matters are of little concern to her and that she has more important personal problems to worry about. It *is* significant to her to see that her daughters have the advantage of living in the U.S., which requires certain cultural adaptations. This was thwarted near the end of the study, when Rosa and her family were deported to Mexico by immigration authorities. One senses, however, that this will be merely one more in a series of round trips, and that Rosa and her daughters will return to the U.S. in the not-too-distant future.

Conclusion

Case material from the two types, *La Raza* and Changing Ethnics, discussed in this chapter are distinctive in comparison to the other types that we have isolated primarily because of their knowledge of Mexican culture and the Spanish language and their propensity for maintaining a Mexican cultural orientation and contact and identification with Mexico and the Mexican people. Most of our respondents who hold either of these two cultural orientations were born in Mexico and received their primary socialization in a Mexican cultural context. However, inclusion in either of these two categories is not confined exclusively to immigrant Mexicans. As we have seen, Dolores Guerrero is a fourth-generation Mexican American who prefers to identity herself simply as a "*mexicana*" and whose ethnic social orientation and loyalty are to Mexican people.

Mexican cultural maintenance requires considerable contact with others of Mexican descent, not only in childhood but in adult life. In many ways, these traits come rather matter-of-factly to individuals involved in the case studies. Hermila, for example, feels simply that she is Mexican because she was born in Mexico, and although she can "pick up American ways," she will always "feel like the same person basically . . . I feel Mexican in any situation." Dolores, on the other hand, associates only with Mexicans and claims to have always had only Mexican friends. This is true despite her relatively high level of acculturation in comparison to other Mexican friends for whom she serves as a broker in the community because of her bilingual skills.

The difference between the two types in this chapter has to do primarily with the individuals' attitude toward American culture and people, and their perception of discrimination against people of Mexican descent in the U.S. For example, Dolores (Type I) reports many personal experiences with ethnic discrimination, and her attitude toward Anglo Americans and their culture is succinctly captured in her consistent reference to them with the derogatory term *gabacho*. On the other hand, Hermila (Type II) admires Anglos and American culture in many ways, and while she acknowledges the existence of ethnic discrimination she feels that it is not much of a problem where she lives and that it should decrease even further as Mexicans acculturate. In sum, Type II individuals retain strong positive feelings about their own Mexican culture and Mexican people; but they have also developed a positive attitude toward American culture and people, which is correlated with a lessening perception of discrimination in the U.S.

6

Cultural Blends

THE THREE CASE STUDIES PRESENTED in this chapter represent individuals who are aware of both their Mexican cultural heritage and their American roots. At the same time, they demonstrate patterns of ethnic loyalty that fluctuate between Mexican and American traditions. We have chosen to label these individuals as *Cultural Blends*. Other writers have used the term *bicultural* to identify individuals who manifest joint cultural traits that characterize the type illustrated in our case descriptions. However, for several reasons, we believe that *bicultural* is an inappropriate label for *Cultural Blends*. First, as currently conceptualized, *bicultural* implies a point midway between two cultural poles on a unidimensional space (see the discussion of biculturalism in chapter 2). This conceptualization is too simplistic from both a measurement and psychological perspective. Second, the state of biculturality is far more complicated than it has been envisioned. Our Cultural Blends are not always comfortable in their bicultural role, and they are even more troubled by the biethnic loyalties they are sometimes called upon to demonstrate. In other words, biculturality is not the ideal state that some social scientists have depicted it to be; it sometimes involves difficult decisions and conflicts that keep an individual in a state of turmoil in attempting to resolve questions of culture and ethnic loyalty.

In consideration of the ambiguities surrounding the term *bicultural*, we have chosen to use *Cultural Blend*, a label which is free of earlier connotations associated with the term *biculturalism*. Further, we feel that Cultural Blend more accurately represents what our individuals were communicating to us during the interviews. Let us now turn to our first case.

Magdalena Rivera

Magdalena (Lena) Rivera is thirty-seven years old, a second-generation Mexican American and a native of rural south Texas. Lena has been through two divorces, and currently lives with four of her seven children in a four-bedroom home in South Oxnard. Educated through the eighth grade, she works as an unskilled laborer in an electronics plant, earning the minimum wage.

Lena has struggled through a very hard life. As Lena describes it, there has never been a time when she has not experienced some serious difficulty, nor has she experienced any stable or very emotionally rewarding social relationship. Lena says that she puts her trust in God (recently becoming a member of Jehovah's Witnesses). She determinedly works to overcome repeated adversities, seemingly because she has no sense of defeat, and she characterizes herself as possessing no aspirations greater than keeping her head above water—both financially and emotionally—and hoping that her children will settle down to hard work and honest lives.

Lena has never given a great deal of thought to her ethnic identity. She considers herself "Mexican American," saying that she has always felt that way, from childhood through adolescence to adulthood. She makes no distinction between "Mexican American" and "Chicano," nor does she feel that "American of Mexican descent" signifies anything different from "Mexican American." To Lena, all three of these identities mean that a person is born in the United States of Mexican parentage; as that circumstance applies to her, she reasons that "Mexican American is what I am and what I'm proud to be." Lena does not consider herself "*mexicana*" because a "Mexican is someone born in Mexico," and similarly, she does not consider herself "just plain American" because "American would mean that your ancestors are already Americans."

According to Lena, her family did not emphasize any particular Mexican customs or beliefs. She learned to speak Spanish at home, but her father and stepmother never spoke much about Mexico, did not teach her Mexican history nor Mexican legends or folktales, and did not observe Mexican religious practices. Concerning music and dance, for example, Lena says that her stepmother, Aurelia, never allowed her to participate in festivities or attend dances. Nor did Aurelia teach Lena how to make Mexican food, which Lena says she learned from her first mother-in-law. Aurelia and Felipe, Lena's father, did not celebrate Mexican holidays; and to this day, Lena says that she does not make a point of observing them, nor does she know the historical significance of Mexican holidays.

Concerning religion, Lena says that her real mother, Dahlia, had her baptized as a Catholic. But Dahlia died, and since Felipe was Lutheran instead of Catholic, Lena did not mark her first communion or her confirmation. She recalls attending Lutheran services with her father, and the people in the church were very friendly. Lena feels that this early exposure to Protestantism has made her receptive to the Jehovah's Witnesses in recent years. Now as an adult, Lena's religious orientation is mixed. She considers herself a Catholic, and she has had her children receive the principal Catholic sacrament of baptism; otherwise, however, Lena has not instituted any religious instruction for her children, and Lena herself is not much of a churchgoer.

Lena says that her exposure to American customs was confined to her schooling, learning English and learning about American holidays, music, dance, legends, and even cooking. Lena is certain that "whatever I learned [about American culture], I learned at school." With regard to her own children, Lena says that she has raised them as Americans because "I'm here [in the United States]." Her children speak only a little Spanish; eat Mexican food appreciably less often than American food; know only about American music and dance; and with Lena, celebrate only American holidays. Lena notes that though her children call themselves "Chicanos," their network of interpersonal associations is mixed, including Chicano, Anglo, and Black friends. Her sons, she says, almost exclusively date Anglo girls, although her daughter married a Chicano. Either way, according to Lena, it is of no importance to her since she believes that her children should have friends and spouses based upon mutual attraction rather than ethnic considerations. In sum, Lena concludes that her children are more American than she is.

Lena says that she has raised her children primarily as Americans because the United States is their home and not because she rejects Mexican culture. She considers herself "proud" of her Mexican heritage, but she claims to know very little about it that she could teach to her children. She does hope her children will travel to Mexico and learn about their heritage. In general, Lena feels that children of Mexican descent in this country should learn Spanish and be taught Mexican history in the schools.

As a child, Lena says that she felt pulled between the Mexican and American cultures. In Texas, where Lena went to the "Mexican school" through the third grade, she became fluent in English. Because she was one of the first children to be transferred to the "white school," she says that the other Mexican children "disliked me" and tried to "push me into being Mexican." Lena resisted this pressure by considering herself more intelligent than the other Mexican children, and interpreting their criticism of her as jealousy. She also sought to minimize ethnic differences by considering herself "equal with whites" and believing that "we were all the same," aside from differences in skin color. Significantly, Lena says that neither she nor her parents were greatly concerned about discrimination in the educational system because segregated schooling was the natural order of things where she grew up.

As an adult, Lena now says that she feels equally comfortable with Mexicans and Anglos. Her feeling of ethnicity is situational, "depending on where I'm at." When she is at a Mexican social gathering, she feels Mexican; and when she is with Anglos, she feels American—"if I'm in a place where there's whites then I feel the same, I feel white or half-white," she explains. While Lena's network of friends is predominantly Mexican American, and her two former husbands and her current boyfriend are Mexican American, she also has several Anglo friends. She says that her pattern of association does not mean that she discriminates against Anglos; she simply has had greater contact with other Mexican Americans during the many years she has lived in *La Colonia*. Lena says that she has no preference, one way or the other, concerning associating with Mexicans or Anglos, or participating in Mexican or American festivities and other social events.

Although Lena feels equally comfortable with Mexicans and Anglos, she is very aware of problems of discrimination. She recalls that when she was young there was a lot of discrimination in Texas, which included the segregated schools and problems of job discrimination. Lena feels that discrimination is not as bad in California and that problems of discrimination have decreased in recent years, but she knows that discrimination still exists. Lena feels employers in Oxnard refuse to hire Mexicans; she believes that teachers show favoritism to Anglo students; she imagines that many Mexicans are automatically suspected of being illegal aliens; and she considers the local police to be very prejudiced in feeling that "if you're Mexican, right away you're supposed to be guilty of something." Lena says that the only discrimination she has experienced personally as an adult concerned job refusals, but otherwise she has not suffered discrimination in restaurants, in getting loans, or as a renter. Her greatest concern is that her children have suffered from discrimination. Lena feels there is some discrimination by teachers in local schools, but she is sure that the police are the worst offenders and have unjustly troubled her own children. The arrest and imprisonment of her oldest son, following a knifing, was unfair she claims, because he was fighting in self-defense; and on another occasion, her daughter and son-in-law were hassled by police at the scene of a street fight, although they were innocent bystanders. Such experiences have caused Lena to "hate" the police.

On the other hand, Lena admits there is discrimination by Mexicans against whites: "If I was white I couldn't go into the *Colonia* at night." Her children tell her of fights at school, and she reads newspaper stories about Mexican–white gang fights and about white teenagers beaten in the *Colonia*. To Lena, both groups are at fault, and she wishes there were no discrimination by any group against others. Lena feels that she does not discriminate against anyone.

Lena believes that many similarities exist between the two ethnic groups, and that there are as many good and bad Mexicans as there are good and bad Anglos. Still, she recognizes some major differences. Her major complaint with Mexicans is that the men are demanding, drink too much, and are spendthrifts. In contrast, she feels that Anglo husbands are much more understanding of and helpful to their wives. Lena also feels that Mexicans are more strict with their children, and she does not like what she deems a lack of morality among Anglo young people. According to Lena, the Mexican family has closer ties, whereas in the Anglo culture, "once the kid reaches a certain age, then you're gone and you don't get in the house no more."

In her behavior, Lena is basically a mix between being very

Mexican and very American, which she recognizes, in a sense, by identifying herself as Mexican American. She says that she gets along with both groups, does not discriminate, and has no preference for associating primarily with Anglos or Mexicans. At work and during social activities, she says that she prefers to be involved with a mixed group, as opposed to one that observes strict ethnic separation. Lena was raised in Texas, where there was considerable discrimination, in her opinion. Thus, as she grew up, she was very aware of her Mexican status, but she received little instruction in her home about Mexican customs and history. She seems to have developed most of her identification with Mexican culture by associating primarily with Mexican Americans all of her life. She learned about American culture through her schooling experience, and she has raised her children principally as Americans because the United States is their homeland. Still, she feels "proud" of her Mexican heritage, and she wishes her children could learn more Spanish and more about Mexican culture. Lena is aware of discrimination in Oxnard, but she feels that she has seldom experienced it personally. Although the discrimination suffered by her children is what most concerns her, she believes that it is balanced by her children's ability to maintain friendships with Anglos and Blacks as well as Chicanos.

In sum, Lena is both Mexican and American. She speaks both languages; she enjoys participating in both cultures' social activities; she has Anglo and Mexican friends; and she feels comfortable with both ethnic groups. While she felt "pulled" between the two cultures when she was young, she feels no such conflict as an adult. She is now at ease with her mixed heritage and her dual identification.

Anthony Reyes

Anthony (Tony) Reyes is a college-educated, thirty-six year-old family man. He holds a well-paying administrative job, and lives in a pleasant hillside home in an attractive, primarily Anglo-American residential area overlooking downtown Santa Barbara. Both of his parents were migrant farm-workers from Mexico who settled in Santa Barbara when Tony was an infant, and they provided him and his four siblings with a secure, if not affluent, home life. They encouraged the educational efforts that enabled Tony to achieve a good measure of socioeconomic success.

After college, Tony was strongly influenced by the student political and social activism of the late 1960s and early 1970s, and he became deeply involved in the Chicano movement. Although Tony feels that the enthusiasm of the movement has ebbed, he remains concerned about Chicano affairs, participates in several Chicano organizations, and is still politically active.

Considering his involvement in the movement, it comes as no surprise that Tony prefers to be identified as "Chicano," which, to him, is both an ethnic and political designation; importantly, it is a label created in the U.S. by the Mexicans themselves, and not one applied to them by Anglo society. Tony, however, did not always identify as "Chicano." When he was growing up, he considered himself Mexican American, a label that he still uses at times. Tony eschews the other possible ethnic labels. He is not "Mexican," he says, because he was not born in Mexico. He does not like the phrase "American of Mexican descent" because it sounds to him as though "you're trying to impress the dominant Anglo people." Tony does not resent or reject the label "just plain American," but he prefers not to use it. He likes "Chicano" because it indicates that a person is American without denying his Mexican heritage. He states what he believes about Chicanos by saying:

> I think "American" means that you're just like everybody else,
> and you don't have any roots, any heritage, any special things. I
> think that the roots that Chicanos have are good, and I wouldn't
> want to see them lose that identity just to be like everybody else.

In spite of this ethnic identification, Tony recognizes that he does not fully adhere to Mexican cultural traditions. He admits that his parents are much more Mexican than he is: "They speak Spanish a lot better than I do, and they still have a lot of the customs from Mexico, where me, I'm the opposite. I'm more comfortable with the English language." He explains that his parents speak Spanish and he answers them in English. He says that he avoids speaking Spanish in front of his parents because his Spanish is not very good, and they would probably criticize him. He has had this problem at work, where people from Mexico have made fun of him; but, interestingly, he rationalizes that Spanish fluency is not that significant for his sense of ethnic identity.

In some ways, Tony prefers Mexican culture. He enjoys the music and he definitely prefers Mexican food. He likes to celebrate in the Mexican fashion, whether it is a Mexican wedding or a holiday like *Cinco de Mayo*. At parties or in restaurants or night clubs, he prefers to associate with Chicanos because he feels more comfortable with them and finds them livelier than Anglos. In general, Tony feels that his orientation in life is more Mexican than Anglo, for he has a strong attachment to his family and eschews material gain in favor of being contented with life and forming good interpersonal associations.

However, Tony rejects the other aspects of Mexican tradition. He learned from his parents Mexican legends such as "*La Llorona*," but they are not important to him and he has not taught them to his daughters. He does not believe at all in Mexican "superstitions," and in general, he puts little credence in Mexican folk healing. However, he did grow up exposed to such beliefs because his mother "couldn't afford doctors" and would take Tony and his siblings to *curanderas* (folk healers). Tony's father, who knows a lot about sore muscles, is informally considered a *sobador* (masseur) among his circle of family and friends. Today, however, Tony totally accepts American medical beliefs, and he relies entirely upon doctors for medical treatment.

Tony has also rejected Catholicism. His parents, who are still strong Catholics, raised Tony as a Catholic, with *padrinos* for the sacraments of baptism, communion, and confirmation. Tony indicates his lack of attachment to Catholicism by no longer associating with nor even remembering the names of his *padrinos*. Tony explains that he turned away from the Catholic church because it was too "dogmatic." Furthermore, he says,

> I've done everything a Catholic isn't supposed to do. I married a Methodist, I never go to church, and my first child was baptized into the Methodist church.

Jane, his Anglo wife, has raised their two daughters as Methodists, and the influence of Jane's very religious mother has been strong. Thus, Tony attaches little intrinsic importance to the Mexican custom of *compadrazgo*. While he has *compadres*, Tony views *compadrazgo* as a means of "making a friendship stronger," but he attaches no ritual or religious significance to the custom.

In his ethnic identification as Chicano, Tony expresses sentiments of attachment to both Mexico and the United States. He feels Mexican when he is with his Chicano friends, especially in Chicano group meetings, and also when he attends Mexican fiestas and holidays. But because he was born in the U.S., Tony has no national loyalty to Mexico ("I've never felt like a Mexican citizen"); and he says that though his parents "strongly identify with Mexico, they still see themselves as American citizens." As a Chicano, Tony feels "very American." To Tony, the Chicano movement is a typical American political movement.

> I like America. But at the same time that we look at the good things of this country we also have to look at the bad things and try to change them, especially for Chicanos and other minorities. I think it's very American to look at the plight of the minority people. And in that sense, I feel very American, because what we're doing [Chicanos] is no different from any other ethnic group in the country.

Tony admits that he has not done much at home to instill Mexican traditions in his children, a situation which reflects an informal agreement between him and his Anglo wife, Jane.

> I'm not trying to make her a Chicano and she's not trying to make me Anglo. And I think what we're trying to do with our kids is give them some of both cultures.

They did have "some problems" with their daughter, Maria, who did not like people to speak Spanish in front of her "because she didn't understand it." Tony says that she is now in a bilingual–bicultural program at elementary school and is "accepting it more." Tony places a great deal of emphasis upon the bilingual program at school because he admits that he has not been consistent in reinforcing the Mexican language or culture with his children at home.

> I'm sure we're passing on some Mexican things to the kids, but not as much as I'd like. Well, just little things like a *piñata* at a birthday party, and we expose them to some of the food and some language. And like what I try to do is give them Mexican toys. Or like for *Cinco do Mayo*, Maria will get dressed up in a pretty Mexican outfit. We're just trying to get Maria to get some

pride in Mexico, so that she'll feel she comes from an interesting culture, that both cultures are interesting.

Tony's pattern of interpersonal associations is confined principally to Chicanos, with the exception of his wife and in-laws. All his close friends at work, for example, are Chicanos; and throughout his life, Tony's closest friends have always been Chicanos like himself, what he calls "Americanized Chicanos." Tony does not go to bars or night clubs very often, but when he does he goes to Mexican establishments. Similarly, he much prefers Mexican social activities, like parties and wedding fiestas, to Anglo social functions. He does not avoid Anglo social events or night clubs, but he would rather attend Mexican activities, which he feels are more enjoyable and more comfortable for him.

Tony's ambivalent feelings about Anglos stem from an awareness of discrimination. He agrees that many employers refuse to hire Mexicans, and he believes that when he was working for a government agency he had difficulty in getting promotions because he was Mexican American. He feels that government agency employees, in general, whether in public service agencies or the police department, do not show Mexicans much respect and give preferential treatment to Anglos. He feels the same way about school teachers, and he knows from his own school experience that there is ethnic discrimination in the schools.

On the other hand, he states that "Mexicans from Mexico" denigrate and "make fun" of Chicanos, to some extent. Furthermore, when he was involved in Chicano politics, Tony was subjected to some abuse from other Chicanos; for example, he was chastised for being married to an Anglo. Tony's response has been to minimize the importance of the opinions of others, to limit his interactions to relatives and Chicano friends with whom he feels most comfortable, and to attach primary importance to his own feelings and self-identity. As he explains, "I'm happy with what I am, and I'm not going to apologize to anybody."

Thus, Tony is proud and identifies with his Mexican heritage. Yet, he does not speak Spanish very well, and he rejects outright many aspects of Mexican culture. Moreover, he is married to an Anglo, and he has been inconsistent about teaching Mexican culture to his children. He has become somewhat ambivalent about Chicano politics, and has experienced problems in his associations with Anglos, Mexicans, and even Chicanos. Nevertheless, Tony has a strong ethnic identity as a "Chicano," and he prefers to associate with Chicanos, with whom he feels more comfortable. His closest friends are all Chicanos. Although Tony says that he gets along well with Anglo Americans, and his successful working career and marriage attest to this, his intimate social life is primarily bound up with other "Americanized Chicanos" like himself. Tony recognizes his acculturation and the fact that he is different from "Mexicans from Mexico," but at the same time, he remains closely tied to others who share his ethnic background.

Anna Fuentes

Twenty-three-year-old Anna Fuentes is a second-generation Mexican American, born in Santa Barbara. She grew up in a middle-class family in the eastside *barrio* where her father still runs a business. She and her husband, Ruben, also a second-generation Mexican American, were married immediately following her graduation from high school. They live in a small one-bedroom apartment in a mixed-ethnic residential neighborhood. Ruben works as a cook in a cafeteria, while Anna is a bilingual clerk–typist. They have no children, but they plan to begin a family soon.

Prior to her marriage, Anna's home life was a mixture of Mexican and American influences. She learned both languages at home; her father, born in Santa Barbara, spoke mainly English, while her mother, born in Mexico, spoke only Spanish. She learned both Mexican and American cooking from her mother. She learned to love Mexican music because of her mother's preferences, but the influence of radio, television, and her friends led Anna to an equal preference for American music and dances. From her mother she learned about Mexican folklore, and remembers listening often to her reflections about life in Mexico. But Anna says that more substantive Mexican traditions were not part of her childhood. She learned nothing of Mexican history; herbal teas were the only aspects of folk medicine she learned, for the family relied primarily upon doctors; and in her home, only American holidays were celebrated. This mixed bag of cultural elements neither disturbed or created confusion for Anna, for, as she explains, it was all she knew and was accustomed to in childhood: "I never gave it any thought because on the eastside . . . we were all the same."

Anna's religious training was mild. Her parents made certain that she and her siblings received the appropriate sacraments (baptism, communion, confirmation) sponsored by *padrinos*; but the custom of *compadrazgo* is not a particularly important part of her family life, and Anna was never close to her *padrinos*. Moreover, her parents were not very religious, and in spite of insisting that their children attend Mass each Sunday, they almost never went to church. Anna has followed her parents' pattern, only rarely going to church since her graduation from high school.

In Catholic elementary school, the majority of Anna's friends were her cousins, whose ethnic background is similar to her own. The insularity of that home and early school environment did not become evident to Anna until ninth grade, when she attended a Catholic high school dominated by Anglos. She disliked that school so much that she transferred to the public high school in the *barrio* the following year, where once again she was with her cousins and other Mexican American girlfriends.

Anna's employment history also reflects her sense of estrangement from Anglos. In high school, she had no aspirations for college; instead, she enrolled in vocational classes. One class offered an "exploratory job" at City Hall, where Anna worked three months "for experience." Only Anglos worked there, and she found herself feeling uncomfortable.

> At City Hall there were no Mexicans when I worked there, and you kind of feel the tension—like the Anglos [are thinking] "oh, she's nothing but a dumb Mexican."

After high school, she worked part-time as a receptionist for a physical therapist, a job she says she enjoyed because the therapist was Mexican. However, her sense that Anglos are prejudiced was again evident in her perception of the therapist's patients: "I could feel it sometimes, like they thought, 'I don't trust you with my pocketbook.'" The job as receptionist helped her through City College, where she took business courses because she wanted to be a secretary, finally receiving a two-year degree. The job for which she was then hired—and which she still has—was based on her Mexican background: she is a bilingual clerk—typist in the civil service. She feels this job is "great!"—partly because most of her coworkers are minorities, either Mexican American like herself or Black.

Anna identifies herself as "Mexican American"; that is, she considers her principal ethnic identity to be Mexican, and she defines a Mexican American as "a Mexican person born in the United States." Moreover, she explains, "I've always been raised hearing 'Mexican American' and I never doubted it." However, the apparent simplicity of this identification obscures several complexities.

As a child, when Anna identified herself simply as "Mexican," this was due to her mother's influence: "When they asked us we always said we were 'Mexican' because my mom was from Mexico and that's all she ever talked about." On the eastside, she adds, "we were all Mexicans so we never gave it any thought." In high school, she began identifying herself as "Chicana," largely because of the social influence of her peers, and perhaps due to the discrimination that she felt at the Anglo high school she attended briefly in the ninth grade.

> When I was in high school I thought I was a real radical. I guess I thought of myself as Chicana and I used to cause a lot of fights at home. I used to call myself a Mexican and my dad would say 'you're Mexican American,' and I'd say, 'no I'm not, I'm not white!'

Eventually, however, Anna says the "middle class" or conservative nature of her personality led her to disassociate herself from Chicanos. In contrast to Tony Reyes, Anna now feels that Chicanos are too "radical" and too violent for her taste. Finally, Anna decided to call herself "Mexican American" because "Mexican American I guess has always been the preferred identity in my family."

Anna's sense of identity also reflects a reaction against Anglo society. She says that she chooses not to consider herself simply "American" because "when I think of American I think of Anglo." She also chooses not to consider herself "American of Mexican descent" because she does not think of herself as "American first." "My Mexican heritage is still very important to me," she declares. Nevertheless, Anna considers herself as much American as Mexican. As she says, she feels "in between" the two cultures.

This in-between status is reflected in Anna's personal preferences, attitudes, and styles of behavior. Although fluent in both languages, Anna prefers to carry on conversations in English and to read and write in English; however, she chooses to watch Spanish television programs. Anna speaks only English with her friends and coworkers, but she speaks both languages with her family. Concerning her attitude about Mexico and the United States, she feels that there is more discrimination in the U.S. than in Mexico and that Mexicans can count on help from each other more than Anglos can. However, she believes that a person has a better chance of getting ahead in the U.S. than in Mexico; that the Mexican government does not help its citizens very much in comparison to the U.S. government; and that a child born in the U.S. is much luckier than a child growing up in Mexico. Anna has a preference for American food, and yet on holidays her family usually eats Mexican food. She has no preference for Mexican music over American music, but she much prefers Mexican parties and dances to American ones. In sum, there is no simple pattern in Anna's cultural orientation. Her tastes are partly Mexican and partly American, and as she explains, her choice of either is as much a function of her mood as that of the social situation in which she finds herself.

Anna's sense of discrimination and her perceptions of Anglos and Mexicans also reflect the mixed nature of her ethnic identity. At times, she has experienced prejudice. However, she believes that discrimination is not a major problem in Santa Barbara. Anna believes that there are few differences between Anglos and Mexicans in their social behaviors. At dances both ethnic groups behave essentially the same, although Mexicans are "more lively." At public places, such as nightclubs and bars, as well as in their own homes, Anna feels that Anglo men and women "pretty much act the same as we do, as Mexicans do." The only general differences Anna sees are that, first, "Anglos are more starchy, more stand-offish, and less affectionate" than Mexicans. Secondly, she feels that "appearances are everything" to Anglos, "and they kind of like to show off all the ritzy stuff they have." In contrast, Mexicans are, in her opinion, "sort of brought up to share things"; they are more affectionate, and they emphasize respect and loyalty to their elders much more than Anglos do. In sum, according to Anna, Anglos are very "materialistic," so that "you are what you have"; whereas Mexicans are more prone to "live for the day and we'll see about tomorrow later." Anna, of course, prefers the

Mexican orientation in these things, and she feels more comfortable with Mexican Americans. She would like her children (when she has some) to associate primarily with Mexican Americans. Anna admits that she has a strong preference for her children-to-be to marry Mexican Americans; "It's just a feeling I have," she said, "but I think my child would be happier with a Mexican."

To summarize, Anna's ethnicity includes a mixture of cultural elements, but a mixture which is not entirely without paradox. In childhood, the ethnicity stressed by her mother was simply "Mexican"; however, Anna's father stressed the idea that the family was Mexican *and* American. Her preferences are for the English language and American food and customs, yet she chooses Mexican social events and Mexican social values. While she feels that discrimination is not significant in the town in which she lives, she would much prefer to limit her own and her future children's interpersonal associations to other Mexican Americans. Thus, Anna appears not to be fully integrated into either culture; she seems to be American in some ways, but she has a negative opinion of Anglos, and while she has a preference for Mexicans she knows little about Mexico and its customs. In her own words, she is "in between" these two cultures; and yet she is fully integrated into, and secure in, a kin-based ethnic social network.

Conclusion

The three cases presented here demonstrate that Cultural Blends show no simple pattern in their cultural orientation. All three individuals are proud of their Mexican heritage, but they do not identify as Mexican. They participate in Mexican customs, but recognize their limitations in Mexican cultural awareness. At the same time, they participate in American cultural practices and interact extensively with Anglos on a daily basis. Yet they maintain a preference for Mexican American friends. Furthermore, they hold different opinions about the term *Chicano*. Thirty-seven-year-old Lena makes no distinction between the terms *Chicano* and *Mexican American*, using the latter term as her preferred ethnic label. Anthony, on the other hand, identifies as *Chicano*, and comments that the term signifies both an ethnic and political designation. Yet he recognizes the impact of acculturation on his own behavior and on that of his Chicano associates. In addition, while he articulates a clear ethnic preference for Chicano friends and activities, he is interethnically married to an Anglo.

Our youngest respondent, twenty-three-year-old Anna, states that a Mexican American is "a Mexican person born in the United States." She says that though she identified as *Chicana* not too long ago, she no longer uses that term to describe herself because she feels it is too radical for her. Interestingly, Anna, like the other two individuals, is selective about which cultural patterns—Mexican or American—she participates in. She makes distinction between ways in which Mexican Americans and Anglos behave, and has preferences which fluctuate between the two cultural orientations depending upon the circumstances.

Also important is the fact that Cultural Blends comment on the discriminatory practices of Anglos directed against Mexican Americans. Lena, for example, believes that the police are the biggest offenders. But at the same time, Lena recognizes that Mexicans discriminate against Anglos. Similarly, Anthony comments on discrimination against Chicanos practiced by employers, the police, and teachers, and yet he is sensitive toward discrimination by Mexicans against Chicanos. More interesting still are Anthony's reactions toward intragroup discrimination, especially when it is directed toward him because he is married to an Anglo.

An important consideration in our summation of Cultural Blends is that they are not marginalized members of their ethnic group, nor are they *bicultural* in the sense in which the term has frequently been applied. These individuals participate selectively in both cultural orientations, but they are not equally proficient in both cultures. They recognize that they are not Mexicans, and they do not identify as Mexican, noting, for example, their lack of fluency in Spanish or their nonacceptance of some Mexican cultural practices. At the same time, Cultural Blends draw a clear distinction between themselves and Anglos, and although they appear comfortable in many aspects of American life, they have many ethnically based preferences that keep them separated from Anglos.

7

Americans . . . Set Apart

IN THIS CHAPTER, WE PRESENT four case studies of individuals who differ from our other informants in the extent of their Mexican cultural orientation and their loyalty to their Mexican background. Although they display a varied knowledge of Mexican culture, these informants are clearly more versed in American values and customs. Perhaps more important is their marked preference for being identified as Americans of Mexican descent, which signals their internalization of American values. This process is best illustrated by respondents who indicate that they are Americans first, and only then identify themselves as of Mexican descent. Furthermore, with few exceptions, these individuals maintain that it is essential to socialize their children to be Americans.

An interesting aspect of the cases to be discussed here is that in spite of the acculturation and/or Americanization of our respondents, they have not yet achieved complete status as Americans, at least not in their own view. For this reason, we were prompted to title this chapter "Americans . . . Set Apart," which is intended to suggest (with its associated punctuation) the separation that still exists between our informants and mainstream Americans.

The first two cases are individuals who scored within Cluster Type IV. After studying the cases, we felt that this type characterized a group best depicted as "Emerging Americans," and we have designated them as such. The final two cases fell in our Cluster Type, V and are labeled "New Americans." In reading the case material, it is important to contrast these informants with those presented in chapters 5 and 6. The differences between types are sharp and unambiguous on some issues; for example, in ethnic identification and in perception of discrimination by Anglos against Mexican Americans. However, along other dimensions the distinctions between types are not so clear. Even our New Americans have many vestiges of Mexican culture and customs that align them closer to Types I and II than to Anglo Americans. Let us turn now to our final set of case studies.

Emerging Americans

Celia Torres

Born in Santa Barbara, Celia Torres is thirty-five years old and a second-generation Mexican American. She has been married since her graduation from high school, and she has three children. Her thirty-seven-year-old husband, Gil, was born and raised in Mexico City, and came to the United States at age sixteen. Gil worked as a restaurant cook until ten years ago, when he became an American citizen expressly for the purpose of obtaining a high-paying factory job in an electronics assembly plant. Celia is enterprising in contributing to the family income; and because Gil has not wanted her to work outside the home, she runs a small beauty shop for relatives and friends in her garage.

Gil's job classifies him as blue collar, but his income and family home reflect a more affluent life style. There are no Mexican artifacts or furnishings in their home, and by all appearances it is typically American and middle class. The Torres family lives in a neighborhood with a mixture of Anglo and Mexican American families. Celia was born and raised in the *barrio* on the eastside, where her parents and Gil's still live, and where Celia and Gil lived until five years ago. Because they perceived the eastside as "rowdy" and in other ways not beneficial to their children, Celia and Gil moved to this "nicer" neighborhood.

Celia's parents have their roots in Santa Barbara. Her father was born in Santa Barbara and educated through the tenth grade in local schools. He speaks both English and Spanish quite well. Her mother, Trinidad, was born in Mexico, but immigrated to Santa Barbara with her family at the age of two. Trinidad speaks English substantially better than she speaks Spanish.

According to Celia, her parents did not emphasize Mexican traditions in the home. For example, they did not celebrate any Mexican holidays, whereas an American version of Christmas, Thanksgiving, and the Fourth of July have remained their main celebrations to this day. Throughout her school years, the majority of her friends were Mexican American, and Celia explains that this was not a matter of selection, but simply a product of the high concentration of Mexicans on the eastside. While growing up, Celia gave almost no thought to Mexico or to ethnicity in general "because most of my friends were just like me." She did not speak Spanish or know about Mexican customs or cooking until she married Gil; now she takes considerable pride in her cooking and in her Spanish fluency.

Celia does not feel so positive about other Mexican traits. For example, she portrays herself as "working on Gil" to diminish what she perceives as some of his Mexican attitudes of male dominance. She has interceded on her daughter's behalf when Gil has tried to curtail the girl's freedom, and she has continuously fought against the double standard in her own marriage. Gil no longer goes "out with the boys (and perhaps with the girls)" as much as he once did, whereas Celia has won for herself some freedom to go out with her girlfriends once in a while. Still, she feels that jealousy and the double standard are the major problems for Mexican couples, and they have engendered conflict in her own marriage. In addition, she has successfully demanded that Gil never verbally abuse her in public like so many Mexican men do to their wives, in her opinion. To Celia, a husband berating and belittling his wife in public is an unforgivable offense.

On the other hand, Celia states that she has accepted what is essentially the Mexican role of wife and mother. The responsibility of home and family are of paramount importance to Celia. Marriage is a lifelong commitment, and infidelity is virtually unthinkable to her. She put up with Gil's carousing in their early years, even though she resented it. She enjoyed working, but she says she acquiesced obediently when Gil insisted that she stay home to mind the house and children. Gil is the recognized head of the household, and Celia insists that her children respect their father, but she points out that "I manage to get my two cents in when we're alone." She considers her greatest sacrifice to the marriage to be her attempt to tolerate and to be accepted by Gil's family (his mother and seven siblings), all of whom live in Santa Barbara. In her eyes, his family are chauvinistic Mexicans, intolerant of Americans, and she has never felt accepted by them.

Celia claims that she has never felt confused about her ethnic identity, but in other statements it is evident that she experiences ambivalence. In spite of her parents' Mexican heritage and the fact that they lived on the "Mexican side of town," Celia was raised essentially as an American, learning very little about Mexico and its customs from her parents. Presumably, if she had married an Anglo like her siblings, she would have remained very American, but she married into a Mexican family, and that forced her to confront a new set of values and customs. Basically, Celia's response has been to accept and appreciate much of Mexican culture, while struggling to maintain her deeply ingrained American values and attitudes.

Celia states that she considered herself "*mexicana*" when she was a child. But that seems to have been a product of her surroundings; as she says, "All of my friends were just like me, they had Mexican parents." As a result, she says she never had to think much about ethnic identity. Not until high school, when she saw students who were newly arrived from Mexico, did Celia begin to recognize ethnic differences and come to understand how American she really was, which prompted her to change her self-identity to "Mexican American." As an adult dealing with her "very Mexican" in-laws, Celia has developed an even greater consciousness of her American identity.

> I'm an American of Mexican descent. I feel that anybody born
> here is American, but I have Mexican descent as far as my
> mother and her parents are concerned. But I'm American first! I
> guess I'm prejudiced because I'm proud of where I was born.

On the other hand, Celia states that she is proud of herself for learning Spanish as well as proud of her Mexican heritage. She feels good about having successfully adapted to Mexican culture. Because of her fluency in Spanish, she has been "mistaken for Mexican" by some of the clients in her beauty shop. With regard to her and Gil's Mexican friends, she says, "I could go over to some friend's home where they're all very Mexican—like the food, language, music and drinks are all Mexican—and I feel just as Mexican as they are."

Celia's ambivalence is particularly noticeable with regard to her feelings about her children's ethnicity. She feels that all Mexican children in this country should be taught Spanish, and she is proud that her two oldest children are fluent in the language. In the same vein, she has been quick to scold her children for expressing bigoted feelings about Mexicans, such as the time when she caught them referring to recent immigrants from Mexico as "broncs." Yet Celia has strong feelings that her children should be American first, with their Mexican heritage serving as an important but only secondary element in their lives. For example, she is basically opposed to the Chicano movement:

> This thing about 'La Raza,' big deal! It's mainly just kids running around with a chip on their shoulder—but why?! There's so many Mexican people here now. They're bringing over their customs and holidays. How many of their holidays do we celebrate now that we didn't years back? They should celebrate *our* holidays! They're not in Mexico now, they're in the United States. If I was in Mexico on the 4th of July, who the heck is going to blast and toot and have a parade for me?

Celia says she has never personally experienced discrimination. She has several Anglo relatives and one Anglo friend, but she considers them in no way different from her other relatives and friends. She has never been reluctant to visit, nor has she ever felt uncomfortable, in Anglo homes, parties, nightclubs, or recreational areas. Gil, however, feels uncomfortable in these Anglo places, which has made their visits to such places relatively infrequent. As a result, Celia believes that it is the "Mexicans from Mexico" who set themselves apart from Anglos, not vice versa. And because Celia dislikes discrimination in any form, the problem that most bothers her is to hear Mexicans criticize the United States, which is what makes life with Gil's family so difficult for her.

> Gil's relatives complain so much about having to work so hard here. If they have to complain so much, what are they doing here?! Why don't they go back? I feel strongly about this. My mother-in-law, when she's in the mood, 'The United States is great!' But other times she says, "Oh, everything is so expensive," and she complains and complains. But in Mexico it's just as bad. Yet they're here now because there is more opportunity

here, and this is where they've gotten everything they have. That really bugs me! To me, that's being ungrateful. Maybe I'm just being super extra loyal to my country. But here they have everything, where over there they had nothing, nothing! I mean, that's what gets me!

Celia has become increasingly upset with Gil's family and with "Mexicans from Mexico" in general. She avoids her husband's family as much as possible and works to increase her network of associations to include Mexican Americans and Anglos.

I think this is awful to admit, but I should be honest about it. It's gotten to be lately that more of our friends and more of our social things are Mexican, I think mainly because my husband has such a big family. And I've noticed that a lot of our friends are Mexicans from Mexico. But I want to have a large variety of friends. I want to have friends that are the same as myself. But if they associate me with Mexicans—like that lady in my beauty shop who thought I was Mexican—then other people are going to think I'm Mexican. I don't know, it's hard to explain, but it bothers me. Maybe that's being prejudiced, I don't know.

In summary, Celia grew up in the *barrio*, but her parents appear to be quite acculturated, and her friends seem ethnically quite similar to herself. Although she grew up considering herself Mexican and had no appreciation for Mexican culture, she realized how American she really was once she gained exposure to native Mexicans. In marrying into a Mexican family she has tried hard to adapt to Mexican culture, and has succeeded well: she now speaks Spanish fluently, cooks Mexican food, enjoys the music, and generally feels that she fits in well with her Mexican friends. At the same time, however, she has become increasingly aware of her American values and her strong loyalty to her native country and culture. Finally, although her social network is almost exclusively made up of people of Mexican descent, she would prefer more of a balance between Mexican and Anglo friends.

Catarina Machado

Catarina "Kate" Machado is a fifty-two-year-old native of Santa Barbara County. She is a second-generation Mexican American. As teenagers, her parents migrated from Mexico to Santa Barbara County, where her father became a miner. As an infant, however, Kate went to live with her baptismal *padrinos*, who were childless. Kate was never estranged from her parents, who lived only a few blocks away, and she saw them and her brothers and sisters often. This was significant in Kate's enculturation, for her *padrinos* were more American in their ways than her parents. Although her parents were bilingual, they preferred to speak Spanish in the home and to eat Mexican food every day; in contrast, her *padrinos* preferred to speak English, eat American food, play American music, and so on. In general, Kate explains, they tried to raise her to be an American. When she was eight years old, her *padrinos* moved away and Kate returned to her parents. However, she attributes much of her later ethnic orientation to this early experience. For example, Kate says that due to her *padrinos'* Americanizing influence, she had no trouble in adjusting to public school. She spoke English fluently, and she learned all the basic skills, such as reading, very rapidly. Kate also adjusted socially, becoming friends with many Anglos. Even as a child in school, Kate considered herself American, not Mexican, and she was quick to battle against any ethnically derogatory comments.

> I went to kindergarten and I learned right away how to salute my flag and the fundamentals of being an American. So naturally, if some guy called me a "dirty Mexican." . . . I used to really sock it to them; they found out they better not call me one again! Maybe [it was] because I was brought up early feeling American.

Kate has had a hard life. She was married at the age of seventeen, after completing the tenth grade, and soon she had two children. Then, a bout of tuberculosis put her in a sanitarium for five years, and her marriage fell apart. To support her children, she worked for several years at two jobs, sixteen hours a day. Finally, suffering from physical exhaustion, she quit working and moved in with her mother. At this point, she met and married her current husband, Paul, and they had a third child, Andy. Kate has worked part-time since her remarriage, but she has adopted the primary role of housewife and mother.

At this time in her life, Kate admits that she is reasonably secure. Paul is a traveling salesman and earns a good living. Right after their marriage, he purchased a nice four-bedroom home situated in a predominantly Anglo residential area overlooking the Pacific Ocean. To say that Kate's life with Paul has been secure is not to say, however, that it has been serene. Kate has a quick temper, as does Paul, and they have fought many times over numerous problems, including her alcoholism. Recently, Kate suffered from a variety of physical problems, and ultimately from what she is sure was a case of *embrujo* (bewitchment) (see Keefe 1981).

When asked her ethnic identity, Kate declares, "I consider myself very much American . . . because I was born here . . . and I live very much like my American friends." Technically, she admits she is "Mexican American" because her parents were Mexican, but she feels that the term does not really apply to her since she has never felt herself to be Mexican.

In probing the issue, Kate says she feels no loyalty to Mexico, although she has enjoyed her trips there and has even thought of moving there when she and Paul retire. Her loyalty has always been to the U.S. Kate believes that the Mexican people are "very different" from her. For example, she explains, "I'm very outspoken; I'll come right out and say whatever I feel, where Mexicans might hold back." Kate continues:

> I could care less what my neighbors next door think about what I do. But I think if I were from Mexico then I would think "Oh, I'm gonna be different if I don't keep my lawn trim; my neighbor is gonna think I'm Mexican if I let it grow." But I couldn't care less because we're equal. Another thing I've noticed about true Mexican people is that they apologize too much if they do the wrong thing. Where, to me, if I do the wrong thing I just forget about it. And I've noticed that Mexican people are too proud of themselves, bragging about things. I couldn't care less!

Kate prefers to live with Anglo neighbors rather than with Mexican Americans. She also says that she prefers Anglo restaurants and night spots to Mexican ones, and she even has a negative attitude about attending Mexican fiestas and parties:

> I prefer going to an American party rather than a Mexican party. Because I've found that in going to Mexican things there's always bickering, fighting, violence, and what have you. Where, at American parties I find that you don't have this.

Finally, in comparing the two countries, Kate feels that people are friendlier in the United States than in Mexico, that a child in America is luckier than one in Mexico, and that a person has a much better chance to achieve material success in the United States than in Mexico. In sum, Kate says she likes Mexico, considers it a beautiful country and has enjoyed her two or three visits, but the United States is her homeland and the object of her loyalty.

Kate says that she raised all three of her children to be American. She spoke only English in the home, celebrated all the American holidays and none of the Mexican ones, and, in general, never exposed her children to many Mexican influences. Yet there was no way for them to avoid some involvement with their Mexican heritage. For example, Kate does speak Spanish occasionally, and she prepares Mexican food regularly. She is a practicing Catholic; she chose *padrinos* for each of her children's baptism, communion, and confirmation; and she provided her children with a Catholic education. Of her children, the oldest son, David, has proven to be the most involved in his Mexican heritage. "In fact," Kate declares, "he's more Mexican than I am." David married a girl from Mexico, has learned to speak Spanish, and has learned many Mexican customs from his wife. Kate's daughter, Alice, is, like Kate, "not very Mexican," although she did learn Spanish in high school. Kate says that Alice's children are all very American and do not understand a word of Spanish. Finally, Kate's youngest son, Andy, is the least Mexican of her children, which she says is largely due to Paul's influence. Although Paul is of Mexican descent, he does not like to display his Mexican heritage. Paul speaks no Spanish, and he is resentful if anyone calls him Mexican. "Paul," Kate pauses to explain, "he'll knock you down if you dare call him a Mexican!" Kate says that when she occasionally attends Mexican festivities, she has to go without Paul because he refuses to accompany her. In particular, Paul is very critical of the current Chicano movement, and he "hates" the Chicano cultural center in town.

In some ways, there are strong Mexican influences in Kate's life. She is very attached to her family and kin, a trait that she considers more Mexican than American. She also emphasizes her love of Mexican music. Kate says that the only time she "feels Mexican" is when she is listening to her Mexican records; in particular, she says that the Mexican music makes her feel so good that she always plays it to lift her spirits when she is feeling depressed. Another influence comes from her brother-in-law, Juan. Kate is very close to her sister, Silvia, and as it happens, Silvia's husband, Juan is very much involved in Mexican American social activities, especially at the Chicano cultural center. Over the years, Kate has attended various "Mexican American doings" at the center with Silvia and Juan, including the *Cinco de Mayo* celebrations; and a few times she has accompanied them to see Spanish-language movies playing at the Mexican theater in town. It was Juan who convinced Kate that she was *embrujada* (bewitched) three years ago, and who succeeded in curing her of the condition. Since then, Kate has developed an interest in Mexican folk medicine, although she says she would only go to a *curandera* for treatment if repeated visits to physicians proved to be unsuccessful.

Kate says that she gets along well with other Americans, including Anglos. In social interaction, she does not emphasize her Mexican background and those things that set her apart from Anglos. "I'm not ashamed of my Mexican heritage because there's no denying that I'm Mexican; but I don't go down the street with a Mexican flag saying 'I'm Mexican!.' " Instead, Kate accepts the Mexican side of her heritage, but she puts more emphasis on her American traits. She says she has always felt certain about her identity: "I know where I fit . . . I'm very much American." Apparently, she has had little difficulty in being accepted as one. She has always gotten along well with Anglos. Throughout school, most of her friends were Anglos; most of her boyfriends, she recalls, were Anglos; she has always worked with Anglos; and in adulthood, the majority of her friends and neighbors have been Anglos. Kate also says she has never experienced discrimination as an adult in any way.

Kate generalizes from her own experience in saying that Mexican people are not discriminated against. She does not believe that local employers refuse to hire Mexicans; she disagrees with the notion that school teachers pay more attention to Anglo than Mexican children; and she also doubts that Mexicans are treated badly by government agencies, such as the welfare office or the police department. Instead, Kate firmly believes that discrimination is brought on by the Mexican people themselves:

> If Mexicans are discriminated against, it's because they feel that they are discriminated against, not because they are in fact dis-

criminated against. They just feel that way. I believe they are
picked on because of who they are as individuals, and they think
it is because they are Mexicans.

These statements indicate that while she recognizes the Mexican
influences in her life, Kate is not involved with—nor is she particularly sympathetic to—Mexican American people as a group.
Moreover, Kate says that she has felt this way all of her life. Even
though she speaks Spanish, occasionally attends Mexican festivities,
and has many Mexican American friends and relatives, these influences mean less to Kate than her sense of being American. For this
reason, Kate chooses not to call herself a "Mexican American;"
instead, in emphasizing her attachment to the American side of her
ethnic identity, she considers herself an "American of Mexican descent." Kate has been influenced by the two cultures, but she has never
felt pulled between them, and in the end, her preference is to be an
American and to participate primarily in the American way of life.

New Americans

Kathy Marquez

Kathy Marquez is a thirty-one-year-old housewife with five children. She was born in Ventura, but now lives in Santa Barbara. After
completing the ninth grade, Kathy dropped out of school to get
married. Her husband, Al, is a warehouseman. Kathy does some
child care, but otherwise she does not work outside the home.
Strictly speaking, Kathy is a second-generation Mexican American
because her father was born in Mexico. However, he left the family
when she was quite young, and the stepfather who raised her was
born in the United States. On her mother's side, her grandparents
were also born in the United States.

Kathy's life has not been easy financially. When her father de-
serted the family, she and her two brothers as well as her mother had
to work for years as farm laborers in order to make ends meet. After
her mother's remarriage, Kathy remembers living in a small two-
bedroom house, which must have been quite cramped considering
the fact that two half-brothers and a half-sister also lived there.

The Marquezes live in a mixed-ethnic neighborhood with some

well-kept, medium-sized homes and smaller, more rundown ones. Their two-bedroom home is one of the smaller ones, and it is very worn and in need of paint. While some of the nicer homes have fairly well-kept yards, Kathy's front yard is dirt, devoid of lawn or greenery. Inside, her living room shows the wear and tear of five children and a less than fastidious approach to housework. One of the walls of the living room is decorated with a huge tapestry depicting Christ's Last Supper. Throughout the house, there is no other evidence of Mexican cultural influence either in the decor or in any other aspect of the house.

Kathy reports that things are very difficult financially for her family. In remembering the efforts that her own mother went through to provide for holidays, Kathy tries to do the same within the confines of her tight budget. But for some of the lesser holidays, like Easter, she finds that she cannot do very much. On Easter, she remembers that her mother used to buy complete outfits for the children. Kathy explains that she just cannot afford it for her own children. Kathy complains about the high cost of living and the need for her eldest son to get his dishwashing job.

Kathy's husband, Al, is a third-generation Mexican American. Kathy reports that Al considers his role as husband to include a good deal of decision making and direction shaping for his wife, such as determining with whom she socializes, when she uses the car, and whether or not she continues her education. Enforcement of these decisions is not always achieved by overt sanctions. When she began to frequent night spots with friends, he simply forbade her to do so; and as a result of a disagreement over the use of the car, her access to it diminished considerably. His opposition to her returning to school, however, was more subtle; Al simply discouraged her and would not contribute to child care, car use, or other logistic support. Al probably also had something to do with Kathy's early termination of the interviews, which she suddenly cut off after several meetings.

Kathy grew up in Ventura County, where she married Al and where they continued to live for seven years. Kathy is very close to her family and kin, and when Al's employer transferred him to another store in Santa Barbara she hesitated to leave Ventura. But her husband gave her an ultimatum: either she would come with him or they would get a divorce. Kathy decided, with some later regret, to move with him. She still sees her siblings and her parents on a weekly basis, and she values her close kin ties.

Kathy's ethnic identification is remarkably inconsistent. She states that ten years ago she identified as "American," as well as the first time she was asked in this particular study. In our second interview conducted with her a year later, she said that she identified as "Spanish." She also recalls identifying as an "American" when she was a child. However, she would like to be considered an "American of Mexican descent" by other Mexican Americans, and as "Chicana" by Anglos. Finally, if she were traveling in Mexico, she would like to be identified as "Spanish" by Mexicans. This variation in ethnic identity, when considered in conjunction with her almost complete lack of appreciation of ethnicity in other parts of her life, is puzzling at first. Instead of making a fine discrimination in ethnic identification across several situations or showing a pattern of evolution, it appears to be a function of her lack of knowledge about or sensitivity to the connotations and meanings of the various terms.

Mexican and/or Mexican American culture does not influence Kathy's life in many direct or perceptible ways. She is unaware of many of the events and ideas that play an important part in the lives of other more culturally oriented Mexican American families. For example, she does not celebrate *Cinco de Mayo*, the Twelfth of December, or the Sixteenth of September, and she could not say exactly what they signify. While the use of *curanderos* is consistently low among the Mexican Americans we interviewed, most can identify the term; Kathy was completely unfamiliar with it. In addition, if she were given the choice she would travel in the United States rather than in Mexico. Furthermore, she had never heard of a *Quinceañera* until her oldest son was invited to participate in one. When asked for the rationale or purpose for such an event, and the possibility of her daughter having one, she replied in the following way:

> To me, it's advertising that the daughter is available for marriage. That's what I feel . . . I'm not going to pay out money, like that. I'll save it for her wedding. I didn't have one. If I was real Mexican, I would have heard about it.

Her eldest son, who was present, retorted, "It's when a girl turns into a woman," and "Yes, Sarah will have one, I'll pay for it!" In any case, knowledge of celebrations and events and their deeper and more fundamental meanings are not important dynamics in her life. This is understandable, considering her generational distance from Mexico and enculturation. For most of her life, there were no monocultural Mexican experiences. She can speak Spanish, but only in a limited way. She has had Anglo and Mexican American friends, and she has operated in both cultures. What perhaps affects her more profoundly is her continued membership in a lower-class culture and all its associated manifestations. Recently, she attended a wedding reception for one of her in-laws, and she was very surprised that there were only Mexican American people there. She had never experienced a similar situation. "It was the first time [for me] there were not white people there, they were all Spanish." She has apparently been accustomed to the presence of both groups.

Although she does not seek out or prefer only people of Mexican descent in such places as a restaurant or in her neighborhood, she does prefer going to parties where most of the people are of Mexican descent. She also hopes that her children will ultimately marry others of Mexican descent. The strength of this wish is not so great as it might be, for she does have Anglo in-laws and shares good relationships with them. Her two close friends are of Mexican descent, and the neighborhood in which she lives is populated by a large percentage of Mexicans and Mexican Americans. Also, since many of her social contacts are with her own family, many of her social activities are with other Mexican Americans. But this appears to be happenstance rather than an actual search for persons of similar ethnic orientation.

Kathy does not report any incidents of discrimination, either in her own life or in her children's lives. She does not recognize discrimination in the school system, in public agencies, or with the Immigration and Naturalization Service. She has "no opinion" about discrimination by employers, in overall general opportunities or with the police force. She could not recall experiencing any difficulty, due to her Mexican heritage, in getting a job, renting or buying a house, applying for a loan, or receiving commercial service. Either she has not been the victim of overt or subtle discrimination or she has not been sensitive to it.

In sum, Kathy's ethnicity is a minor aspect of her day-to-day life. Instead, there is a myriad of daily hassles arising from the cramped quarters, the lack of money, and the consequent lack of material goods. In addition, because her children are also being raised in a lower socioeconomic milieu, she has concerns about their finishing school and their exposure to drugs and juvenile crimes. Class, then, rather than ethnicity plays a much more important role in her life and in her children's lives. Although she acknowledges her Mexican heritage, she makes no conscious effort to maintain it, and except in certain gender-linked behaviors and familial relations, it is hardly visible. She has no consistent identification, and those that mark her Mexicanness are as acceptable to her as those that do not. Her social relations happen to be primarily with others of Mexican descent, and probably this, more than anything else, reinforces her limited Mexican orientation.

Margaret Camacho

Margaret (Marge) Camacho, thirty years old, is a fourth-generation native of Santa Barbara. She is of mixed ancestry, four generations removed from Mexico on her mother's side, and five generations removed from Ireland on her father's side. That mixture, in conjunction with her birth in the United States, makes Marge, by her definition, an "American." Only nominally does she recognize her Mexican heritage by identifying, if asked, as "American of Mexican descent." But she knows little of Mexico or its customs, she speaks no Spanish, and she has no feeling of attachment to the Mexican people. Perhaps her sense of identification may be understood more clearly if it is kept in mind that while her married name is Camacho, her maiden name is Callahan, reflecting her father's Irish ancestry.

During Marge's childhood her family was somewhat poor, and they lived in several homes in the eastside *barrio* of Santa Barbara. Marge liked the area then, describing it as "a fairly decent neighborhood." Most of her neighborhood and school friends, she says, were Mexican American. When Marge was thirteen years old, the family bought a large house on a ten-acre plot in a foothills area, where their neighbors were primarily Anglo Americans. James and Martha still live there, but Marge left home and school at age sixteen, after completing the tenth grade, to marry twenty-six-year-old Ernie Camacho, a third-generation Mexican American born in Santa Barbara.

Marge, Ernie, and their two boys and baby daughter live in an old Spanish-style three-bedroom house in a residential area comprised fairly equally of Mexican American and Anglo American lower-middle-class families. There is no apparent Mexican influence in the furnishing of their home. To maintain the basic expenses of the house rent and the support of three children, both Marge and Ernie must work. Ernie is a janitor, while Marge is an assembler at an electronics plant. They have a small supplemental income: Ernie is in the California Army Reserves, and he participates one weekend a month in training exercises.

In Marge's opinion, she was raised as an American, with some Mexican influence from her mother. Martha, her mother, speaks a little Spanish and cooks Mexican food regularly, but that is the extent of her Mexican traits, according to Marge. Her father, James, considers himself an American of Irish descent, and has little or no affinity with Mexican culture. Marge even says that James would consider it an insult if someone suggested that he was Mexican; and probably a significant correlate of James's attitude is Marge's statement that between her Mexican and Irish heritages, she is most proud of being Irish. The anomaly here is that Marge has dark brown skin, while her siblings are all fair, as is her father who has red hair. So Marge on occasion has been "mistaken" both for being Mexican and American Indian. Marge says that her father legitimates her skin color by referring to her as "smoked Irish." But skin color notwithstanding, Marge considers herself an American whose heritage happens to be partly Mexican.

Marge did not learn to speak Spanish as a child, for the language which Martha and James speak almost exclusively is English. Marge developed an ability to understand some Spanish primarily through exposure to her Spanish-speaking grandmother. Otherwise, there was no instruction in Mexican customs during Marge's childhood, neither in Mexican history nor in proverbs, legends, music, or dances. The family never celebrated Mexican holidays, only American ones. As Marge explains, "my parents, me, and my children we're all born and raised in Santa Barbara, so there's no need to go digging into Mexican history." While growing up and attending school, a number of Marge's neighborhood and school friends were Mexican American, but she describes them as being very Americanized, like her. Besides, Marge points out, many of her other friends were Anglos; and now, as an adult, most of her friends are Anglos, almost all of whom are members of a voluntary organization in which Marge and Ernie are very active.

Marge's religious instruction was Catholic, but basically in the American fashion. Although she had *padrinos* for baptism and confirmation, the bond was not significant to Marge. Marge and Ernie were married in church, but they followed the American custom of having a "best man" and "maid of honor" instead of having a coterie of *padrinos* and *madrinas*. Marge's interest in ritual kinship was renewed after the birth of her children. Each child has been baptized, and Marge has chosen *compadres* for each occasion. She considers these *compadres* good friends (some are relatives), and she feels that there is some obligation between *compadres* to be of help to one another in time of need. Specifically, she believes that it is the godparents' obligation to look after the child if the parents die, and she considers this a useful function.

Marge's preference in identifying herself as "American" or as "American of Mexican descent" reflects her lack of involvement in Mexican culture. She says that as far as she is concerned, there is no appreciable difference between the two terms. She feels American because she was born in the United States, and she states that "though I look like one [with dark skin], I don't feel like a Mexican." She emphasizes that her lack of identification with Mexico is due to the fact that she was not born there and "wasn't raised like Mexicans are raised."

In keeping with this pattern of identification are Marge's attitudes about the relative merits of Mexican and American culture. She believes that people born here should learn about the United States, and so she disagrees that Mexican American children should learn Spanish and Mexican history in public schools. She considers American music and food to be appreciably better than Mexican music and food. She believes that a person born in the United States is luckier than one born in Mexico, and in general, she feels that a person living in the United States has a better chance of getting ahead than one in Mexico.

Marge's primary attachment to American culture is even more strongly evident in her negative attitude toward the Chicano movement. She declares that "I don't believe in that brown-power stuff." She adds, vehemently:

"La Raza," that's a bunch of garbage! And Ernie feels the same way. Why live here in the United States and bitch about this and

that? I don't even understand why they do it. If they want to believe in all that Mexican [stuff] then they can go back to Mexico!

Marge's sympathies are at the other end of the pole, as is evident in
her statement that she always identifies herself as "white" on job
application questions asking for ethnicity. She also says that this has
never been a problem in her marriage, for although Ernie is Mexican
American, he "doesn't relate to the Mexican people" and "doesn't
speak any Spanish." Yet he has been exposed to more Mexican
traditions than Marge.

Marge has not emphasized any Mexican customs in the rearing of
her children, nor do her children speak Spanish. Marge does cook
Mexican food periodically. However, the only Mexican trait she
strongly advocates is what she feels is the Mexican value of respect for
parents; in this vein, she feels that American children are too dis-
respectful in the treatment of their parents, and Marge says she will
not tolerate that in her children. At times, Marge has told her sons
that they are more Mexican than she is, due to their "blood line" from
their father; nevertheless, she says that her boys identify themselves
exclusively as American.

Marge claims to have never experienced any confusion or other
problems about her sense of ethnic identification. She says that
"Mexicans are not my people"; all of her life, many of her friends have
been "white," and she has never "been treated like a Mexican." Nor
does she associate very often with Mexicans: "I don't even mingle
with Mexicans, like I won't go to a Mexican dance."

Finally, reflecting Marge's orientation is her belief that discrimination stems from Mexicans' dislike of Anglos, not vice versa. Specifically, Marge recognizes three different ethnic groups in Santa Barbara: "Mexican Mexicans" (from Mexico), "Mexican Americans that
are in between," and "Anglos." Marge identifies more with Anglos
than with the two Mexican groups; and when asked to explain this
identification, she says that more precisely she is an American who is
"part-Mexican but doesn't identify as Mexican at all." Concerning
relations between these three groups, she feels that Mexican Mexicans are the most prejudiced: "The Mexican Mexicans don't recognize the Mexicans from here [Mexican Americans], so if you're part
Mexican, the Mexican Mexicans will spit on you just as if you were

Black." Marge describes the Mexican Americans as being "in between."

> Well, the middle group, the Mexican Americans, they tend to lean toward the whites, but they're Mexican at the same time. They're easily offended at Mexican insults, and I think that's where all this Chicano stuff comes from—because they're just halfway in between and they're never accepted by one group or the other.

In contrast, she believes that Anglos are not prejudiced: "I think Anglos get along better with Mexicans than Mexicans get along with Anglos." Thus, Marge concludes that in Santa Barbara most of the ethnic discrimination "comes from Mexicans against Anglos," and not vice versa.

Given this attitude, Marge feels that there is no discrimination against Mexicans by Anglo employers, school teachers, or government agency personnel. She suggests that if police treat Mexicans on the east side of town badly, it is because there is a lot of violence and crime on that side of town. Marge feels quite strongly on this point, explaining that there are many juvenile gangs in the *barrio*, and she would never want to raise her children in that area. Finally, Marge says that she herself has never suffered from discrimination by Anglos. Instead, she says that she has discriminated against Mexicans; for example, when she was an apartment manager for a time, she would not rent to Mexicans.

To summarize, Marge has virtually no conscious attachment to the Mexican people or to Mexican culture. She considers herself American, and she identifies only nominally as an "American of Mexican descent." She feels that she was not raised as a Mexican, and she has not raised her children as Mexicans. Most of her friends are Anglos, and she says she feels much more comfortable in socializing with Anglos. Moreover, she would not like to live in a very Mexican neighborhood or to even attend such social activities as a "Mexican dance." Finally, she says that she has never suffered from discrimination, but she has discriminated against Mexicans; and, in general, she believes that the problem of discrimination in town comes from the Mexicans and not from the Anglos. And yet Marge is not completely divorced from her Mexican heritage because she married a Mexican

American and she is tied to a large Mexican American social network through their combined kin groups.

Conclusions

The case studies presented in the last three chapters demonstrate a gradual acculturation in many aspects of the Mexican American way of life. Certain traditional traits, such as an orientation toward Mexico as one's homeland or passing on folktales and folk remedies, seem to decline within a generation, and in some ways, there is a gradual replacement with American cultural traits. For example, American holidays quickly replace Mexican ones, and English fluency is more common than Spanish fluency. Much of this comes as a result of the cultural homogenization process in American schools. As Lena Rivera says, "Whatever I learned of American customs, I learned at school." Immigrants, if they arrive as children in the U.S., can quickly become Americanized in this sense.

It is inaccurate, however, to infer that Mexicans simply become more American from generation to generation. The case of Dolores Guerrero, a fourth-generation *La Raza* type, obviates that conclusion. Moreover, many Mexican cultural patterns are held fast across generation and ethnic type. For example, despite a decline in Spanish language fluency and preference, 96 percent of our respondents in the second survey speak some Spanish. The vast majority (81 percent) eat Mexican food daily, and Mexican Americans (89 percent) tend to remain Catholic from generation to generation. Furthermore, in some ways Mexican culture adapts to the American experience by producing new forms or functions, such as the development of a new and separate identity as "Chicano." In any case, it is clear that Mexican culture persists in the U.S., perhaps changing in character, but such is the fate of culture in general. The last two cases in this chapter illustrate the inherent retention of certain aspects of Mexican culture, especially strong family ties. Even those individuals who marry out of their ethnic group or are the product of an interethnic marriage and no longer bear a Spanish surname (and thus would not appear, for the most part, in our sample) would maintain the attachment to a Mexican extended kin group. Chapters 9 and 10 explore in more detail the importance of kinship in Mexican American life.

Similar to cultural awareness, ethnic loyalty displays no simple continuum from Mexican to Anglo. Most of the individuals in the case studies feel that Mexican people and Mexican culture are good in some ways and that Anglo Americans and American culture are good in other ways. The significance seems to be in the emphasis on self-identification with one group and culture or the other. Here again, there is no clear indication that Mexican identity ultimately declines and disappears for any great number of people of Mexican descent. Celia Torres and Kate Machado recognize with pride their Mexican heritage, while simultaneously cultivating their American identity. Even Kathy Marquez and Marge Camacho exhibit a certain felt affiliation with Mexican people. Kathy Marquez, for example, feels more comfortable with other Mexican people and hopes her children will marry within their ethnic group. Marge Camacho verbally denies her Mexicanness ("Mexicans are not my people"), and yet she married a Mexican American and socializes within a huge local extended kin network made up mostly of other Mexican Americans.

Perhaps the aspect of social interaction is the key to understanding the complex relationship between cultural awareness and ethnic loyalty in the case studies. As the informants imply over and over again, their consciousness of their own ethnicity came in response to their exposure to others who were different from themselves. Carmen Muñoz (chapter 5) was struck by the unfriendliness of Anglos when she was kept waiting on a neighbor's porch. Celia Torres (in this chapter) began to realize in high school that while she was of Mexican descent, she was not like the newly arrived immigrant students. Her differentness was confirmed after her marriage to a foreign-born Mexican whose values and behavior still disturb her in many ways. Obviously, there are more than two ethnic reference groups. As Marge Camacho summarizes, there are Mexicans from Mexico, Mexican Americans, and Anglos.

Even these categories fail to tap the complexity of ethnic social organization that exists. For example, Kate Machado's *padrinos* and Celia Torres's mother were born in Mexico and yet spoke English and interacted with Anglo Americans. Tony Reyes (chapter 6) primarily interacts with other politicized Chicanos. Clearly, individuals seek out others like themselves, people with similar values and cultural heritage, and people with whom they feel most comfortable. Here again is where kin groups become significant because (as will be discussed in chapter 11) family members tend to make up a large portion of all Mexican Americans' social networks. Thus, while Tony Reyes socializes with Chicano friends, his family is less politicized and aligns him with a larger, more inclusive ethnic reference group. It is through ethnically enclosed friendship and kinship groups that individuals' cultural awareness and ethnic loyalty are maintained and where the tangible evidence of being somehow "Mexican" is undeniable.

8

Ethnicity: Variation and Change

ONCE HAVING ESTABLISHED MEASURES of acculturation (Cultural Awareness), social assimilation (Ethnic Social Orientation), and ethnic identity (Ethnic Loyalty), we can now turn to an examination of factors related to these three processes of sociocultural change. Researchers have suggested that acculturation is affected by several factors, with generation as one of those most commonly mentioned. It is only logical that immigrants would possess more knowledge of traditional culture and less about the host culture. Also observed frequently is a positive association between socioeconomic status and acculturation. Gordon (1964) specifically isolates education as the key to the Americanization process. Other factors believed to be associated with the acculturation process include Protestantism; residence outside of the ghetto or *barrio*; an urban background; and youth. A relationship between sex and acculturation also has been suggested, but authors differ on whether women or men acculturate more rapidly.

The process of social assimilation is generally discussed in conjunction with the same variables associated with acculturation, which is largely due to the assumption that acculturation must precede assimilation (Gordon 1964; Teske and Nelson 1974), as well as the assumption that ethnic minority members who more closely resemble the majority in their socioeconomic status and those who live outside *barrios* are more likely to associate with Anglo Americans on a personal basis. Some researchers, on the other hand, find that upward mobility and residence outside the *barrio* do not necessarily result in social assimilation. Gordon (1964) refers to this phenomenon as an ethclass consisting of ethnic minority group members who have been upwardly mobile, but remain socially tied to their ethnic group. Finally, studies of intermarriage suggest that the relationship between sex and intermarriage varies by ethnic group (Fitzpatrick and Gurak 1979). Among Chicanos, it appears that women are more likely to marry members of the majority group, which implies greater interethnic social interaction for females generally (Mittelbach and Moore 1968). However, recent research has also demonstrated that intermarriage itself is not necessarily a good index of acculturation. Rather, the findings show that Mexican Americans, in spite of marrying outside their ethnic group, maintain cultural ties as well as an ethnic identity (Salgado de Snyder and Padilla 1982).

Less attention has been given to the investigation of factors affecting the process of ethnic identification. Several authors suggest that upward mobility results in the loss of ethnic identity as well as in acculturation and social assimilation (Grebler, Moore, and Guzman 1970). Clark, Kaufman, and Pierce (1976) state that there is no relationship between age or generation and ethnic identity in their data. They offer a number of possible explanations for variation in ethnic identity, many of which are incorporated in our model of Cultural Awareness and Ethnic Loyalty (for example, perceived discrimination and family members' level of acculturation). In contrast, Dashefsky and Shapiro (1974) find that generation is indeed related to ethnic identification; they also conclude that ethnic identity is associated with maintenance of the ethnic religion.

Factors Related to Cultural Awareness, Ethnic Loyalty, and Ethnic Social Orientation

The Pearson correlation coefficients for Cultural Awareness, Ethnic Loyalty, and Ethnic Social Orientation and the variables reviewed above are presented in table 8. Since generation is significantly intercorrelated with all of the variables except those denoting religion, the correlation coefficients for Cultural Awareness, Ethnic Loyalty and Ethnic Social Orientation were also computed while controlling for generation.

Cultural Awareness is very highly correlated with generation. It is

Table 8 Pearson and Partial Correlation Coefficients for Cultural Awareness, Ethnic Loyalty and Ethnic Social Orientation

Descriptive Variables	Cultural Awareness r	Ethnic Loyalty r	Ethnic Social Orientation r	Control for Generation		
				Cultural Awareness r	Ethnic Loyalty r	Ethnic Social Orientation r
Generation	-.74***	-.26***	-.33***			
Socioeconomic Status						
Respondent's education	-.65***	-.32***	-.44***	-.54***	-.26***	-.40***
Family income	-.25***	-.15***	-.16***	-.31***	-.18**	-.19**
Head of household occupation	-.37***	-.25***	-.36***	-.41***	-.21***	-.33***
Head of household SEI[a]	-.35***	-.23***	-.34***	-.38***	-.21***	-.32***
Socioeconomic Mobility						
SEI change, first job to present	-.23***	-.15**	-.24***	-.23***	-.11*	-.21***
SEI change, father's job to son's	-.23***	-.11*	-.24***	-.24***	-.11*	-.20***
Religion						
Catholic	.10*	.05	.20***	.17**	.06	.15**
Protestant	-.10*	-.06	-.21***	-.16***	-.05	-.17**
Agnostic/atheist	-.03	.02	-.01	-.06	-.03	.02
Barrio residence[b]	.35***	.37***	.49***	.34***	.37***	.49***
Urban background	-.17***	-.15***	-.12**	-.18**	-.23***	-.13*
Age	.23***	-.05	-.02	.04	-.02	-.14*
Female Sex	.02	-.09*	.07	.16**	-.04	.14*

Source: Second Mexican American survey.
[a]Duncan's Socioeconomic Index (SEI).
[b]Ethnic density greater than 40%.
Signficance levels: .05*, .01**, .001***.

also highly and negatively correlated with all of the indicators of socioeconomic status, but most especially, the respondent's education ($r = -.65$, $p < .001$). In addition, Cultural Awareness is negatively related to socioeconomic mobility. Urbanism is negatively associated, and *barrio* residence (defined here as residence in census tracts with an ethnic density greater than 40 percent) is positively associated with Cultural Awareness. All of these relationships hold when controlling for generation. As table 8 also shows, there is a weak relationship between religion and Cultural Awareness, which becomes more significant when controlling for generation. The apparent correlation of age and Cultural Awareness disappears, while female sex and Cultural Awareness appear to be correlated when generation is controlled.

A stepwise multiple regression analysis was computed for Cultural Awareness by using the same independent variables. According to the results, 85 percent of the variance is accounted for by five of the variables: generation (74 percent); education (8 percent); and the combination of *barrio* residence, head-of-household occupation, and rural background (3 percent). In sum, unacculturated respondents are most likely to be first generation, less educated, lower in socioeconomic status, less socioeconomically mobile, and *barrio* residents who have not lived in large cities during most of their lives. In contrast, the more acculturated respondents are likely to be native born, better educated, higher in socioeconomic status, more socioeconomically mobile, and non-*barrio* residents with urban backgrounds.

None of these findings is surprising, considering our familarity with the process of acculturation. The correlation coefficients for Ethnic Loyalty are weaker, but they indicate similar relationships with most, if not all, of the variables (see table 8). Perhaps most interesting, however, is the difference between the correlations of Cultural Awareness and Ethnic Loyalty and generation. Ethnic Loyalty has a significant but much weaker negative relationship with generation when it is compared to Cultural Awareness (-.26 vs. -.74). Thus confirming other analyses in chapter 4, identification with the ethnic group is less affected than the process of acculturation by exposure or length of exposure to another culture. The comparatively lower correlation of Ethnic Loyalty and education also supports this conclusion, since respondents with higher levels of education have generally attended school in the U.S. Nevertheless, there is a negative association between Ethnic Loyalty and the indicators of socioeconomic status and mobility which parallels the correlations for Cultural Awareness. Similarly, Ethnic Loyalty is positively correlated with *barrio* residence and negatively correlated with an urban background. As with Cultural Awareness, these relationships hold when controlling for generation. In contrast to Cultural Awareness, however, there is no correlation between religion or age and Ethnic Loyalty. Finally, although Ethnic Loyalty and female sex is weakly and negatively correlated, this correlation disappears when generation is controlled.

By using stepwise multiple regression analysis, fewer variables account for the total explained variance of 49 percent for Ethnic Loyalty. These variables are *barrio* residence (40 percent), education (6 percent), and rural background (3 percent). Thus, while foreign-born and lower-class Mexicans are much more likely to be unacculturated, they are only somewhat more likely to identify with their ethnic group. Actually, *barrio* residence is the variable most strongly associated with Ethnic Loyalty, as was shown in both statistical analyses. But it is impossible to say whether *barrio* residence reinforces one's ethnic identity or whether those with loyalty to the ethnic group choose to live in the *barrio*, or if both are true. Other factors that have not been tapped must be involved in the maintenance of ethnic identity. In any case, the two different patterns of correlates for Cultural Awareness and Ethnic Loyalty further demonstrate the semiindependent nature of the two processes.

The question of formation and maintenance of ethnic identity is an interesting one. Why, for example, should two of our case studies, Dolores Guerrero (Type I) and Lena Rivera (Type III), express such different reactions to overt discrimination against Chicanos? Also, why do they have different perceptions of discriminatory practices directed at Chicanos? Both women remember attending segregated schools, but Dolores is pained by the memory, while Lena is proud of her ability in advancing quickly to the "Anglo" school. Both live in Oxnard, but Dolores recalls numerous instances of local discrimination affecting her and her family, while Lena is less convinced that she has been the object of much discrimination and believes that both ethnic groups are at fault. Certainly, personal experience and discrimination has much to do with its perception, but clearly there are more factors that contribute to feelings of ethnic attachment.

The life histories of Dolores and Lena are remarkably similar and reveal few answers. They are almost the same age, were born in Texas, grew up in poor farm-labor families, and experienced turbulent family lives during their childhoods. The differences in education, socioeconomic status, and generation are not what one would predict from the statistical findings; for Dolores has more education, a higher income, and is further generationally removed from Mexico than Lena. On the other hand, the correlation with *barrio* residence holds true; Dolores lives in *La Colonia*, while Lena lives in a south Oxnard neighborhood, where less than 25 percent of the residents are other Mexican Americans. Instead of providing a determinant of ethnic identity, however, their choice of residence seems to simply reflect other attitudes and attachments. Lena, for example, did live for several years in *La Colonia*, and while Dolores identifies strongly with her ethnic group, her husband (and coresident in the *barrio*) has little pride in his Mexican heritage.

The process of ethnic identification is complex. Many of our informants spoke of differences in the ethnic affiliation of their own children, who would have similar social characteristics. Personality, special talents and skills, physical features, parental influence, experience with discrimination, and variety of contact with Anglos, among other things, may contribute to ethnic identification. The life histories indicate that the process of ethnic identification begins early in childhood. However, it is also subject to modification, as when Anna Fuentes (Type III; see chapter 6) changed from a rebellious Chicana in high school to a less chauvinistic Mexican American in her twenties. Clearly, the topic of ethnic identification deserves greater attention in future research.

Our measure of interethnic interaction (Ethnic Social Orientation), which is one subfactor contributing to the factor patterns for Cultural Awareness and Ethnic Loyalty, is interesting when examined separately because of its implications for the related process of social assimilation. Ethnic Social Orientation is comprised of variables that identify the ethnicity of associates such as friends, neighbors, church members, and leisuremates, as well as other variables that identify ethnic food preferences. A high score on Ethnic Social Orientation denotes ethnic enclosure. Social assimilation is, of course, a much more complex and extensive process than the measure of Ethnic Social Orientation would indicate. Nevertheless, by tapping interethnic interaction in intimate primary relationships,

Ethnic Social Orientation should prove to be a sensitive measure of the completeness of integration of the ethnic groups.

As table 8 indicates, Ethnic Social Orientation has correlational patterns similar to Cultural Awareness in some respects, and to Ethnic Loyalty in others. Most notable is the fact that Ethnic Social Orientation, like Ethnic Loyalty, is not as highly related to generation as Cultural Awareness. The relationship between Ethnic Social Orientation and the measures of socioeconomic status generally resembles that of Cultural Awareness, although both Ethnic Social Orientation and Ethnic Loyalty are less responsive to differences in family income. Ethnic Social Orientation also tends to resemble Cultural Awareness in its strength of association with the measures of socioeconomic mobility. All of these associations hold when controlling for generation. Ethnic Social Orientation is similar to Cultural Awareness in the relationship with religious affiliation, positively correlated with Catholicism ($r=.20$) and negatively correlated with Protestantism ($r=-.21$). Also, like Cultural Awareness, a relationship (albeit weak) between female sex and Ethnic Social Orientation emerges when controlling for generation. Ethnic Social Orientation is more highly correlated with *barrio* residence, and has a lower correlation with an urban background than either Cultural Awareness or Ethnic Loyalty. Finally, a weak negative relationship between Ethnic Social Orientation and age appears when generation is controlled. A stepwise multiple regression analysis indicates that *barrio* residence is the most significant variable associated with Ethnic Social Orientation and accounts for 48 percent of the variance. In addition, education accounts for another 11 percent of the variance. None of the other variables, except Catholicism and head-of-household occupation (2 percent, when combined), emerged as significant predictors of Ethnic Social Orientation.

In descriptive terms, Chicanos who interact with Anglos in personal relationships tend to be generationally removed from Mexico. As we will see in chapter 11, the primary distinction exists between the foreign born who predominately live in *barrios*, and who tend to interact primarily with other Mexicans, and the native born who tend to incorporate some Anglos into their personal networks. The association with generation is not as high as that found with Cultural Awareness because social assimilation, unlike acculturation, appears to level off substantially after the second generation. Socially assimilated Mexican Americans are more likely to be Protestants and non-*barrio* residents, who tend to be higher in socioeconmic status and education as well as more socioeconomically mobile.

In sum, while the process of social assimilation shares much with the related process of acculturation, it has a unique pattern of correlates that sets it apart. It demonstrates a definite relationship with social class and socioeconomic mobility. But its strongest association, like that of Ethnic Loyalty, is with *barrio* residence, which holds when controlling for generation. Again, the question is whether *barrio* residence primarily shapes ethnic social interactions, or whether the choice to live in the *barrio*, especially, among post-immigrant generations, is made first, and if so, what factors affect this decision. Future studies of social assimilation must focus on the dynamics in individuals lives that result in increased interaction outside the ethnic group. For example, Anna Fuentes (Type III; see chapter 6) appears to have experienced, as a high school student, an unfavorable initial exposure to Anglos, which negatively colored her subsequent feelings about and interaction with Anglos. Kate Machado (Type IV; see chapter 7) remembers being called a "dirty Mexican" in school, but still got along well with Anglos, having Anglo school friends and boyfriends, and presently continues to claim several Anglo friends. Personality, self-concept, peer-group attitudes and behavior, and individual talents and opportunities undoubtedly have much to do with the outcome for individuals, but it is apparent that we have much to learn about the process of social assimilation and its determinants.

Conclusions

Our data support many of the findings of previous research on cultural change. A relationship between all proposed variables (except age) and acculturation is confirmed. The pattern of correlations for our measure of social assimilation is somewhat similar to that for acculturation. However, generation has a weaker association and *barrio* residence a stronger association with social assimilation than with acculturation. In sum, our study indicates an important qualification for previous research because we find little support for a gradual and combined acculturation–assimilation model. Instead, it is evident that increased social assimilation occurs primarily in the second generation, leveling off thereafter. Furthermore, our data support, in a way, the idea that movement outside the *barrio* is associated with increased interaction with Anglos. However, as we shall see in chapter 11, this interaction occurs mainly in less intimate kinds of relationships, and Gordon's (1964) concept of the ethclass is accurately applied to Mexican Americans.

Our analysis of ethnic identification confirms a relationship between generation, socioeconomic status and mobility, and ethnic identity, but the correlations are not strong. Like Clark, Kaufman, and Pierce (1976), we find no relationship between ethnic loyalty and age. And unlike Dashefsky and Shapiro (1974), we find no relationship between religious affiliation and ethnic loyalty. The strongest relationship which emerges in our analysis of Ethnic Loyalty is with a factor that has gone unmentioned in research on ethnic identity: *barrio* residence, which deserves greater attention in future research.

9

Family and Ethnicity

FAMILY STRUCTURE IS AN IMPORTANT ASPECT of ethnicity, and this is particularly true among Chicanos who—as researchers always point out—are very family oriented. Because family structure is essential to understanding the three processes of culture change (acculturation, assimilation, and ethnic identification), we have isolated it for special attention in the following two chapters. In previous studies of Mexican Americans, researchers consistently contrast kin relations with those of Anglo Americans, in order to highlight the significance of ethnic background in determining aspects of social structure. In this chapter, we turn to an examination of family data collected from both Anglo Americans and Mexican Americans and provide some detailed comparisons of family structure in the two ethnic groups.

Although it is rarely mentioned, there are actually many similarities between Mexican American and Anglo American kinship patterns. Anglo American kinship, like that of Mexican Americans, is founded on the bilateral kindred and affinal extensions. The nuclear family is the basic and most significant familial unit and normally constitutes the household. Relatives in the kindred sometimes interact as a social group and are often relied upon for assistance in times of need. Likewise, relatives are visited frequently, in some cases more frequently than friends and other non-kin. Moreover, the distinction between more important primary kin (parents, siblings, and children) and less important secondary kin also applies among Anglo Americans. Not found in the Anglo American kinship system, on the other hand, is a pattern of fictive kinship.

Typically, the Chicano extended family also includes *compadres*, or fictive kin. As godparents (*padrinos*) of a child, *compadres* or coparents have a special link with the real parents of the child. *Compadres* tend to be close friends or relatives of the real parents, and the relationship of *compadrazgo* is expected to last a lifetime. Rituals that commonly formalize the relationship include baptism, confirmation, and first communion. In addition, *compadres* are chosen for marriage; however, for these ties the bride and groom usually choose their own *padrinos*, and thus the most significant relationship is not between the parents and coparents as in the other forms of *compadrazgo* (Carlos 1972). Researchers have found that fictive kin fill the same role as real kin in the extended family (Clark 1959; Madsen 1964; Rubel 1966). They are accorded the same attention and affection, and they have similar rights and obligations. *Compadres* as well as relatives are expected to render mutual aid when it is needed.

Students of Anglo American kinship in the past twenty years have documented the retention of kin bonds by urban Anglos despite social and geographic mobility. Working separately, Marvin Sussman (1959) and Eugene Litwak (1960) have persuasively called attention to the maintenance of an "extended family network" among Anglos, which does not entail geographic propinquity. On the other hand, researchers working with Mexican Americans have long referred to the comparative weakness of less extensive Anglo kin ties (González 1969; Madsen 1969; Moore 1970). Mexican Americans are believed to value familism more highly than Anglos and to know more relatives, see them more often, and rely on kin more extensively for mutual aid. It is important to point out that these two views of Anglo American extended-family ties are not necessarily contradictory. Both recognize that the tendency for substantial geographic mobility among Anglos reduces the importance of the localized kin group, but does not necessarily eliminate periodic visiting and mutual aid over distances. The difference, then, is one of emphasis; research with Mexican Americans tends to exaggerate the Anglos' lack of local kin groups, while research with Anglo Americans tends to emphasize the retention of a far-flung kin network.

Despite the fact that the importance of the Mexican American extended family has always been discussed in contrast to Anglo

American family patterns, few studies provide empirical data on both groups. In a comparison of Anglo and Mexican American *attitudes* toward familism, Farris and Glenn (1976) found some statistically significant ethnic differences; unfortunately, however, no questions about actual behavior were asked. Yet, it is well known that vast differences may exist between ideal values about familism and real behavior concerning relatives. Without behavior data on a comparative sample of Anglo and Mexican Americans, any statements about ethnic differences in extended family structure amount to guesswork. Mindel (1980) presents data on Anglo, Black, and Mexican American local extended-family networks, concluding that Anglos are likely to be "isolated" from their kin while Mexican Americans have the largest and most socially integrated extended families. Mindel provides no information, however, on relations with kin outside the local area, and his conclusion that Anglos are "isolated" from kin is premature. In this chapter, interethnic comparisons are presented in order to document differences and similarities between Anglo and Mexican American kinship ties.

While descriptions abound in which the Mexican American family is judged to be "stronger" than the Anglo family, this is nevertheless generally coupled with the notion that the Mexican American extended family is declining with acculturation, assimilation, and urbanization. However, as we shall see, the local extended family actually becomes larger and more integrated even as the individual family members are themselves becoming acculturated. One simple way of dealing with this important variation among Mexican Americans is to carry out a generational analysis, since two key indicators of extended familism (migration and socioeconomic status) are highly correlated with generation. In this chapter, therefore, the comparisons with Anglo Americans make use of generational analyses of the Mexican Americans. Using a generational breakdown, it becomes clear that there is no single relationship between the two ethnic groups with regard to extended kin ties. Anglo Americans resemble the immigrant Mexicans in some ways and the native-born Mexican Americans in other ways; in still other ways, the Anglo Americans differ from all three Mexican American generations. The need for multidimensional comparisons is evident throughout the following discussion of ethnicity and kinship.

Ethnicity, Kinship, and Social Correlates

Analysis of Social Spheres

Analysis of kinship was undertaken as part of an overall factor analysis of social interaction with relatives, fictive kin, friends, co-workers, and neighbors. The purpose was to evaluate the independent strength of these social spheres, determine their interrelationship, and examine relationships with ethnicity.

Since it was assumed that primary and secondary kin would constitute distinct dimensions of extended family structure, aspects of these two types of relationships were measured separately. Four basic aspects of kinship were measured: (1) the total number of adult kin outside the household living in town, in the county, in the United States, and outside the United States; (2) the total number of kin seen daily, weekly, and less than weekly; (3) the total number of kin never seen; and (4) the total number of kin exchanging goods and services including advice, child care, financial help, household labor, and brokerage. There were seventy items used to measure the primary kin domain, and eighty-six items for the secondary kin domain. All of the aspects were measured as continuous variables, according to the number of kin indicated by the respondent.

Less intensive measurement was applied to the remaining four social sphere dimensions, but the general aspects of number, interaction, and exchange were preserved. Forty-four items were used to measure the fictive-kin domain, twelve for friends, four for neighbors, and four for coworkers.

The final social sphere analysis was to be based on both Mexican American and Anglo American responses. However, Mexican American responses were first analyzed independently in order to determine the significance of fictive kin (the only social sphere not applicable to Anglos). In this analysis, fictive kin did not emerge as a factor leading to the conclusion that, contrary to popular belief, *compadrazgo* is currently of limited importance as a means of extending kinship ties among Chicanos. Attention was turned, therefore, to the remaining social spheres. Five factors appeared in the following analysis: Primary Kin, Secondary Kin, Friends, Neighbors, and Widespread U.S. Kin. Coworkers did not emerge as a factor because of the large number of respondents not employed. The factors of Friends and Neighbors are discussed more thoroughly in chapter 11. The factor of Widespread U.S. Kin was primarily the result of Anglo responses concerning the distant geographic location of primary and secondary kin. Mexican Americans score above average and Anglo Americans score below average on the Primary Kin factor ($M=51.71$ vs. 45.55; $p<.05$) and the Secondary Kin factor ($M=51.82$ vs. 45.69; $p<.05$). On the other hand, Mexican Americans score below average and Anglo Americans score above average on the Widespread U.S. Kin factor ($M=48.58$ vs. 53.24; $p<.05$). These finds coincide with the general notion that the Chicano family is more strongly integrated than the Anglo family. Averages tend to obscure the fact, however, that considerable variation can exist within an ethnic group. We will now turn to a closer examination of variation in family structure among Chicanos and between the two ethnic groups.

Ethnic Comparisons

A review of the findings concerning markers of primary, secondary, and widespread U.S. kin networks among the two ethnic groups indicates important similarities and differences. Statistical analysis of our data, shows that geographic mobility is the most important trait associated with primary kin and widespread U.S. kin group formation among Anglo and Mexican Americans. Ethnic group members who migrate are less likely to have a local primary kin network, and more likely to have relatives out of state with whom they maintain contact. It would seem that the outstanding significance of this simple relationship is not given the attention in the literature that it deserves.

There is no indication, on the other hand, that urbanism bears any significant relationship to extended familism. The urban–rural residential history of respondents in either ethnic group is not associated with the kin factors, except for a very weak positive correlation with Secondary Kin among Mexican Americans. Furthermore, the kin-factor averages for each ethnic group indicate no significant relationship with the extent of urbanization within the three towns. Among Mexican Americans, those in Oxnard have the lowest and those in Santa Barbara have the highest Primary Kin–average ($M=49.68$ vs. 53.32, $F=4.66$, $p<.01$) while among Anglos, those in Santa Barbara have the lowest and those in Oxnard have the highest Widespread U.S. Kin factor average ($M=51.10$ vs. 56.22; $F=6.52$; $p<.01$). In both cases, the two large towns are at opposite poles with the small town in the middle. The historical development of the specific community is obviously more important than urbanization per se. Finally, as we shall see, the data indicate that these two ethnic groups sharing the trait of urban residence have fundamentally different kinship patterns that are due more to ethnic culture than to urbanism.

Acculturation appears somewhat related to kinship, but in a direction opposite to that hypothesized in the literature. The more acculturated Mexican American has a stronger primary and secondary kin network as well as being somewhat more likely to have a widespread U.S. kin network. More important for both Anglo and Mexican American kinship, however, are other factors such as birthplace, geographic mobility, and socioeconomic status, which are nonetheless intimately related to the acculturation process.

Socioeconomic traits are less important for extended familism than a review of literature would indicate. Only two very significant relationships appear in the data; Mexican Americans of high socioeconomic status are more likely than those of low status to have secondary kin networks ($r=.35$, $p<.001$) and Anglos who are socioeconomically mobile are more likely to have a widespread U.S. kin network ($r=.20$, $p<.01$). It is important to note that in both of these cases the socioeconomic traits are positively related to maintenance of kin networks, a relationship which contradicts many researchers' claims that the poor or working class are most familistic.

Of the social demographic characteristics, age and marriage are most important for kinship. Younger people in both ethnic groups are most likely to have a local secondary kin group. Older Mexican Americans, on the other hand, are more likely to have a widespread U.S. kin network. Marriage increases the secondary kin group among both ethnic groups and sexes through the addition of in-laws to the extended family. This process is rarely discussed in the literature, which tends to focus specifically on the kindred rather than the extended family. The idea that women maintain closer kin ties, which has received more attention in the literature, is not supported by our findings.

In order to test the comparative significance of the impact of ethnicity, migration, and other traits on kinship networks, stepwise multiple regression analysis was undertaken employing all variables applicable to both ethnic groups. In the analysis of Primary Kin, three variables account for 57 percent of the variance. Migration proves to be most important for Primary Kin; the two key measures of migration are the geographic distance between the respondents' birthplace and his or her current residence (38 percent) and the number of years of residence in town (12 percent). In addition, ethnicity as Anglo versus Mexican American accounts for 7 percent of the variance.

With regard to the Secondary Kin factor, ethnicity is most significant, while socioeconomic status, marriage, and age are also important variables. Stepwise multiple regression indicates that 50 percent of the variance is accounted for by five variables: ethnicity (34 percent), education (9 percent), marital status (4 percent), and the combination of age and family income (3 percent).

Ethnicity per se, on the other hand, does not contribute to the total explained variance (34 percent) in the Widespread U.S. Kin factor. Migration traits are more important, specifically generation (23 percent) and the geographic distance between the respondent's birthplace and his or her current residence (5 percent). Of some additional importance are socioeconomic mobility (4 percent) and age (2 percent). The migration pattern appearing in the data is one in which respondents (whether Anglo or Mexican American) born in the U.S., but outside California, are most likely to have a Widespread U.S. Kin network.

In sum, ethnicity is a significant predictor of two of the kin factors even when taking into account differences between the two ethnic groups in migration patterns, socioeconomic status, and other characteristics. Mexican Americans are likely to have a local extended family, while Anglo Americans are not. These are basic cultural patterns. In addition, migration bears an important impact on kinship in both ethnic groups. Migration is more important than ethnicity in determining the presence of a local primary kin group and a widespread U.S. kin network. Regardless of cultural affiliation, people who migrate logically stand to lose their primary kin group, but contact is nevertheless maintained with relatives over distances. Yet it is the combination of ethnicity and migration which is the key, for Anglos not only have no cultural bias favoring a local primary or second kin group; they are also much more migratory than Chicanos—a factor which works against local kin group formation. Chicanos, on the other hand, have a cultural preference for local kin groups, and are facilitated in their maintenance due to a high degree of residential stability.

Family Structure and Ethnicity

In order to fully appreciate the distinctions between Mexican American and Anglo American kinship, a descriptive analysis of family structure, interaction, and exchange is presented here. Comparisons are made between Anglos and the three generations of Mexican Americans, with some generalizations covering the Mexican American group as a whole.

Respondents were asked about all of their kin, regardless of residence in or out of town; and kin were distinguished as primary or secondary. Table 9 indicates the average numbers of relatives of the Anglos and the three Mexican American generations by geographic location, frequency of interaction, and involvement in exchange of goods and services.

The primary kin data in table 9 follow some similar patterns for the Anglos and all three Mexican American generations. All the groups maintain contact with the overwhelming majority of their primary kin. In addition, goods and services are also exchanged with the majority of primary kin, although this is most characteristic of the native-born Mexican American. There are also the expected differences between the groups. Anglos have fewer primary kin than Mexican Americans, presumably because of a lower birth rate. The data are complicated by the fact that only *living* kin were counted. In any case, Anglos counted an average of only 2.5 siblings, while Mexican Americans had an average of 5 siblings. All three Mexican American generations have more primary kin in town than the Anglos; however, the majority of both the Anglos' and Mexican immigrants' primary kin live outside the local area, a fact that affects the frequency of visiting primary kin. The native-born Mexican Americans see the majority of their primary kin at least weekly, while the Anglos and immigrant Mexicans do not.

In table 9, the secondary kin data exhibit patterns of similarities and differences much like the primary kin data. Interaction with secondary kin is much less common than with primary kin among all groups; but it is least common among Anglos, who visit only 12

Table 9   Average Number of Anglo American and Mexican American Generations' Extended Family Ties

Adult Kin Ties[a]	Mexican American Generations						Anglo Americans	
	First (N = 153)		Second (N = 142)		Third (N = 70)		(N = 163)	
	M	%	M	%	M	%	M	%
I. Primary Kin								
Geographic Distribution								
Town	2.7	37	4.4	56	4.0	58	0.8	17
County	0.4	6	0.9	12	0.7	10	0.4	9
U.S.	1.4	19	2.3	29	2.2	32	3.3	72
Outside U.S.	2.8	38	0.2	3	0.0	0	0.1	2
Total	7.3	100	7.8	100	6.9	100	4.6	100
Interaction								
Daily	1.3	19	1.4	19	1.5	23	0.3	7
Weekly	1.8	26	3.3	44	2.3	35	0.7	16
Less than weekly	3.8	55	2.8	37	2.8	42	3.4	77
Total	6.9	100	7.5	100	6.6	100	4.4	100
Exchange goods/services[b]	5.1	70	6.6	85	6.1	88	3.3	72
II. Secondary Kin								
Geographic Distribution								
Town	7.3	12	22.7	26	32.7	37	2.1	3
County	2.3	4	11.1	12	12.9	15	1.3	2
U.S.	13.6	23	32.5	37	37.5	42	55.2	83
Outside U.S.	35.5	61	21.9	25	5.2	6	8.0	12
Total	58.7	100	88.2	100	88.3	100	66.6	100
Interaction								
Daily	3.3	16	7.6	23	10.7	29	1.2	15
Weekly	2.3	11	3.1	10	5.2	19	0.5	6
Less than weekly	14.9	73	22.1	67	20.9	57	6.3	79
Total	20.5	100	32.8	100	36.8	100	8.0	100
Exchange goods/services[b]	8.4	14	12.2	14	11.4	13	4.8	7
III. Total Kin								
Geographic Distribution								
Town	10.0	15	27.1	28	36.7	39	2.9	4
County	2.7	4	12.0	13	13.6	14	1.7	3
U.S.	15.0	23	34.8	36	39.7	42	58.5	82
Outside U.S.	38.3	58	22.1	23	5.2	5	8.1	11
Total	66.0	100	96.0	100	95.2	100	71.2	100
Interaction								
Daily	4.6	17	9.0	22	12.2	28	1.5	12
Weekly	4.1	15	6.4	16	7.5	17	1.2	10
Less than weekly	18.7	68	24.9	62	23.7	55	9.7	78
Total	27.4	100	40.3	100	43.4	100	12.4	100
Exchange goods/services[b]	13.5	20	18.8	20	17.5	18	8.1	11

Source: Second Mexican American and Anglo American surveys.

Note: Analysis of variance indicates F values for the three generations and the Anglos are significant for all extended family variables at the .05 level except for "total secondary kin," which is not significant.

[a]Adult is defined as twenty-one years of age or older.

[b]Measured as giving and/or receiving one or more of the following: babysitting, advice, money, household help, and brokerage.

percent of their secondary kin, compared to the three Mexican American generations, who see 35 percent or more of their secondary kin. The majority of secondary kin visited are seen less than weekly by all groups. Moreover, exchange of goods and services with secondary kin is infrequent among all groups.

At the same time, there are sharp differences between the groups concerning other secondary kin characteristics. Despite the lack of statistical significance, native-born Mexican Americans appear to have more secondary kin than Anglos or immigrant Mexicans. It is perplexing that the immigrants count the fewest secondary kin, considering the fact that the birth rate for Mexicans in Mexico should be as high or higher than for native-born Mexican Americans. Evidently, the immigrants have lost track of, or forgotten, many secondary kin as a result of migration. The tendency to have locally residing secondary kin increases from generation to generation among the Mexican Americans; more than half (52 percent) of the secondary kin of the third generation live in the town or county. Anglos are least likely (5 percent) to have local secondary kin. The same pattern is evident for interaction with secondary kin. More secondary kin are seen more frequently as one moves from Anglos (21 percent) through the first- (27 percent), second- (33 percent), and third- (48 percent) generation Mexican Americans. Finally, Mexican Americans exchange aid with two to three times as many secondary kin as Anglos.

In sum, primary kin are the most significant family ties for both Anglos and Mexican Americans. Interaction and exchange are maintained with the vast majority of primary kin, while respondents are much more selective with secondary kin. Foremost in the secondary kin network of both ethnic groups are the spouse's primary kin (the respondent's parents-in-law and brothers- and sisters-in-law). Also included regularly are the spouses of the respondent's siblings and children. More choice occurs in relations with distant consanguines and other affines. Despite the fact that primary kin as a group form the core of the respondent's extended family, secondary relatives among both ethnic groups dominate numerically as local kin and in the respondent's network of interaction and exchange.

Evident from the summary of data on total kin in table 9 is the vast difference between Anglo and Mexican American kin structure. The native-born Mexican Americans have far and away the largest and most integrated extended families. The native-born Mexican Americans count more relatives than the Anglos or immigrants, and they interact and exchange aid with more relatives. While the first-generation Mexican Americans have much smaller kin networks, the networks are relatively well integrated through visiting and mutual aid. Anglos count a good many relatives, but the number of kin included in interaction and exchange networks is comparatively small. Anglos have an average of only twelve relatives with whom they visit, less than half the number visited by first-generation Mexican Americans and less than one-third of the number seen by the native born. The Anglos also exchange aid with the smallest number (eight) of kin, compared to between thirteen and nineteen for Mexican Americans, depending on generation, of course. Thus, not only are Anglos less likely to have a local kin network than Mexican Americans; their full kin network is smaller and more selective than the Mexican Americans' kin network. Apparently, kinship as a social system is less important for Anglo Americans.

On the other hand, it is significant to note that the Mexican American kin network becomes more and more localized from generation to generation; more than 50 percent of the third generation's relatives live in the town or county. Very few of the kin recognized by the third generation live outside the United States. In fact, Anglo Americans recognize more relatives living outside the U.S. than do third-generation Mexican Americans! Above all, kinship among Mexican Americans is a *local* network of social interaction and exchange.

Before continuing with the comparison of Anglo American and Mexican American family structure, let us briefly examine the system of *compadrazgo* as practiced by the three Mexican American generations. The overwhelming majority (90 percent or more) of all three generations have *compadres*, and more than half of each generation have *compadres* living in town. While *compadrazgo* survives from generation to generation, the system is strongest in the first two generations; but considerable change occurs in the third generation. For example, the first and second generations have, on the average, fourteen coparents compared to nine in the third generation. Choosing baptismal *compadres* is almost universal (98 percent or more) for all three generations, but the practice of choosing *compadres* for other rituals declines from generation to generation. Although 70 percent of the first generation have chosen *compadres* for confirmation, for instance, only 52 percent of the second generation and 36 percent of the third generation have done so. The practice of choosing coparents from outside the family also declines from generation to generation. Only 13 percent of the third generation have chosen all of their *compadres* from among friends instead of relatives, compared to 22 percent of the second generation and 26 percent of the first generation. Choosing relatives as *compadres* is one way of reinforcing the kin network, and this appears to be the strategy used by the third generation, rather than adding to the network by bringing in non-kin. Of course, the third generation already has extremely large local kin networks, and they have much less to gain by incorporating fictive kin than, say, the first generation, which has comparatively small kin networks. Indeed, the first generation adds an average of eleven fictive kin to their kin network through *compadrazgo*, compared to ten for the second generation and six for the third generation.

The preceding analysis indicates several things. First, there is a significant difference between Anglos' and Mexican Americans' extended-family structure, which is due to cultural preferences regarding kinship and migration. Anglos are more mobile and tend to have a very small local kin group or none at all. However, they maintain ties with a selected number of kin over geographic distances. Anglos are not isolated from relatives, but neither are they especially kin oriented. Mexican Americans, on the other hand, tend to be more kin directed, particularly the native born. Moreover, the kin group tends to be a local one, rather than a network covering geographic distances. The immigrant Mexicans have a larger and more local extended family than the Anglos, although it is smaller than the local kin group of the native-born Mexican Americans. The immigrants also maintain ties with many relatives still living in Mexico. Native-born Mexican Americans who are least migratory have extremely large and integrated local extended families. They are also likely to have some relatives living elsewhere in the U.S. with whom they maintain contact, but very few outside of the country.

The significant differences within the Mexican American ethnic group demonstrate the importance of conducting subgroup analyses before making generalizations for the ethnic group as a whole. Surprisingly, the first-generation Mexicans resemble the Anglos;

both have experienced kin group disruption due to migration, yet both continue to maintain kin ties over distances. Nevertheless, the immigrant Mexicans demonstrate other cultural patterns not found among Anglos, such as having relatively large local secondary kin networks and more frequent social interaction with kin, which come into flower among the native-born Mexican Americans.

Family Organization and Sociocultural Change

Four sociocultural processes are regularly suggested in the literature as having a significant impact over time on extended familism among Mexican Americans: acculturation, social assimilation, economic assimilation, and urbanization. The relationship between extended familism and ethnic identification has remained unexplored.

Many authors see a combination of two or more of the four processes involved in promoting change within the Mexican American extended family. With a few notable exceptions, most see acculturation, social assimilation, and economic assimilation as associated with the decline of the extended family. The process of urbanization, on the other hand, has provoked more controversy in its relationship to extended family change. Researchers appear to see urbanization as the causal variable, but the nature of the resultant change in the family is characterized variously as breakdown, persistence with modification of functions, or increased reliance on extended family ties. It is difficult to separate the four processes involved in change within the extended family because they so often occur simultaneously, and this is probably why researchers frequently lump two or more processes together in ascribing causality; but there is danger in this, because no definite relationship has been established between each singular process and extended family change. There is little empirical data to indicate if and how change occurs, and whether or not it is unilineal; nor do we know, for certain, the direction of change. For this reason, each process and its interrelationship with the extended family must be examined independently before assuming congruency in the effects and the associated rate of change.

Our analyses of kinship patterns show that the cultural emphasis on kinship is retained and strengthened by Mexican Americans, despite Americanization in other ways. Furthermore, there is no decline in extended familism with social and economic assimilation and urbanization. All four sociocultural processes, plus change in ethnic identification, are associated with intensive local kin networks. Acculturation is also somewhat related to the increasing presence of kin networks spread over geographic distances. Thus, while acculturated Mexican Americans put an emphasis on having kin nearby, there is no lack of interaction with relatives living in other areas of the United States.

While the kinship factors are related to the four sociocultural processes, there are other variables more important for extended familism. These relationships are sufficiently different for each kin factor that each one requires separate discussion.

The process of primary kin group formation can be described as follows. Mexicans immigrating to the United States generally leave many of their primary kin in Mexico. Those who come as children (less than sixteen years of age) migrate with their parents and most or all of their siblings, bringing their primary kin with them. When these individuals marry, their own children add to their primary kin network. Thus, the longer they remain in the United States, and particularly in the same community, the larger their primary kin group grows. Mexicans who emigrate as unmarried adults are more likely to journey alone. Parents and siblings are likely to be left in Mexico, although one or more may already be living in the United States as the first link in the "migration chain." If married, the adult immigrant usually emigrates alone, seeking employment and living accommodations, then attempting to bring his or her spouse and any children to the U.S. Once in the United States, older immigrants may establish a primary kin group with their children, and possibly assist other primary kin, such as parents or siblings, in emigrating to the same area. Nevertheless, older Mexicans who are recent immigrants, irregardless of marital status, are least likely to have primary kin nearby.

In contrast, native-born Mexican Americans, especially those born in and around the town where they now live, have a readily available primary kin group. Most important in maintaining their primary kin network is the tendency to put down roots and remain in the same community for many years or several generations. Our data suggest that this residential stability is a common trait among Mexican Americans. Native-born Mexican Americans exhibit extreme residential stability; 32 percent of the second-generation and 43 percent of the third-generation respondents were born in the city in which they were interviewed. The rest of the native born had lived an average of twenty-one years in town. Residential stability has an obvious impact on the potential for relationships among primary kin.

The formation of secondary kin groups is a different process. First-generation Mexicans tend to immigrate to areas in the United States where relatives are located. The general processes involved in such chain migration networks have been described in the literature (Graves and Graves 1974; Moore 1971). However, as time goes by and the migrant becomes adjusted, secondary kin may become less significant. Among Mexican Americans as a whole, relationships with secondary kin depend for the most part on age, marital status, and socioeconomic status. As young adults, respondents have a wide range of secondary kin available: grandparents, aunts, uncles, cousins, and so on. In addition, marriage brings a spouse and in-laws into the secondary kin circle. With time, however, older relatives with whom strong relationships were established die or move away, and close secondary kin become more limited in number. Moreover, ties with secondary kin are not as strong as those with primary kin, and secondary kin ties lose some importance over time, perhaps inevitably as ties with primary kin intensify, especially relations with adult children and grandchildren.

This process is mitigated, however, by socioeconomic status. Regardless of the respondent's age, it is those of higher socioeconomic status who are most likely to keep up secondary kin interaction. This finding contradicts the assumption of many observers of Mexican American culture who believe that the extended family primarily serves as a large mutual aid group for people living in poverty, a utilitarian function obviated with economic mobility. On the contrary, much empirical cross-cultural research demonstrates that the poor are likely to have relatives who are equally as poor, with few resources to support visiting and exchange, while the middle and upper classes have the surplus resources necessary to fully engage in extended family interaction (Jacobson 1970; Rosen and Berlinck 1968).

The Widespread U.S. Kin factor forms yet a third pattern. Most importantly, the maintenance of a Widespread U.S. Kin pattern is not very strongly correlated with any other variables. In general, the presence of a widespread U.S. kin network is found primarily among Mexican Americans who were born elsewhere in the United States and migrated to California, and specifically, to the town in which they were interviewed. This pattern of residential movement was true for only 16 percent of our second survey sample. In addition, there has been either some out-migration of relatives of respondents who are older, more acculturated, and socially assimilated, and who maintain less of a Mexican identity, or else these respondents are simply more likely to keep in contact with U.S. relatives. Among first-generation Mexicans, the pattern of immigration has had an important impact on the development of widespread U.S. kin networks. Immigrants who move to the U.S. late in life and have not lived here long are least likely to have kin elsewhere in the U.S. with whom they interact. Immigrants who came to the U.S. at a young age (before reaching thirty) and have lived here twenty-five years or longer are most likely to have a dispersed kin network, due to their or their relatives' pattern of migration within the United States.

Conclusions

The Chicano family is far from being a declining institution. It persists as a local extended kin network in which parents, siblings, and adult children form the core for interaction and exchange. In addition, large numbers of affinal and consanguinal secondary kin and some fictive kin are included. This contrasts with Anglo American kinship patterns, which are less localized.

One important conclusion reaffirmed as a result of these analyses is that acculturation among Mexican Americans is not a single interdependent process. The cultural trait of local extended familism does not appear to change in the same direction as either Cultural Awareness or Ethnic Loyalty. Nor are kinship patterns necessarily shaped by these two measures of ethnicity. Instead, it is suggested that the formation of primary and secondary kin groups operates as two additional independent processes in sociocultural change.

A second major finding is that the local extended family grows stronger despite the impact of many processes assumed to promote family breakdown: acculturation, social and economic assimilation, and urbanization. There is a weak tendency for acculturation to be associated with having kin living at a distance, but this tendency exists in addition to the maintenance of a local kin network rather than operating as a pattern of replacement.

Other social processes, which are rarely given their due in discussions of changing Mexican American family organization, are found to be the most important indicators of variation. Primary kin patterns are most responsive to the individual's history of migration. Secondary kinship reflects socioeconomic status and the life-cycle markers of age and marriage. Maintenance of widespread kin networks in the United States tends to be associated primarily with native-born respondents who have migrated to California and away from kin; although with increasing age, acculturation, change in ethnic identity, and social assimilation, there is also an increase in the maintenance of widespread U.S. kin ties.

Finally, the variation in kinship patterns among Chicanos indicates that there is no *one* type of ethnic family structure. Patterns of variation are complex, and a simple analysis is impossible. Perhaps one of the most important distinctions within the Mexican American population, however, is between the foreign born and the native born. This intraethnic distinction is intimately tied to population differences in acculturation, ethnic identification, socioeconomic status, and migration—all of which are associated with variation in kinship organization. The Mexican immigrants have a much more restricted pattern of kinship organization than either the second- or third-generation Mexican Americans. Moreover, internal variation in the first generation further demonstrates the consequences of migration in the formation of kinship groups. Immigrants who came to the United States at a young age (before age sixteen) have a primary kin group and a widespread U.S. kin network which are similar to the average for the native-born Mexican American sample. This is also true for immigrants who have lived in the United States for twenty-five years or longer. In contrast, immigrants who have lived in the United States less than twenty-five years tend to have a secondary kin network that is more important than their primary kin network.

10

Case Studies in Chicano Family and Ethnicity

GENERATIONAL ANALYSIS IS IMPORTANT because it allows us to examine subcultural differences in Chicano extended-family structure. Generation as an index combines indicators of migration and socioeconomic status as well as acculturation, ethnic identification, and assimilation. In order to examine the relationship between ethnicity per se and kinship, the cluster analysis discussed in chapter 4 will be reintroduced here. One case study for each cluster type has been selected to illustrate variation in extended familism. Some expected relationships emerge given the close association between generation and the clusters types.

An analysis of the data demonstrates that *La Raza*, or Type I, have a local secondary kin network, but are unlikely to have a local primary kin or a widespread U.S. kin network. The Changing Ethnics in Type II differ because a widespread U.S. kin network is likely to be present. The Cultural Blends (Type III) have a strong local primary kin group, an average local secondary kin group, and an average widespread U.S. kin network. The Emerging Americans in Type IV have a strong local primary and secondary kin group as well as a widespread U.S. kin network. Although the New American group (Type V) possesses a strong local primary and secondary kin network, it is unlikely to have a widespread U.S. kin group. There emerges a tendency, as in the previous analyses, for the more acculturated Mexican Americans (Types IV and V) to reveal the strongest extended family organization. The less acculturated Mexican Americans show a stronger secondary than primary kin group, while those individuals who appear to be midway in the process of acculturation put more effort into building up their local primary kin group. None of the cluster types are very likely to have a large widespread U.S. kin network.

The Case Studies

La Raza / Type I

Carmen Muñoz, who migrated to the U.S. as an adult, left most of her family in Mexico, and her ties with kin there are negligible because she has never returned during the twenty-two years she has lived in the U.S. Both of her parents are dead. One of her sisters is living in San Diego, and the other is in Tijuana, a Mexican border town. Only recently, her brother moved back to Mexico after having lived in southern California. She sees her siblings only rarely now, but her sister in San Diego helped Carmen when she originally migrated to the U.S. Carmen cannot remember many of her other relatives and old friends still living in Mexico, for she lost contact with most of them long ago. Her second husband, Miguel, has many relatives in Mexico, including his mother and siblings, and his ties to kin living there are much stronger than Carmen's. Miguel's mother came to live with them for several years, but then moved back to Mexico. Carmen has met few of Miguel's other Mexican relatives, and she does not feel close to any of them.

When they were living in Mexico, Carmen and her first husband chose *padrinos* for all of their children, and she sees some of them occasionally on their rare visits to the United States; basically, however, she no longer has contact with those *compadres*. But she does have *compadres* in town, her youngest child's baptismal *padrinos*, whom she sees regularly.

Carmen's close social network consists primarily of her children and her children's families. She sees her five married children almost daily, and exchanges a high level of goods and services with them. For example, when she became critically ill several times, her sons or daughters accompanied her and her husband to the emergency room. When one of her daughters was hospitalized, Carmen spent most of her time at the hospital. Presently, another daughter is having many financial difficulties, and Carmen has taken in all four grandchildren for a while to help in alleviating some of the burden.

Carmen's children frequently give her rides to the market, to church, and to run other errands, since she does not drive and Miguel often works the night shift, sleeping during the day. But this type of exchange seems to be limited to her children. Although she knows a few of her neighbors, she does not exchange favors, advice, child care, or money with them. Her exchange with her *compadres* in town is also minimal.

Changing Ethnics / Type II

Hermila Gutierrez left most of her relatives in Mexico when she migrated to the U.S. Unlike Carmen, she still maintains close contact with many of them as well as with several of her siblings living in Texas. Hermila is very close to her mother and one of her sisters in Mexico, and says they are the most cherished people in her life outside of her own nuclear family. Her parents have come to stay with Hermila for several weeks at a time, and Hermila manages to visit them in Mexico at least once a year. She also visits her siblings, who were of great help the last time she traveled to Mexico for an extended visit following a brief separation from her husband; they presented her with gifts, offered her advice, and provided her with child-care help.

Hermila's local network in Santa Barbara, however, is quite limited. She sees frequently an aunt and cousin living in town, to whom she feels very close. In fact, it was in visiting these relatives that she first came to the U.S., where she met her husband. Hermila does not get along with her husband's Santa Barbara relatives, who are all native-born Mexican Americans, speak English, and are culturally different from Hermila. When her mother-in-law was alive, the two of them had frequent disagreements.

Half of the Gutierrezes' eighteen *compadres* are their primary kin, and they are the only ones to whom Hermila feels strongly attached. The other compadres are Mexican American couples in Santa Barbara, but Hermila seldom sees them. Hermila has two or three Mexican friends in town with whom she maintains some contact, including visits on a monthly basis and an exchange of small talk. Nearly as often, she sees another close friend with whom she also discusses her personal problems. During the course of this study, she also came to know a Mexican woman in her Anglo-dominated neighborhood, and their families occasionally got together for barbecues and trips to the park.

In sum, Hermila socializes with a few secondary kin and friends in town, but her strongest attachments are with her primary kin in Mexico and Texas. Geographic distance obviously prevents more interaction with them.

Cultural Blends / Type III

Anna Fuentes, a native Santa Barbaran, has a large local kinship network and very close relations with her primary kin. Specifically, Anna's parents and one sister and one brother live in town, while a second brother lives in nearby Oxnard. Her husband, Ruben, has nine siblings, only one of whom does not live in town. Anna estimates that she and Ruben have about forty other relatives in town, and they see at least ten of them monthly. Anna usually takes her mother shopping every Saturday, and on Sunday she and Ruben have dinner at her parents' house. Every Monday night, Anna and Ruben have dinner at his parents' house. These immediate kin are the only individuals whom Anna and Ruben are sure to see socially several times a week. Frequency of contact diminishes rapidly outside of the immediate families, with Anna seeing her closest first cousin an average of only once a month and her aunts and other cousins perhaps two or three times each year.

Anna tends to be self-reliant, rarely asking for help from others; but she says she would rely on her primary kin in a time of trouble. On the other hand, she recalls that she has been of service to several relatives during the past year. For example, her mother and sister confide in her about their problems, and several other relatives have also come to Anna for advice about their personal problems. Furthermore, Anna has loaned some money to one of her sisters-in-law, and she has helped her parents with household chores as well as such tasks as preparing tamales for a party.

Anna feels very close to her family, who are the most important people in her life. She and Ruben have friends, but they are secondary to her relatives. Ruben and Anna have six good friends, all Mexican Americans. Four of these are *compadres*, as Anna and Ruben are *padrinos* to their children. In general, however, Anna does not consider the bond of *compadrazgo* to be very important. For example, she feels that a baptismal *compadre*'s obligation is to care for the child if the parents die, but beyond that there is no expectation on her part that a *compadre* is necessarily a close friend or a source of material or emotional support. Anna sees her friends regularly, and sometimes she has invited them as well as her relatives to gather together at her house. For example, the one large party she hosted during the year of interviews was a barbecue with family and friends celebrating her and Ruben's fifth wedding anniversary. Anna does not generally exchange goods or services with friends, preferring to rely on family when it is necessary.

Emerging Americans / Type IV

Kate Machado, another native-born Mexican American, is also devoted to her primary kin, who dominate her social life. Kate cared for her ailing mother daily until her recent death. She is especially close to her only sister, Sylvia. Kate says that she and Sylvia get together four or five times each week, especially on weekends. Typically, Kate stops over at Sylvia's house for an informal, friendly visit, or they meet downtown and go shopping. All of Kate's seven brothers live in town, and since childhood, she has been particularly close to two of them, Raul and Tony. Kate says she cares for her other brothers (except for one who uses drugs and according to Kate is a "bum"), but they are "living their own lives"; so Kate sees them, at most, only once a month, usually at family get-togethers. But she visits with Tony and Raul at least once a week, and she says that they call her frequently "to see how I'm doing." Usually, she visits Tony and Raul at their homes because they are always working and do not have much time to visit her. In addition to these informal visits ("dropping by for a cup of coffee"), Kate explains that she is regularly involved in the family activities of Sylvia, Tony, and Raul. Raul has five children, Sylvia has four, and Tony has five; consequently, there is "almost always" a birthday party, graduation, wedding, or some kind of family event occurring.

Besides the families of her siblings, Kate is equally involved in the lives of her children's families. Her oldest son, Randy, has three children, and her daughter, Alice, has five. Randy lives in the northern part of the county, yet Kate manages to see him several times a month since he visits her regularly. Alice lives in town, not far from

Kate, so they can easily get together a couple of time a week. Moreover, Kate is kept busy with her eight grandchildren's birthday parties, baptisms, graduations, and "what-have-you."

Kate has one very close friend in town, Dorothy, a Mexican American who is Sylvia's next-door neighbor, which enables Kate to see Dorothy nearly every time she visits her sister. Kate's relatives who are *compadres* are the *compadres* closest to her. Kate has not kept in contact with *compadres* who have moved out of town, and she feels, in general, that a *compadre* is "just a friend" and nothing more. Kate has a number of other friends she sees frequently. In particular, Kate says she has known five "little old lady" neighbors since she moved into her present neighborhood eighteen years ago. Kate met these neighbors, all Anglo women in their sixties and seventies, "because they were walking by while I was out watering my lawn or something and we'd get to talking." Kate got into the habit of dropping by to visit them once or twice a week for "chats." The ladies are widowed and live alone, and Kate enjoys keeping company with them and occasionally running errands for them. Significantly, however, these friends are not involved in Kate's family interaction. They have met some of Kate's relatives, but they are not invited to the parties and other get-togethers that Kate has with her family.

Like Anna Fuentes, Kate claims to give more aid than she receives. Almost all her exchange is with relatives. She has asked advice from the individuals closest to her, including her sister, her daughter, her brothers Tony and Raul, and her oldest friend Dorothy. She says she has "plenty of money" and never asks for financial assistance. In fact, she often loans cash to others, such as her son and daughter and some of her siblings. Kate also needs little help with chores and other day-to-day labors, although occasionally her sister or daughter will lend a hand in cleaning house or cooking food for a party. On the other hand, Kate says she is the one who usually helps with chores for others, running errands for her "little old lady friends" or helping with the house-cleaning when visiting her siblings.

New Americans / Type V

Margaret Camacho claims to be extremely independent, but she is actually involved with a very large kin network. She says she tries to limit her contact with her relatives, and yet she gives evidence of considerable interaction with them. Her parents and two sisters live in Santa Barbara. When Marge and her husband Ernie moved to San Jose early in their marriage, Marge's mother suffered a stroke and refused to go to the hospital for weekly treatments unless Marge was present. With increasing frequency, Marge had to drive from San Jose to Santa Barbara just to take her mother to the hospital. When it reached the point where Marge was making the trip almost every weekend (a distance of several hundred miles), she and Ernie decided that they had better move again to Santa Barbara.

Marge visits her parents perhaps once a month, and she says that they call her about once a week and frequently ask her to come to see them more often than she does. She is not close to her sisters, seeing them only once every few months, and usually at her parents' home. Marge says that she and her sisters never telephone each other, and they exchange little aid. This appears to be a recent development. Marge mentions that her sisters, especially Penny, are having personal problems continually and frequently appeal to Marge for advice and other forms of help. In Penny's case, the problems concern her marriage to a Black man, subsequent ostracism by her family, and later a painful divorce. At this point, Marge can no longer tolerate the incessant problems, and so she has disassociated herself from her sisters.

In contrast, Marge has no problems with Ernie's family. She gets along well with his mother and stepfather, and she sees them once every week or two. In addition, she sees Ernie's brother, Carlos, who lives in town, several times a week, since Ernie and Carlos are very close.

Because her roots in Santa Barbara go back several generations, Marge has many relatives in town on both her parents' sides of the family. Ernie also has a large family network in Santa Barbara. Thus, Marge recognizes at least fifty other relatives in town, including affinal and consanguinal kin. However, Marge says she exchanges no help with these secondary kin, and she sees them only a few times a year, on holidays such as Christmas when her parents host a family gathering at their home or at family events such as weddings, baptisms, or funerals.

Marge and Ernie have a small circle of friends whom they see quite often. Specifically, there are four married couples (one couple are *compadres*) with whom she and Ernie regularly socialize. Two of these couples are members of a social club with the Camachos. The wives of the other two couples are old school friends of Marge. Two of the four wives in this group also happen to be coworkers with Marge. It is a mixed-ethnic social group. The club members are Anglo, with the exception of Betty, who is a Mexican American; Marge's school friend, Barbara, is Mexican American; and her closest friend, Janice, is Apache. Marge's friendship network is an integrated one, in which each of the couples know the others. They all generally get together on weekends for an afternoon barbecue or a nighttime party. Quite a bit of exchange goes on between the friends, and Marge claims to give to them a lot more than she receives. All four couples know Marge and Ernie's close primary kin, having been invited to many of the same social gatherings.

Conclusions

As the case studies demonstrate, familism is a pervasive Mexican American trait, irrespective of their level of acculturation. Those who immigrate to the U.S. must leave their relatives in Mexico, and their interaction with them obviously must decline. But, like Hermila, they tend to remain close emotionally to their parents and siblings left behind. The few relatives who happen to live in town become important. As the immigrants grow older, time and energy is invested in maintaining a primary kin network which, like Carmen's, is based on adult children and their families. Importantly, fictive kin, friends, neighbors, and coworkers do not figure significantly in their social life.

For the native born, the extended kin group becomes large and cohesive. Most significant are the primary kin: parents, siblings, and adult children. Certainly, Chicano kinship retains a voluntary nature to some extent. For example, Kate Machado avoids one of her brothers, who is a drug addict, and Marge Camacho has tried to stop seeing her sisters, who have had numerous personal problems. But the break with kin is hard to maintain when they live in town and are certain to be seen eventually. Friends and other non-kin are likely to be integrated into the social networks of the native born, but never to the exclusion of relatives. For most native born, like Anna Fuentes or Kate Machado, the kin group is the core of their social life, which means an ethnically enclosed social life because relatives tend to be Mexican American. Even Margaret Camacho, who emphasizes her Anglo associates, has a network that is predominantly Mexican American, which is due primarily to her large affinal and consanguinal kin group. These case studies nicely demonstrate the continued importance of the family in the life of Chicanos, despite extensive acculturation. This finding supports the long-held belief that close familial relationships constitute a core Mexican value—one that persists even with immigration and acculturation. In the next chapter, we will look more closely at the non-kin relations of Mexican Americans and the makeup of the ethnic community in general.

II

The Ethnic Community

ONE OF THE FUNDAMENTAL QUESTIONS about American ethnic groups concerns the impact and interrelationship of two major processes of change stemming from culture contact: social assimilation and acculturation. Most researchers agree that extensive acculturation has taken place among American ethnics, but there is less agreement about the nature of social assimilation. In the early twentieth century, social scientists such as Park, Burgess, and MacKenzie (1925) and Wirth (1938) envisioned the rapid acculturation and assimilation of the immigrant ethnic groups whose separate way of life, it was felt, could not be maintained in large, impersonal cities. The community studies by W. Lloyd Warner and his associates in the 1940s emphasized a more gradual but nevertheless progressive acculturation and assimilation of ethnic groups, particularly the European immigrants (Warner and Srole 1945).

As we pointed out in chapter 2, the persistence of ethnic minority groups into the 1950s and 1960s, and their continued socioeconomic and political disadvantages when compared to mainstream Anglo Americans, produced revisions in the acculturation–assimilation model. Milton Gordon (1964) argued that despite acculturation and some assimilation in secondary relationships (the more impersonal, formal, and single purpose ties such as those present at work or in school), ethnic minorities in America have not been accepted into the mainstream's primary sphere of family and close friendship ties. Even with socioeconomic mobility, minorities remain separate as an ethclass or socioeconomic segment within the ethnic community. While Gordon emphasized discrimination and exclusion as reasons for the lack of assimilation, other researchers have focused on the benefits of ethnicity. Glazer and Moynihan (1963), for example, developed the concept of the ethnic group as a political interest group.

New models emerged in the 1960s which better reflected the ethnic persistence observed. The model of pluralism, as developed by M. G. Smith (1960, 1969) and others, defines the nature of the coexistence of ethnic groups as one of competition for resources. The internal colonialism model, on the other hand, emphasizes the domination of ethnic minority groups by a majority group (Fanon 1968; González Casanova 1965).

Along with new models, researchers have begun to investigate positive ethnic factors to account for ethnicity. While not denying discrimination by Anglo Americans, it is further argued that ethnic groups do not assimilate because members find it psychologically rewarding to be with "their own kind"; because ethnic loyalty and identity is promoted by group members; and because the benefits of assimilation are regarded by group members with some skepticism (Greeley 1974; Williams 1975). Instead of assimilating, American ethnics continue to form their own communities. These communities may not encompass the entire ethnic group; rather, there are separate communities for specific segments. As Kramer (1970) points out, acculturated minority group members come together to form their own acculturated communities. Furthermore, these communities may not be spatial, and are perhaps better characterized as "networks of informal social relationships" (Williams 1975). Within these separate communities, cultural differences are perpetuated so that acculturation is never complete, and these cultural differences serve to reinforce ethnic stereotypes and boundaries (Suttles 1968).

Given the persistence of ethnic boundaries, acculturated ethnic-group members tend to lead a "double life," living in an ethnic community at home while assuming Americanized behavior at work, at school, and in the public mainstream. This situational ethnicity makes it difficult to categorize individuals on a one-dimensional model of assimilation. The pluralism model, on the other hand, recognizes different types of pluralism (social, cultural, and structural) and, therefore, the possibility of different levels of assimilation in various spheres of activity (Smith 1969). Unlike the colonialism model, pluralism accepts the potential for socioeconomic mobility among ethnic minorities. However, the assumption is that mobility is limited and that minority groups will continue to be economically and politically disadvantaged relative to Anglo Americans.

Studies of Chicanos have reflected these changing perspectives on ethnicity. Studies done prior to the 1970s tend to cite growing acculturation and assimilation (see, for example, Clark 1959; Graves 1967; Madsen 1964). This perspective culminated in the massive UCLA Mexican American Study Project and publication of *The Mexican American People* (Grebler, Moore, and Guzman 1970). The analysis suggested that Mexican Americans experience acculturation and assimilation, especially in Los Angeles where the "permissive climate" results in high rates of intermarriage and movement out of the ethnic community. The majority group is depicted as the primary cause of limited assimilation.

A restudy of the respondents in the UCLA project, on the other hand, produced contrasting results. Ambrecht and Pachon (1974) found that the respondents were not assimilationist, although they had experienced selective acculturation. In another study, Salgado de Snyder and Padilla (1982) found that Mexican Americans married to Anglos maintained their cultural orientation and ethnic identity even after nearly two decades of intermarriage. More interesting, perhaps, is the fact that the offspring of these interethnic marriages identify strongly with their Mexican origin cultural group (Salgado de Snyder, Lopez, and Padilla 1982).

Other studies confirm variation in assimilation patterns. The internal colony model has been applied to Chicanos by several researchers who emphasize discrimination and domination by Anglo Americans (Acuña 1981). Factors internal to the ethnic group are stressed by other investigators. For example, Teske and Nelson (1976) report that an assimilation orientation among Mexican Americans is the product of early familial socialization and the formation of self-identity. They argue that those who desire to assimilate are not blocked by Anglos. The implication, then, is that many Chicanos do not desire to assimilate.

These findings pose important questions for Chicano studies. What is the relationship between acculturation and social assimilation among Mexican Americans? How do patterns of social assimilation vary within the ethnic group? Can general patterns be observed, or is social assimilation simply an idiosyncratic matter of individual choice? What internal and external factors affect the social assimilation process? And does the Chicano ethnic community decline with acculturation and social assimilation, or does it persist in new forms? These topics are discussed in this chapter in the context of analyzing additional data on social interaction.

Friends, Neighbors, and Coworkers

The significance of kinship in ethnic social organization was emphasized in the last two chapters. In order to further appreciate the relative significance of kinship for Mexican Americans, it is necessary to compare kin and non-kin ties. Moreover, cross-cultural comparisons with Anglo Americans again demonstrate important differences in social organization between the two ethnic groups.

Ethnicity and Non-kin Ties

Due to the importance of kinship among Mexican Americans, little attention has been given to other social relationships in Chicano studies. Some researchers state that Mexican Americans interact with relatives almost to the exclusion of non-kin. For example, Rubel (1966) finds that the practice of visiting neighbors is discouraged, while most socializing is between relatives and fictive kin. On the other hand, studies taking a quantitative approach report a good deal of interaction and exchange with friends, neighbors, and other non-kin. Ramirez (1980) reports that 37 percent of a sample of Detroit Mexican Americans visit with friends several times a week. Moore (1971) states that between 10 percent and 25 percent of a sample of Los Angeles Mexican Americans would consult first with a friend or neighbor for help with a problem.

Our data indicate that Chicanos are likely to interact with non-kin, but not as extensively as Anglos tend to do. Respondents were asked specifically about relationships with friends, neighbors, and coworkers. Table 10 summarizes the information on numbers of non-kin ties, frequency of visiting, and exchange found among Mexican American respondents by generation, as well as among Anglo Americans.

Chicanos, in general, are likely to have friends in town and to visit

Table 10 Anglo American and Mexican American Generations' Friend, Neighbor, and Coworker Ties

Non-Kin Ties	Mexican American Generations			Total[a]	Anglo American
	First (N = 153)	Second (N = 142)	Third (N = 70)	(N = 381)	(N = 163)
I. Friends					
Mean number in town	4.1	7.2	6.1	5.9	10.7
Percent without friends	37	25	17	28	15
Percent visiting friends weekly	63	52	59	58	55
Percent who exchange with friends	43	49	60	49	71
II. Neighborhood Friends[b]					
Mean number of well-known neighbors	1.6	2.6	2.5	2.2	4.3
Percent without well-known neighbors	35	32	34	33	25
Percent visiting neighbors weekly	60	40	52	51	41
Percent who exchange with neighbors	43	48	47	46	63
III. Coworker Friends[c]					
Mean number of coworker friends	3.1	4.3	4.5	3.9	8.7
Percent without coworker friends	70	49	44	55	19
Percent visiting coworkers weekly	15	31	29	26	15
Percent who exchange with coworkers	23	50	67	46	68

Source: Second Mexican American and Anglo American surveys.

[a]The total sample also includes 16 respondents for whom generation could not be determined.

[b]Neighbor is defined as someone living on the respondent's street block.

[c]The data on coworkers is analyzed on the basis of the subsamples of respondents who work: Mexican American first generation, N = 69; second generation, N = 70, third generation, N = 43; total, N = 193; Anglo, N = 78.

them frequently; they have fewer numbers of friends, however, than Anglo Americans, and they are less likely to exchange goods and services with their friends. As in kinship relations, there are variations by generation among the Mexican Americans. First-generation Mexicans are most likely *not* to have friends (37 percent), and they have the smallest average number of friends (4.1); but visiting and, to some extent, exchange are sustained within the friendships that exist. Second- and third-generation Mexican Americans, who tend to resemble one another, have more friends than the immigrants, but they have fewer friends than the Anglos. The tendency to have friends and to exchange with friends increases with each generation. Anglos have the largest number of friends ($M=10.7$) and are most likely to exchange with friends (71 percent). The tendency to visit friends, on the other hand, is fairly consistent across generations and ethnic groups.

Mexican Americans are also likely to know some of their neighbors well and to visit them frequently, but they have fewer numbers of neighborhood friends than Anglo Americans and are less likely to exchange with them. All three generations are fairly consistent in their degree of neighborliness, except that immigrants have somewhat fewer neighborhood friends and are likely to visit with them somewhat more. Anglos are most likely to have neighbors they know well, and they are most likely to have the largest number of neighborhood friends, with whom they are most likely to exchange. Visiting, however, appears to be more characteristic of Mexican American neighbor ties.

As mentioned in chapter 9, factor analysis of social interaction, in general, resulted in two non-kin factors (Friends and Neighbors), in addition to the three kinship factors. In comparing Friend-factor means, we find that foreign-born and native-born Mexican Americans differ in friendship patterns. Immigrants ($M=45.95$) score significantly lower on the Friend factor than the second and third generations ($M=49.38$ and $M=50.24$, respectively). Anglos ($M=53.80$) score significantly higher than first- and second-generation Mexican Americans. Although there is no statistically significant difference between Anglos and third-generation Mexican Americans, the third generation appears to resemble the second generation more than it does the Anglos. We can conclude that networks based on friendship are least important or more difficult for immigrant Mexicans and most important for Anglos, with native-born Mexican Americans midway between the two in maintenance of friendship ties.

Generational patterns do not appear with regard to neighboring. There are no significant differences between the Neighbor-factor mean scores of first- ($M=47.39$), second- ($M=49.67$) and third- ($M=49.51$) generation Mexican Americans. On the other hand, there are significant differences between the scores of the first two generations and Anglo Americans. ($M=53.11$). While there is again no significant difference between Anglos and third-generation Mexican Americans, the third generation appears to resemble the other Mexican Americans more than it does the Anglos, leading to the conclusion that neighbors are more important social ties for Anglos, in general, than for Mexican Americans.

No factor could be generated in the analysis of coworker data, due to the large segment of the sample which is not employed. Table 10, however, provides descriptive data on coworker ties for employed respondents. Mexican Americans, as a whole, are less likely to have coworker friends, than Anglo Americans, have fewer coworker friends, and are less likely to exchange goods and services with them. On the other hand, Mexican Americans are more likely than Anglos to socialize outside of work with coworker friends. The pattern for immigrant Mexicans differs from that of the native born. First-generation Mexicans are least likely to have coworker friends, most likely to have the smallest number of friends at work, and are unlikely to visit or engage in mutual aid with coworkers. Native-born Mexican Americans are more likely to have friends at work and to visit and exchange with them. The native born tend to lie midway between the immigrants and Anglos in number of coworker friends and the tendency to have them. The data are complicated, however, in that the tendency to exchange favors with coworkers increases with generation, so that there is no difference between Anglos and the third-generation Mexican Americans. On the other hand, both second- and third-generation Mexican Americans are more likely than Anglos to visit frequently with friends outside of work. Nevertheless, in general, the coworker pattern can be characterized much like the one for friendship. That is, the immigrants socialize least with coworkers, the Anglos socialize most, and the native-born Mexican Americans tend to fall in between.

In summary, non-kin ties are more important for Anglos than for Chicanos. Anglos are most likely to have non-kin relations. They also have the largest average number of friends, neighborhood friends, and coworker friends; and they are most likely to exchange favors with them. Anglos are likely to visit friends and neighbors fairly frequently, but interestingly, social interaction with non-kin is somewhat more characteristic of Chicanos.

Generational analysis indicates heterogeneity among Mexican Americans. First-generation Mexicans are most socially isolated from non-kin. They are least likely to have friends and coworker friends, and they have the smallest number of non-kin ties. Although they socialize frequently with friends and neighbors, they are least likely to exchange favors with non-kin. Native-born Mexican Americans fall between the immigrant Mexicans and the Anglo Americans in the character of their non-kin ties. They have more friends, neighborhood friends, and coworker friends than the immigrants, but they have fewer than the Anglos. They engage in frequent visiting and exchange with friends and neighbors, but they do not socialize as frequently as the immigrants, nor are they as likely to participate in mutual aid as the Anglos. There are a few ways in which Mexican Americans become more like Anglos from generation to generation (for example, the increasing tendency to have friends and to exchange with coworkers). But, in general, native-born Mexican Americans differ both from the immigrants and from the Anglos. There is little evidence that Mexican American non-kin social relations become more like those of Anglos. Instead, a new pattern of non-kin relations emerges among native-born Mexican Americans, which shares some attributes with immigrants and some with Anglos but which is best depicted as having a unique character.

Ethnic Networks

Comparison of kin and non-kin ties leads us to conclude that there are not simply two ethnic group patterns, but *three*. The three patterns have different characteristics, and they are shaped by different experiences and cultural propensities. Furthermore, the three patterns do not fall along a single continuum from Mexican to Anglo. With regard to some *traits* in the patterns, there is such a continuum, but for most of the traits there is not. The data demonstrate the need for more complex, multidimensional models of acculturation. The data also call attention to the fact that ethnicity is not a homogeneous nor irreducible entity, but is perhaps best conceptualized as "nesting" segments arranged hierarchically. Keyes adopts this notion of ethnic groups which he states "are structured in segmentary hierarchies with each more inclusive segment subsuming ethnic groups which were contrastive at another level" (1976:208). Thus, foreign-born and native-born Mexican Americans contrast with one another at one level, while Mexican Americans (including both foreign born and native born) contrast with Anglo Americans at a higher level of inclusiveness. These findings lend support to the notion that there is a separate Chicano culture which is something more than just an amalgamation of Mexican and American cultures. In addition to the cultural gap between immigrants and the native born, indications abound in the case studies that their social communities are quite separate. Not only is there a lack of close identification with one another, but relations between the subethnic communities can frequently be hostile. This division reflects differences in life experiences and opportunities.

The immigrants' social network is structured by the migration experience and cultural preferences. They favor kin ties, but they tend to have few kin in the U.S. because of their recent arrival. They tend to be drawn to those cities where they have secondary kin who help them in adapting to their new life. However, once they stabilize their residence and begin to establish a primary kin network, their attention turns to these more important relatives. They visit and exchange goods and services with their primary kin in town, who are also their most important social contacts. They also visit frequently a number of secondary kin whom they rely upon for mutual aid. These secondary kin form an important back-up support system for the immigrants. Non-kin make up a relatively large segment of immigrant networks because of the small number of kin who live nearby. The proportion of non-kin in the first generation's local networks is indicated in table 11, which presents the mean number of contacts in town named in several social categories and defined as mutually exclusive categories progressing from kinfolk to *compadres*, to friends, to coworker friends, and to neighborhood friends. A slight majority (52 percent) of the immigrants' social contacts are non-kin, and friends and neighbors are important for socializing but not for exchange. Accordingly, for the immigrants, non-kin have different obligations than kin. They are not interchangeable entities.

Our evidence shows that the social networks of the foreign born change over time in the U.S. However, they do not become more like the Anglos' networks, but more like those of the native-born Mexican Americans who have established large local kin networks as well as strong social and exchange ties with a healthy number of non-kin. Immigrants who migrated to the U.S. before the age of sixteen and who have lived in the U.S. for more than twenty-five years have a local primary kin network and relations with friends and neighbors much like the native born. Similarly, they are likely to have kin living elsewhere in the U.S. with whom they maintain contact. They differ from the native born only with regard to secondary kin, who become less significant to immigrants as time goes by. Those few relations who were called upon for support early in the migration process are gradually replaced by primary kin. Due to their relatively low socioeconomic status, immigrants cannot afford to maintain close ties with secondary kin as well as their growing primary kin network.

Table 11 Mean Number and Percent of Potential Social Relations in Town

| | Mexican Americans | | | | | | | | Anglo Americans | |
| | First (N = 153) | | Second (N = 142) | | Third (N = 70) | | Total[a] (N = 381) | | (N = 163) | |
Relationship	M	%	M	%	M	%	M	%	M	%
Total kin	9.9	48	26.8	59	50.0	76	24.8	62	3.0	11
Primary	2.6		4.4		4.0		3.6		.8	
Secondary	7.2		22.3		46.0		21.2		2.1	
Compadres (non-kin)	2.1	10	4.7	10	2.4	4	3.3	8		
Friends	4.1	20	7.2	16	6.1	9	5.9	15	10.7	40
Coworker friends[b]	3.1	15	4.3	9	4.5	7	3.9	10	8.7	33
Neighbors well known	1.6	7	2.6	6	2.5	4	2.2	5	4.3	16
TOTAL	20.8	100	45.6	100	65.5	100	40.1	100	26.7	100

Source: Second Mexican American and Anglo American surveys. Adapted from Keefe (1980).

[a]The total sample also includes 16 respondents for whom generation could not be determined.

[b]The number of coworker friends is averaged only for the respondents who work: Mexican American first generation, $N = 69$; second generation, $N = 70$; third generation, $N = 43$; total, $N = 193$; Anglo, $N = 78$.

Native-born Mexican Americans have the same cultural preference as the immigrants for interacting with relatives, and by virtue of
two characteristics (residential stability and higher socioeconomic
status), they are able to fulfill their inclination to maintain strong
extended families. It would seem that one of these characteristics,
higher socioeconomic status, is a product of the greater opportunity
for education, the ability to speak English, and thus, a greater access
to skilled jobs—all of which are the result of the social structure. The
other characteristic, residential stability, is more the result of cultural
values concerning kinship. Once having immigrated permanently to
the U.S., Mexican Americans tend to settle in one geographic place,
where they remain for generations. They generally do not move from
town to town or from state to state in looking for jobs or a "better"
life. Even those who go on to college attend one close to home, or
they return home once they have completed their education. Native-
born Mexican Americans choose to stay in one place in order to be
with their family and kin; and by doing so, they manage to accumu-
late large, integrated kin networks.

Table 11 indicates the extent to which the local networks of
native-born Mexican Americans are kin-based. A majority (59 percent) of the second generations' contacts and fully three-quarters of
the third generations' contacts are relatives. Equally interesting is the
increase in absolute numbers of total local kin across the three
generations: ten for the first generation, twenty-seven for the second
generation, and fifty for the third generation. The increase in every
generation is due exclusively to the growth in secondary kin. While
primary kin are only a small proportion of social contacts, they are *not*
less important than secondary kin. When frequency of visiting and
exchange of goods and services are taken into account, primary and
secondary kin are equally important. Moreover, although detailed
tabulations of the type of secondary kin were not made, the completed questionnaire forms indicate that the secondary kin seen most
often are spouse's parents and siblings and all siblings' spouses.
Other kin, such as aunts, uncles, and cousins, are not consistent
members of Mexican Americans' networks. If they live in town, most
of these relatives are apt to be seen irregularly, mainly on holidays and
special occasions such as weddings or funerals. Nevertheless, these
local secondary kin are important latent contacts which can be acti-
vated if the need or desire arises.

While the social networks of the native born are definitely kin-based, their networks also include a good number of non-kin ties with whom they socialize and exchange mutual aid. For the native born, friendship supplements kinship as a support system. Furthermore, residential stability and higher socioeconomic status facilitate the formation of friendship ties, just as they facilitate kinship ties among the native born.

In general, what emerges from the data on Mexican American networks are two very different styles of social interaction. The immigrants are relatively isolated. They have few nearby relatives, and they rely on these kin almost exclusively for material and emotional support. They do not make friends easily, but they are forced to expand their small networks through friendship, which is due to the relative absence of nearby kin. Nevertheless, these friends do not have the same rights and obligations as relatives; they are primarily social companions rather than dependable allies. The ritual of *compadrazgo* is used to integrate non-kin more fully into the local extended-family network; however, only a few people are added in this way.

The native born provide a striking contrast to the foreign-born Mexican Americans. They have an extensive, wide-ranging social network that includes both kin and non-kin. While relatives dominate in interaction and exchange, friends are important in the same ways. The native born tend not to distinguish between friends and relatives in function, but they retain a preference for relations with kin. And whereas foreign-born Mexicans have been forced to fragment their kin network with migration, the native born have been able to establish and maintain large kin networks through geographic stability. *Compadrazgo* is used by the native born to reinforce these kin ties, rather than to add to an already extensive family network.

Anglos have local networks made up almost exclusively of non-kin. As can be seen in table 11, almost 90 percent of the Anglos' contacts in town are friends, neighbors, and coworkers. The networks are relatively small when compared to those of the native-born Mexican Americans, but they are well integrated. Anglos visit and exchange often with friends who appear to provide, in many ways, the kind of day-to-day support that Chicanos acquire from relatives.

Anglos lack nearby kin because they move frequently. Most of the

Anglo respondents (68 percent) were not born in the state of California. Thirty percent had lived in town less than five years; almost half had lived in town less than ten years. Unfortunately, we did not ask about motivation to move, an important question if we are to make sense of the way in which Anglos structure their lives. What we can conclude, however, is that kin ties do not restrain Anglos from moving. In this respect, Anglos sharply contrast with Mexican Americans, who frequently indicate that strong family ties are the reason that they continue to live in the small cities where they have lived all their lives.

This does not mean that Anglos have no kin network, but simply that it is not a local network. Bonds with primary kin are maintained through visiting, telephone calls and letters, and exchange over distance. This is the "extended family network" spoken of by Litwak (1960), Sussman and Burchinal (1962), and others. Anglos maintain this widespread network despite socioeconomic mobility as well as geographic mobility. The Anglo kin network, however, tends to be limited to parents, siblings, and adult children. Interaction and exchange with secondary kin is limited, and most of it takes place with the spouse's primary kin. Thus, whereas Chicanos interact mostly with primary kin but maintain close ties with a few aunts, uncles, or cousins and remain in contact with many others, Anglos have a more restricted kin network that essentially consists of the primary kin of respondent and spouse.

Clearly, Anglos hold a conception of the meaning of kinship ties different from that of Mexican Americans (Keefe 1984). For Chicanos, kin must live nearby to share the essential daily joys and sorrows of life, which Anglos share with friends. Kin, on the other hand, provide Anglos with the special closeness and love of family members, a family identity ("roots") as part of a personal identity, and the psychological feeling of security and well-being stemming from family members' concern and support—all of which can be satisfied either with or without the physical presence of relatives, and are characteristic of both Anglos' or Mexican Americans' extended-family relations.

A final comparison of the structure of the ethnic communities, which deserves more than brief mention, concerns sociality, or the tendency to associate with others. Mexican Americans are more sociable than Anglo Americans. Not only do they have numerous relatives with whom they visit, but they also visit non-kin more often than Anglos. The survey data and case studies bear out this difference in social relations. Even first-generation Mexicans, on close inspection, maintain somewhat larger social networks than Anglo Americans. Although table 9 indicates that immigrants have an average of 21 people in their local network and Anglos have an average of 27, these numbers merely indicate *potential* contacts. When actual social interaction is measured, immigrants see as many or more people in town than Anglos.

Personal network data were collected from 20 Mexican Americans and 21 Anglos during two to three different weeks of the third-year interview period of our research (Keefe 1980). To collect information about socializing and exchange, informants were asked to name only people eighteen years of age or older, whom they knew fairly well, and with whom they conversed by using more than a few words.

Immigrant Mexican informants averaged 13.1 network contacts, compared to the Anglos' average of 10.0. However, most Anglos in the sample actually have less than 10 people whom they see regularly, while most of the foreign-born Mexicans see more than 10. It should be emphasized that this difference between the immigrants and Anglos holds only with regard to socializing. When exchange is considered, there is no difference in numbers; the Anglos exchange with an average of 6.7 local people, and the immigrants exchange with an average of 6.9. Of course, most of these people are friends for the Anglos and kin for the foreign-born Mexicans.

Native-born Mexican Americans have much larger social networks than the Anglos. As table 11 indicates, their potential number of local social ties is two to three times greater than the ties of Anglos, and according to the network data, the native born also socialize with more people. Most of the native born have more than 15 people whom they see regularly. The second generation averages 17.1 people, and the third generation averages 29.8 people. Moreover, the majority of these ties are also part of an exchange network. The native-born informants exchange with an average of 14.8 people.

The interviewers' impressions confirm this picture of intense social interaction. The interviews with native-born Mexican Americans were constantly being interrupted by telephone calls, by relatives and neighbors dropping in, and by friends who were visiting and decided to stay while the interview took place. The interviewers of Anglos were rarely interrupted by such distractions.

Ethnic Boundaries

The ethnic communities of Anglo Americans and Mexican Americans are not only structured in different ways; for the most part, they are also separate from one another. The boundaries are given substance through the presence of the *barrio*, the heart and soul of the Chicano community, which confirms the reality of the ethnic boundaries in each city. In many ways, however, the significance of the *barrio* is more symbolic. The majority of Mexican Americans in the three cities studied do not live in the *barrio*; they live in ethnically mixed neighborhoods, as do the majority of lower- and middle-class Anglos. This does not mean, however, that interethnic ties abound. For one thing (as we have seen), "place communities" such as neighborhoods are not relatively important for either ethnic group. Instead, the communities in which the city residents interact are "personal communities" or networks anchored on individuals (Keefe 1980). On close inspection, however, these personal communities are as ethnically segregated as any *barrio*.

Respondents in the second survey were asked to identify the ethnicity of their friends, neighbors, coworkers, and the people they see in places where they go for fun and relaxation (parties, dances, picnics, and so on). Table 12 lists the percentage of the Mexican Americans and Anglo Americans who said that the people in these categories are mostly of their own ethnic group. For example, 70 percent of the first-generation Mexicans said that most of their friends are of Mexican descent, while 74 percent of the Anglos said that most of their friends are of Anglo American descent.

Table 12 demonstrates that Anglos and first-generation Mexicans have the greatest ethnic enclosure. Close to 60 percent or more of the Anglos and 70 percent or more of the immigrants have friends, coworkers, neighborhood friends, and leisuremates who are mostly of their own ethnic group. Most of the remaining Anglo and immigrant respondents said that their social contacts in these categories are equally of their own or other ethnic groups. Very few respondents indicate that their relations are mainly with members of other

Table 12 Intraethnic versus Interethnic Social Relations[a]

| Relationship | Mexican Americans | | | | | | Total[b] (N = 381) | | Anglo Americans (N = 163) | |
| | First (N = 153) | | Second (N = 142) | | Third (N = 70) | | | | | |
	Mostly Mexican %	Mostly Non-Mexican %	Mostly Mexican %	Mostly Non-Mexican %	Mostly Mexican %	Mostly Non-Mexican %	Mostly Mexican %	Mostly Non-Mexican %	Mostly Anglo %	Mostly Non-Anglo %
Friends	70	2	49	5	40	15	56	6	74	0
At leisure places	86	1	60	10	56	7	69	6	58	3
Coworkers[c]	71	6	30	34	30	30	46	22	66	2
Coworkers well known[c]	77	5	47	25	26	35	48	22	71	2
Neighbors	48	14	27	27	34	23	37	21	50	12
Neighbors well known	71	13	35	27	44	30	49	24	68	11

Source: Second Mexican American and Anglo American surveys. Adapted from Keefe (1980).

[a]For each relationship and ethnic category, the remaining percentage of respondents stated they interact equally with both ethnic groups. For example, 70% of the first generation Mexicans have mostly Mexican friends and 2% have mostly non-Mexican friends, leaving 28% with equal numbers of Mexican and non-Mexican friends.

[b]The total sample also includes 16 respondents for whom generation could not be determined.

[c]The number of co-workers is averaged only for respondents who work.

ethnic groups. For example, only 2 percent of the foreign-born Mexicans, and none of the Anglos, said that most of their friends are members of another ethnic group. The contact with "other" ethnics tends to mean contact with either Anglos or Mexican Americans; neither ethnic group, as a whole, interacts appreciably with Blacks, Asian Americans, or other groups, although they are present in the three cities.

Compared to the immigrants and Anglos, native-born Mexican Americans interact more outside their ethnic group while still maintaining strong intraethnic ties. Of the six types of relationships, friends and leisuremates are most ethnically exclusive. There is a greater tendency to have some friends and leisuremates of other ethnic groups. Still, only 5 percent of the second-generation and 15 percent of the third-generation Mexican Americans have friends who are mostly members of another ethnic group. Similarly, only 10 percent of the second generation and 7 percent of the third generation go to leisure spots where most of the people are not Mexican Americans. In less intimate relationships (with neighbors and co-workers) native-born Mexican Americans are much more likely to interact with Anglos. Nevertheless, even in these spheres of action, a good proportion continue to maintain ethnically enclosed relationships. Thus, 47 percent of the second generation have mostly Mexican American coworker friends, compared to 25 percent whose coworker friends are mostly non-Mexican; and 35 percent have mostly Mexican American neighborhood friends, while 27 percent have neighborhood friends who are mostly non-Mexican. Similarly, 26 percent of the third generation have mostly Mexican American coworker friends, while 35 percent have mostly non-Mexican co-worker friends; and 44 percent have mostly Mexican American while 30 percent have mostly non-Mexican neighborhood friends.

An acid test for assessing the degree of intergroup contact lies in the extent of interethnic marriage between Chicanos and Anglos. Here again, our data on intermarriage indicate, for the most part, that the kin sphere remains ethnically enclosed for all three Mexican American generations as well as for the Anglos. The first-generation Mexicans are most ethnically isolated. Only 1 percent of the first-generation respondents have married an Anglo spouse, and none of these respondents have an Anglo father, while 1 percent have an Anglo mother. Similarly, the Anglos are unlikely to have parents who are not of Anglo American ethnicity; only 1 percent have a father of Mexican descent, and none have a mother of Mexican descent. Nonetheless, they are somewhat more likely to have a spouse of Mexican descent, as 7 percent are married to Mexican Americans. The second-generation Mexican Americans follow the Anglo pattern: 1 percent of the respondents have an Anglo father, none have an Anglo mother, and 6 percent have an Anglo spouse. The third generation indicates most intermarriage of parents, with 6 percent having an Anglo father and 2 percent an Anglo mother; but interestingly, the proportion married to Anglos (7 percent) remains about the same as the second generation.

Network data collected during the interviews with the Mexican American and Anglo American case studies confirm the impression of ethnic enclosure gained from the surveys (Keefe 1980). The Anglo and Mexican American informants tend to interact mostly with people of their own ethnic group, although most of the Mexican Americans have a few Anglo contacts as a result of their employment. The Anglos are most ethnically exclusive; on the average, 97 percent of the Anglo case-study informants' contacts are with other Anglo Americans. For the Mexican American case studies, an average of 82 percent of their ties are with others of Mexican descent. From another perspective, fourteen of the Anglos interviewed at length (67 percent) have contact with Anglos only, compared to four Mexican American informants (20 percent) who have only Mexican contacts. All four of these are first-generation immigrants. However, there are also three other first-generation Mexicans whose case study networks do include Anglos. The Anglo and Mexican American informants only rarely know people of other ethnic groups, such as Blacks, Asian Americans, Native Americans, and so on. The Mexican American informants tend to acquire their non-Mexican ties in the workplace; 47 percent of the non-Mexican ties are with coworkers.

The ethnic communities, then, are not essentially spatial, but arise out of social interaction. We might expect a large proportion of Mexican Americans' contacts to be with other people of Mexican descent, due to the importance of kinship in their networks. Non-kin ties involve more choice with regard to ethnicity. Native-born Mexican Americans manage to incorporate a number of Anglos into their networks through non-kin ties, which is not necessarily due to any concentrated effort, but exists because of contiguous interaction, especially at work. Nonetheless, native-born Mexican Americans' networks tend to remain ethnically enclosed as a result of a cultural preference for kin ties which are, of course, ascribed. Mexican immigrants, on the other hand, must expand their networks through friendship; but due to their limited acculturation, limited ability to speak English, and greater likelihood of living in the *barrio*, they tend to choose Mexican friends.

Anglos have a great deal of choice, given their friend-based networks and their ethnically mixed neighborhoods and workplaces; but they prefer to maintain ethnically segregated personal communities. Anglos must actively discriminate against Chicanos in personal relations in order to maintain their high level of ethnic enclosure. This might better be characterized as "avoidance," which Blalock (1967) describes as a subtle form of discrimination, the result of a lack of common interests, the need for psychological comfort, and the tendency to avoid others of lower status than oneself. As long as ethnically segregated personal communities persist, it is easy to understand why Chicanos may be acculturated, on the one hand, while not socially assimilated, on the other.

Ethnic boundaries, of course, are not limited to personal communities. Social institutions are also separate, for the most part. Chicanos in the three cities have their own voluntary organizations, churches, and business districts. Many schools are predominantly Mexican American. There are Spanish-speaking professionals and social services located in the *barrio* especially to serve the Mexican immigrant population. Chicanos tend to cluster in certain blue-collar jobs and places of employment. There are night clubs, bars, and neighborhood parks frequented primarily by Chicanos. Finally, educational and political issues often take on ethnic overtones, and the Mexican community is beginning to organize politically on its own behalf.

The structural pluralism in the three cities is based on a historical pattern of Anglo domination, beginning in the last half of the nineteenth century. Mexican immigration in the twentieth century has continued to reinforce cultural differences; nevertheless, native-born Mexican Americans who make up a majority of the ethnic population have experienced a great deal of acculturation. In many ways they are very much like Anglo Americans. However, as we have discussed, the native born remain socially apart from the Anglos.

This ethnic separatism is a direct result of continued discrimination by Anglos at both the individual and institutional levels. To be fair, though, the ethnic separatism is also the result of the Mexican American cultural emphasis on kinship and, thus, ethnic ties. With the maintenance of a separate social community, additional ethnic cultural patterns are supported by native-born Mexican Americans, and such things as enjoying Mexican food and speaking some Spanish further distinguishes them from Anglo Americans.

Cities and *Barrios*

The emphasis in our analysis of ethnic social structure has concentrated on distinctions between Mexican American generations. Two of the other most important structural differences are variation by town and the difference arising from *barrio* versus non-*barrio* residence. Recent studies have demonstrated differences between Chicano communities due to factors that are internal and external to the ethnic community (Camarillo 1979; Gilbert 1980). Throughout their book *The Mexican American People*, Grebler, Moore, and Guzman (1970) make use of comparisons and contrasts between residents of Los Angles and San Antonio. According to Grebler, Moore, and Guzman, Los Angeles Mexican Americans, for example, have more economic opportunities and are marked by greater acculturation and assimilation than Mexican Americans in San Antonio. These authors also make distinctions on the basis of neighborhood ethnic density. They identify "Colonists" as respondents living in census tracts in which Mexican Americans comprise more than 43 percent of the population in Los Angeles and more than 54 percent in San Antonio; "Frontiersmen" are identified as respondents living in census tracts which have less than 15 percent Mexican Americans in Los Angeles and less than 54 percent in San Antonio. Grebler, Moore, and Guzman use the characterizations of Simirenko (1964), a student of Russian Americans, who distinguished between Colonists, or "conservatives who retained loyalty to the ethnic community," and Frontiersmen, "who left the ethnic community both spatially and emotionally in the process of occupational mobility" (1970:319). For the most part, Grebler, Moore, and Guzman see increasing integration and assimilation of Chicanos into mainstream society accompanying mobility out of the ethnic neighborhood.

Our conclusions stand in marked contrast to those of Greber, Moore, and Guzman. As we have shown, there is no strong evidence on the part of our respondents that would support an assimilation perspective. In general, we find a decline in Cultural Awareness and Ethnic Loyalty in respondents moving from *barrio* to non-*barrio* residence. At the same time, however, we find an increase in extended kin networks and the maintenance of large numbers of ethnic social ties. In any case, generalizations about the impact of *barrio* and non-*barrio* residence on ethnicity obscure the significance of the specific character of individual *barrios* and the variation from one Mexican American community to the next. Our previous analysis on the basis of generation contributes to an understanding of the character of the Chicano communities in the three cities studied. Let us first consider the case of Santa Barbara.

Santa Barbara

The city of Santa Barbara was established during Spanish mission rule in the late eighteenth century, and Hispanic influence held sway throughout the Mexican period following Mexico's independence from Spain in 1822. Spanish was the *linqua franca*: all educational instruction and official documents were in Spanish. Persons of Hispanic descent formed the majority of the population, and the government positions were dominated by an elite class of *Californios*, the native-born Californians of Hispanic descent. Some Anglos of American, British, Scottish, German, and French extraction married into the upper class at this time, assuming limited aspects of Spanish culture such as Catholicism and the Spanish language. Along with Los Angeles, Santa Barbara was a cultural, economic, and political center of Mexican influence in southern California. With changes in the nineteenth century—particularly the Mexican American War (1846–48) and the discovery of gold resulting in the migration of easterners to California—Anglos ultimately came to dominate legally, politically, socially, and numerically in Santa Barbara, as elsewhere in the state; and consequently, Anglo acculturation to Hispanic ways ceased.

New arrivals in Santa Barbara from Mexico during the latter half of the nineteenth century were treated with contempt by both Anglos and *Californios*, and separation characterized relations between the three groups. As the *Californios* fell from socioeconomic and political dominance after 1850, they retreated to the Pueblo Viejo *barrio* near the center of town (see figure 5). The Mexican railroad workers brought to Santa Barbara by the Southern Pacific Railroad congregated near the freight depot on the lower eastside of the city, and from this settlement developed the large Mexican *barrio* which exists today. Close to 90 percent of the Mexicans in the first quarter of this century lived in the lower eastside *barrio*. By 1918, several Mexican-owned stores and a Catholic chapel appeared, and during the 1920s the East Side Social Center (later known as Catholic Social Services) was established to care for the social welfare of the self-contained community. In addition, *mutualistas*, or mutual aid societies, were organized to provide life insurance, emergency aid, and social activities. During this period, Mexicans were employed not only in agriculture, but as laborers and construction workers.

The spatial separation of the *Californios* and *Mexicanos* was symbolic of their social separation. While they were members of the same occupational level, there was little interaction between the two groups. There were cultural differences as well; although they both spoke Spanish, the dialect was somewhat different, and their wearing apparel and religious customs also differed. The recent arrivals from Mexico identified as "Mexicans," whereas the *Californios* identified as local natives; and in their attempt to detach themselves from the stigma of being Mexican, the *Californios* did as much to differentiate themselves as possible. Importantly, however, the Anglos seldom made any distinction between the two groups and maintained very little contact with either one. Discrimination prevailed in the schools and recreational outlets. As the *Californio* segment of the population withered in proportion to the influx of *Mexicanos*, it was gradually absorbed by the new group; and today, the separate community has all but disappeared, although many still take pride in claiming an "old" Santa Barbara name and descent from the *Californios*.

Since the 1950s, the greater Santa Barbara area has become extensively urbanized, with most of the county's agricultural production taking place in the northern half of the county. Santa Barbara has not had a proportionately large farm-labor force in recent decades, relying more on tourism and its attraction as a county retail center for employment. Because it is the county seat, government jobs are relatively plentiful; and with its local schools, city college, and the university, education is also a major employer. There is no heavy

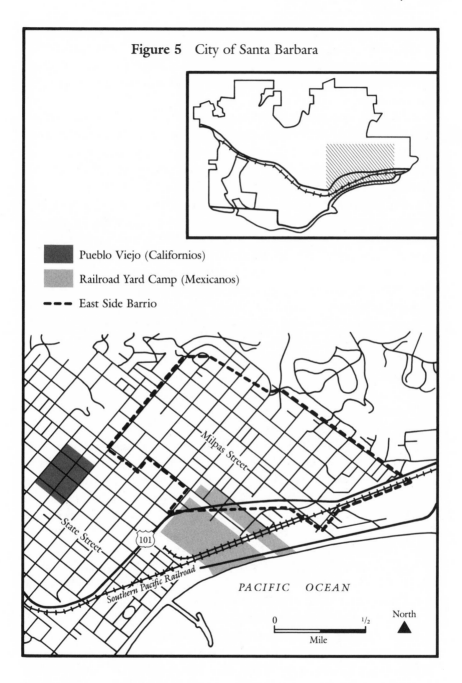

Figure 5   City of Santa Barbara

Pueblo Viejo (Californios)

Railroad Yard Camp (Mexicanos)

East Side Barrio

Milpas Street

State Street

101

Southern Pacific Railroad

PACIFIC   OCEAN

0   ½

Mile

North

industry, but many people are employed in light manufacturing, particularly the assembly of electronic component parts. The Mexican labor force is employed primarily in blue-collar jobs, but these are distributed across the retail, service, and manufacturing occupational arenas.

Given the quality and kind of economic growth in the area since the Second World War, the Mexican population in Santa Barbara has made considerable strides, although it is still socioeconomically disadvantaged when compared to the general population. In fact, Chicanos in Santa Barbara, who make up 27 percent of the population, are better off than they are in the other two cities studied. According to census data, they have a higher level of education, a greater proportion of white-collar occupations, and a lower incidence of poverty than the Spanish-speaking people in Oxnard and Santa Paula. Immigration from Mexico has been proportionately less in Santa Barbara, and the Chicano community is somewhat more stable than in the other two towns. Housing is not as crowded, and it is difficult to find the dismal shacks and slum buildings which are more evident in Oxnard and Santa Paula. Moreover, only 25 percent of the Spanish-speaking population resides within the census tract covering the eastside Mexican *barrio*. In sum, the Mexican American community in Santa Barbara lives under better conditions, as a whole, than in the other two cities.

Our survey data indicate that Santa Barbara also has the least distinctive *barrio* of the three towns. In fact, analysis by census tract indicates a great degree of homogeneity across the three tracts sampled in the city. Regardless of tract, the majority of Santa Barbara Mexican Americans are native-born, long-term residents of the city. Even in the *barrio*, 58 percent of the respondents were either born in Santa Barbara or have lived in town for longer than twenty-five years. This long-term nature of the Chicano population should be expected, given the Mexican history of the city and the absence of an agricultural economy to draw new immigrants. Another historically based feature of the Santa Barbara sample is the presence of a small number of descendants of the nineteenth-century *Californios*, who are represented by the most acculturated cluster (Type V); fifteen of the nineteen respondents making up this cluster were born and raised and continue to live in Santa Barbara. The fact that they are found in almost equivalent numbers in the three census tracts testifies to the disintegration of Pueblo Viejo (the *Californio* neighborhood), as described by Camarillo (1979).

Given the nature of the Mexican American community in Santa Barbara, it is not surprising to find that the town's respondents score relatively low on Cultural Awareness, not much higher on Ethnic Loyalty, relatively high on Primary and Secondary Kin factors, and average on the Friends and Neighbors factors. These are the characteristics of the geographically stable native born. The only index on which *barrio* residents score very differently from non-*barrio* residents is on Ethnic Social Orientation (ESO); but even here, Santa Barbara *barrio* residents score slightly *below* the mean.

Santa Paula and Oxnard

The Chicano communities in Santa Paula and Oxnard are of much more recent origin than in Santa Barbara. Both cities were established by Anglos decades after California was admitted as a state in 1850. Furthermore, both communities were established around an agricultural economy in which the manual labor force was originally made up primarily of Chinese and Japanese. Mexicans began to arrive in the area in great numbers only after 1910, but they eventually became the largest ethnic minority group. In Oxnard, the Mexicans began to settle on the east side of the main road through town, near the sugar beet factory and the railroad tracks (see figure 6). The Mexican *barrio* today, known as *La Colonia*, is located in the same general area. The Mexicans in Santa Paula were housed at first in a labor camp, built by the citrus growers near the railroad tracks on the east side of town (see figure 7). This area is now part of a larger Mexican *barrio* which covers a major portion of the town.

The *barrios* in these two towns developed in much the same way as the *barrio* in Santa Barbara. Small Mexican-owned businesses took hold, and a Catholic church (named after the *Virgen de Guadalupe*, Mexico's patron saint) was established. Schools were segregated, as were many recreational activities. The Mexican population was looked upon with fear and contempt by the Anglos, and social interaction tended to be ethnically exclusive. Thus, ethnic identification was distinct when the Chicano communities were first forming in Santa Paula and Oxnard, and the Mexican population itself was fairly homogeneous.

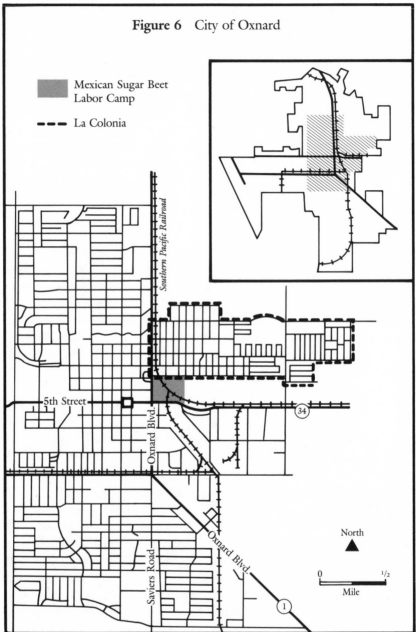

Figure 6   City of Oxnard

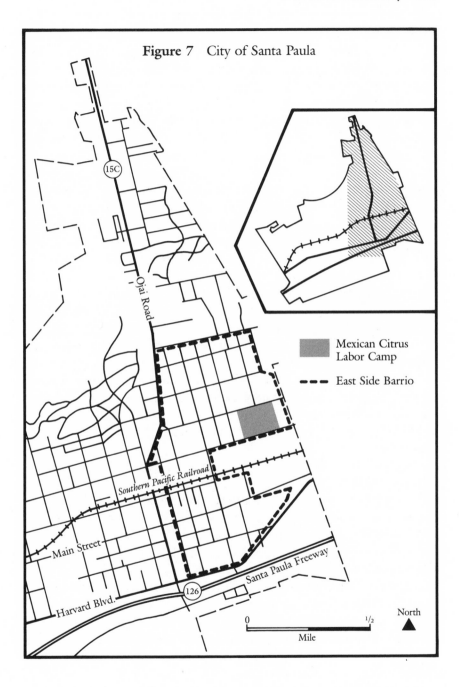

Figure 7   City of Santa Paula

Agriculture reached its peak in Ventura County in the 1940s, when World War II and the subsequent building boom laid the foundation for economic change. Several military facilities were established around Oxnard during and after the war. These military bases brought in new workers, and there were housing shortages for a time. Some settled in other cities, where more housing was available, and for the first time Santa Paula became a bedroom community. Ranches in Ventura County were transformed into housing tracts, especially in the 1950s, when Los Angeles County's population gradually spilled over the mountains. The new residents required more government services and an increase in the tax rates; and when tax increases were combined with the rise in land prices, ranchers were encouraged to sell out. Unemployed agricultural workers became available for industry, which was also attracted to Ventura County because of the area's transportation network and its proximity to the Los Angeles market.

In recent decades, Oxnard has become a large retail trade center, and many residents are employed as civilian workers on the military bases. Agriculture has declined in importance, although it remains a major employer. Still, less than 10 percent of the male labor force were farm laborers in 1980, while food processing and packing houses employed additional workers. Meanwhile, manufacturing has increased dramatically, with the largest companies in the area producing plastic products, electronic components, and electric equipment.

Despite some decline over the years, agriculture remains the primary industry in the city of Santa Paula; two local packing houses are the largest employers. Manufacturing has made small inroads, but only three relatively large firms have been built in the city. Because of its central valley location, Santa Paula has also been a regional trade outlet; but since the completion of the freeway to Ventura in 1963, much of the trade has been drained off by the larger coastal cities. While the local economy is primarily agricultural, many of the residents work in nearby cities and prefer to live in Santa Paula's quiet residential areas. Thus, the occupational distribution of the local labor force is more a reflection of the diversification of the surrounding metropolitan area than an accurate representation of Santa Paula's own economy.

Given its more agricultural basis, Santa Paula as a whole is less well-off economically than the other two cities; and Chicanos, who make up 48 percent of the residents, have suffered the consequences more than the general population. One-fifth of the Mexican American families have an income below the poverty level. Nearly 80 percent of the Spanish-speaking people in Santa Paula are employed as farm workers or as semiskilled operatives, service workers, or laborers. Almost one-half live in the census tract on the east side of town, which covers the core of the *barrio*; and there are more persons per household, more children, and more female-headed households among the Mexican residents of the city.

According to our survey data, the Chicano community in Santa Paula is relatively stable, although a good many immigrants have been attracted by the citrus industry. The *barrio*, however, is not the exclusive domain of the foreign born, who are spread to some extent throughout the three census tracts sampled. In Santa Paula, it is the newer west side of town that is distinctive. The west side, made up of recently constructed housing tracts, is represented in the sample by an upwardly mobile segment of native-born Mexican Americans, who were either born in the city or have lived in Santa Paula longer than twenty-five years. Like Santa Barbara Mexican Americans, they have relatively low Cultural Awareness and Ethnic Loyalty scores, high Primary and Secondary Kin scores, and average Friends and Neighbors scores. Furthermore, their Ethnic Social Orientation score is low, which is true for non-*barrio* residents in general.

The older neighborhoods in Santa Paula, represented by the two remaining census tracts, have fairly mixed populations. About half of the respondents are foreign born, while the other half are native born. Length of residence is variable; about one-third have lived in town for ten years or less, while another one-third are long-term residents or town natives. The sociocultural and social sphere factor scores reflect this diversity. These respondents generally have average Cultural Awareness and Ethnic Loyalty scores, a relatively high Ethnic Social Orientation score, a high Primary Kin score, an average Secondary Kin score, and fairly low Friends and Neighbors scores.

On the whole, the Mexican Americans in Oxnard have done better economically than those who live in Santa Paula. They have a somewhat higher education and income level, and more of them have white-collar jobs than the Spanish-speaking people in Santa

Paula; but they still lag behind the levels for the general population. On the other hand, as in Santa Paula, Oxnard has experienced a consistent influx of Mexican immigrants; and as a whole, the Spanish-speaking people who make up 41 percent of the population tend to cluster in the farm-worker, operative, and service-worker occupational levels. The Chicano population is somewhat less spatially segregated in Oxnard; nonetheless, approximately 40 percent live in the census tracts that encompass *La Colonia*, the Mexican *barrio*.

According to our survey data, Oxnard is the most heterogeneous of the three cities in terms of neighborhood types. Each of the three census-tract samples has distinctive characteristics. *La Colonia*, Oxnard's *barrio*, is the most "Mexican" of the three *barrios* in the study because the vast majority of its residents are foreign-born Mexicans; 72 percent of the respondents in *La Colonia* are first generation. Most of these respondents are fairly recent town residents; 64 percent have lived in town ten years or less. Thus, *La Colonia* is not only geographically isolated from the rest of Oxnard; its residents are also socially isolated, as are immigrants generally. The Cultural Awareness, Ethnic Loyalty, and Ethnic Social Orientation scores in the *barrio* are all extremely high, as one would expect for an immigrant population. The respondents have the lowest Primary Kin and Friends scores of all nine census tracts sampled, with both factors affected greatly by migration. The Secondary Kin score is about average, and the Neighbors score is low, which is true for immigrants generally. *La Colonia* is truly a "colony" set apart from the city, serving primarily as a farm-labor camp for the surrounding ranches.

The mid-ethnic density census tract in Oxnard covers a mixed neighborhood similar to the older neighborhoods of Santa Paula, where the population is equally foreign born and native born and length of residence varies from recent to long term. In this tract, all sociocultural indices and the Primary and Secondary Kin factors are about average, while the Friends and Neighbors factors are low.

Finally, the low-ethnic density census tract in Oxnard is much like Santa Barbara and the west side of Santa Paula. Respondents are longtime residents, and 85 percent are native-born Mexican Americans. Accordingly, they have relatively low Cultural Awareness, Ethnic Loyalty, and Ethnic Social Orientation scores, high scores on Primary and Secondary Kin, and average Friends scores. Neighbors scores, on the other hand, are somewhat low.

Thus, the towns have different neighborhood patterns of ethnicity. On the whole, Santa Barbara is fairly homogenous. In Santa Paula, the newer west side of town is most distinctive. Finally, each of the three neighborhoods surveyed in Oxnard possesses a unique character.

In comparing the *barrios* from one town to the next, we again find striking differences. *La Colonia* in Oxnard best fits the stereotype of an ethnically isolated *barrio*. Over 90 percent of the respondents from *La Colonia* fall into our two "Mexican Ethnics" cluster types (Types I and II). On the other hand, only 23 percent of the *barrio* respondents in Santa Barbara fit these types. In fact, a comparison of the neighborhoods in the two towns shows that the cluster pattern for Santa Barbara's *barrio* is most like Oxnard's low–ethnic density census tract rather than its *barrio*. Moreover, while no respondents in *La Colonia* fit the "Americans . . . Set Apart" Types IV and V, 12 percent of the Santa Paula and 24 percent of the Santa Barbara *barrio* respondents fit these types. Thus, there are real problems in assuming that all *barrios* are alike and in assuming that most *barrio* residents are unacculturated and have high ethnic identity. For example, when using Grebler, Moore, and Guzman's (1970) model, the Santa Barbara *barrio* is more similar to a neighborhood of Frontiersmen than to one of Colonists.

The heterogeneity across high–ethnic density census tracts noted in the three cities is an important finding, and one that has not been noted in previous literature. Collectively, our data demonstrate that both towns and *barrios* are the product of numerous social, economic, and historical factors that create different types of ethnic communities. Some *barrios* are havens for recent immigrants, while others are established communities and neighborhoods. Unlike Grebler, Moore, and Guzman (1970), who speak of the characteristics of "Colonists," we find little cause to generalize about Chicanos on the basis of *barrio* residence. In considering our own data, there is perhaps more reason to generalize about the "Frontiersmen" living in low–ethnic density neighborhoods. However, our interpretation differs from the assimilationist perspective of the Grebler, Moore, and Guzman study. In our study, the Frontiersmen have acculturated to a degree, moved up socioeconomically, and moved out of the *barrio*, but they have not "left the ethnic community." Instead, they have retained an ethnic identity and are fully integrated into an ethnic community; rather than a spatial community, however, it is a personal network of ethnic social ties based mostly on kinship.

12

Recasting

THIS STUDY ATTEMPTS TO UNDERSTAND the dynamics of cultural change and ethnic shift among Mexican-origin respondents in three Southern California communities. To accomplish this goal, we planned a sampling strategy that would be representative of our communities. In addition, we developed data-collection instruments that would provide us with information about a broad spectrum of our respondents' lives. As much information as possible was collected from our respondents over three successive years, beginning with a thirty- to forty-minute interview with over six hundred individuals and ending with countless hours of in-depth interviewing with a small number of respondents. To enrich our study, information was also amassed about the communities where the respondents resided. Finally, we collected information from a large number of Anglo Americans who lived in the same communities. By adding this group, we were also able to make comparisons between the two groups with respect to family organization and social support as well as to intergroup relations. Rarely has such a comparison been made in studies involving Chicanos.

What we have learned is that Chicano ethnicity and its changes over time are not so easily described. Contrary to much of the literature, no single continuum of acculturation and assimilation emerges from our study. Native-born Mexican Americans acculturate, but it is selective; and some ethnic traits, especially the maintenance of family ties, are sustained and surprisingly even strengthened from generation to generation. Social assimilation occurs among native-born Mexican Americans, but this involves only more imper-

189

sonal and formal secondary relations; the primary sphere of family and friends is for the most part ethnically closed. Thus, the ethnic community survives, despite the process of acculturation and the related process of assimilation. For native-born Mexican Americans, the ethnic community is made up of Mexican Americans who have selectively acculturated and interact with Anglos, as well as other Mexican Americans. However, the content and degree of interethnic interaction is governed by time and place, and reflects a situational ethnicity. At times, some of our respondents are Mexican *Americans*, part of the larger society, knowledgeable about American culture, and interacting with the mainstream population. At other times, the same respondents are American *Mexicans*, carrying on traditional culture, taking pride in their heritage, and tied intimately to others of similar ethnicity. At still other times, they are Chicanos, practicing new and emergent cultural patterns and sustaining an ethnic community set apart form both Anglos and recent immigrant Mexicans.

Our understanding of the complexity of ethnicity among Chicanos has emerged from an initial conceptual model that identifies two major processes of sociocultural change: acculturation and ethnic identification. In addition to confirming these two processes, our data analysis indicates that social assimilation, a third related and yet independent process, contributes to ethnic culture change. Furthermore, we have been able to measure these processes by developing scales of Cultural Awareness, Ethnic Loyalty, and Ethnic Social Orientation. In so doing, we find evidence that ethnic loyalty and ethnic social interaction are the persistent components of Chicano ethnicity. Loyalty toward Mexican heritage persists through the fourth generation, although a slight shift occurs between first- and second-generation respondents. Social assimilation follows a similar course, with Chicano interaction with Anglos increasing somewhat in the second generation and no significant change occurring afterward. On the other hand, awareness of Mexican cultural traits declines steadily with each successive generation. For instance, language use and preference, which is the primary component contributing to cultural awareness, shifts dramatically from Spanish to English within two generations.

By means of the statistical procedures used to create our multidimensional model of ethnicity, it was possible to compute composite Cultural Awareness and Ethnic Loyalty scores for our respondents, and, using cluster analysis, to construct a typology of ethnic differentiation. Thus, five ethnic types were produced, ranging from high- to low-average scores on Cultural Awareness and Ethnic Loyalty. If one looked solely at the Cultural Awareness measure, these types would fit a fairly neat continuum model of gradual culture change. When the Ethnic Loyalty measure is taken into consideration, however, the continuum model becomes untenable. Instead, we see culture change *and* ethnic persistence occurring simultaneously.

In sum, our findings do not support the acculturation–assimilation model, which holds the twin processes as inevitably completed at some future point. Nor do our findings fit the internal-colony model, which postulates complete acculturation but continued segregation and domination. The pluralism model is best suited to our findings because cultural, social, and structural continuums are identified, accommodating change occurring at different rates in different life spheres. Nevertheless, given its name and the way in which it has been employed frequently, the pluralism model implies the indefinite persistence of ethnic groups who are, for the most part, separate from one another. Our data, on the other hand, call for a neo-pluralism model that can accommodate concurrent states of change *and* continuity, integration *and* pluralism, in ethnicity. This model would require thinking in terms of a multitude of dimensions, with the possibility of change occurring in each dimension at a different rate and possessing the potential of moving in more than one direction.

Yet no one model, including our own, can be applied in a simple way to the entire ethnic group at large, for there are important variations between segments of the Chicano population. Generation seems to capture many of the variations by culture and class. In many ways, first-generation immigrants fit a colonial interpretation of ethnic relations. They are lower class, ethnically set apart and socially isolated, with their kin networks disrupted by migration. As a result, their ethnic community is not well integrated, which, together with their isolation and lack of acculturation, renders them uncertain and powerless in the larger community. On the other hand, native-born Mexican Americans have the solid backing of an integrated, kin-based community. For the native born, a general pattern emerges of selective acculturation and of somewhat weakened, but persistent,

Mexican identity (described earlier as types called "Cultural Blends" and "Emerging Americans"), as well as assimilation in secondary relations, strong familism, and large ethnic networks. The native born may live to a great extent outside mainstream society; yet they have a well-integrated social organization that can form the basis for competition in the larger society's political and economic arenas.

We believe that the importance of our study will ultimately rest on the fact that we have been able to describe, both conceptually *and* empirically, the heterogeneity that makes up the Mexican American population. By means of our theoretical model and empirically derived typology and case studies, we are able to demonstrate how this heterogeneity operates at both the individual and the community levels. Furthermore, we are able to show why the traditional acculturation–assimilation models are not useful in trying to understand Mexican American ethnic behavior. For instance, we show clearly that generational level is not, in itself, a good predictor of ethnic status. In the development of our typology, and as we demonstrated in our case studies, it is possible to be a late-generation Chicano who is unacculturated and strongly loyal to Mexican culture, just as it is possible to be first generation and more acculturated than one's compatriots.

While our primary intent in this study was not to determine causal factors, we suggest that there are numerous reasons for the persistence of ethnic communities among second- and later-generation Mexican Americans, including factors both internal and external to the ethnic group. First of all, the social gap between Anglos and Chicanos is the product of a long history of ethnic conflict in the Southwest. Many Mexican Americans recall painful events from an era in the not-too-distant past when discrimination was more overt, and revealed in phenomena such as "no Spanish" rules in schools or landlord policies of not renting to Mexicans. Our statistical analysis indicates that perceived discrimination is a major contributory force in the maintenance of ethnic loyalty across our four generations of respondents. The salience of perceived discrimination in the lives of our respondents is further confirmed in our case-study data, which reveal numerous themes of discriminatory practices directed against Mexican Americans.

Although overt social discrimination against Mexican Americans has declined somewhat over the past two decades, it has also become more subtle and indirect, making it difficult to confront. This more covert form of discrimination has been called "institutional discrimination" or "institutional racism" because it cannot be identified as originating from any single individual or group, but appears to be supported by policies that are systematic and endemic to institutions. Regardless of whether Chicanos are confronted by overt or institutional discrimination, the net effect appears to be the same; that is, discrimination continues to structure formal and informal relations between Anglos and Mexican Americans. One aspect of this structure is the persistence of major social class differences between the two ethnic groups, making interethnic social relations on a large scale highly unlikely. Another aspect of the structural pluralism is the persistence of residential segregation in *barrios*, isolating a large segment of the ethnic minority from economic, social, and political benefits. Very striking in our data was the evidence of minimal contact between Anglos and Mexican Americans, which was true even among our most acculturated (New Americans) respondents. It was not uncommon to learn that members of the two ethnic groups did not socialize, even though they were coworkers or neighbors. A mostly peaceful coexistence, with little mixing, seems to define interethnic relationships in the communities we studied. We have no reason to believe that these communities are atypical as far as interethnic relations are concerned.

Although our study was not designed to examine the contact hypothesis (Allport 1954; Stephan and Brigham 1985), it is striking to observe the lack of intergroup contact between Anglos and Chicanos. It appears highly probable that as long as unequal status (majority vs. minority group) and economic competition exists between Anglos and Chicanos, ethnicity will continue to be the major feature separating the two groups.

It is interesting to speculate about what would happen if there were an absence of overt and institutional discrimination against Mexican Americans. Such a situation might hasten both the acculturation and assimilation of Mexican Americans, and it may be that the classical model of acculturation and assimilation of ethnic groups holds when there is little or no structural discrimination leveled at ethnic minorities by the majority group. Through its adherence to social policies that deliberately or inadvertently discriminate against visible ethnics such as Mexican Americans, the majority group may be interfering with acculturation and assimilation of Chicanos, and thus may be responsible to a great extent for this ethnic group's maintenance of ethnic loyalty and pluralism. On the other hand, the personal avoidance in the private sphere of those who are ethnically different seems to be equally important in inhibiting the integration process, which might persist regardless of institutional policies.

On the other hand, the maintenance of the ethnic community is not simply the result of external factors. There are forces within the ethnic group which are also responsible for its persistence. The most significant factor is the emphasis on the extended family. While it is reasonable to assume that family ties might be intensified to counteract discrimination, a strong kinship group is also a core value trait in Mexican culture. The kin ties of our respondents were not spoken of as obligatory, rising out of dependency and exclusion; instead, kin ties are thought of as positive, cherished, and independently worthy in themselves. Perhaps the most important trait developing from this emphasis on kinship is geographic stability. Ties to a town or city give boundaries to the ethnic community, although the structure is better conceptualized as a mesh of personal networks. Importantly, ties to the family and community were strongest among those respondents who were in the best position to break away, that is, to the more acculturated and/or upwardly mobile respondents. Respondents who often fit into our "Cultural-Blend" category had the most resources available to them, and offered more support to their family and community, than respondents in our other categories. This finding points to the pull of the family and the culture, and stands in contrast to popular conceptions of the more able and acculturated members of an ethnic group fleeing to join mainstream society.

The combination of kin ties and place ties ensures the ethnic character of the Chicano community. The interaction with longtime associates guarantees a degree of cultural continuity and, thus, incomplete acculturation and possible consequent assimilation. An ethnic identity may also be maintained within these social boundaries. For the native born, however, it is not likely to be simply an identification with the people and culture of Mexico, but rather an identity which shares something with both Mexicans and Americans, and yet is different, positive, and unique. The biculturalism of the native born facilitates interaction with Mexican immigrants and

Anglo Americans, but the concomitant cultural distinctiveness of the native born results in their maintenance of ethnic communities set apart from both of these groups. It is precisely this cultural blend that serves to identify the main ingredients and forces that give meaning to what some writers have called "Chicano culture."

In this case, Chicano culture is not simply the amalgamation of both Mexican and American culture and ethnic loyalties. As we have shown in our data, awareness of Mexican culture is replaced across successive generations with greater knowledge of American cultural traditions and language, but cultural replacement is not complete even after four generations. Therefore, the variable of generation alone is not sufficient for cultural replacement to occur. However, from our data we are not able to specify with precision the characteristics that describe Chicano culture, since even in the area of language use some Chicanos are fluent in Spanish while others are monolingual in English. More research is clearly needed in order to delineate what cultural traits are included when we speak of "Chicano culture."

No single reason alone accounts for the perpetuation of ethnicity and ethnic communities. Causal factors stem from the ethnic minority group as well as from the majority group and the interaction between the two. The interrelationship of these factors is complex, and makes the theoretical models constructed by social scientists seem highly inadequate. It makes as little sense to attack solely the "oppression" and discrimination of the dominant group as it does to "blame the victim," the minority group and its culture.

A multidimensional model of cultural change and persistence is required in order to account for the variations within the ethnic minority group, in different spheres of social action, and for different cultural traits. At the very minimum, the dimensions of acculturation, ethnic identity, social assimilation, and structural assimilation (including relative economic position and access to political power) need to be examined and measured for comparative purposes. It is only through the study of the interrelationships of cultural, social, and structural factors in historical perspective that a broad understanding of the nature of ethnicity and sociocultural change can be achieved.

The study of Mexican Americans has always been important in understanding the historical development of the American Southwest, but in the twentieth century this ethnic group is significantly changing the landscape of contemporary U.S. society. Because of continued large-scale immigration from Mexico and a high fertility rate, Mexican Americans have shown a dramatic population increase over the past two-and-one-half decades. As the ethnic group has grown in numbers, so have the social problems confronting Chicanos (for example, school dropouts, substance abuse, and single-parent families). By understanding how this group adjusts to mainstream society, it will be possible to institute social policies that may help to alleviate social problems among Mexican Americans today.

The Mexican American population is variously depicted in the press as either an ethnic group on the move or as a group beset by social problems. Both of these depictions have some validity, but in order to understand the direction in which the group is going and how social problems may hinder this movement, we need to have a sound understanding about the place of Chicanos in U.S. society. Only through comprehensive studies combining survey-research and ethnographic methods, quantitative measures and qualitative descriptions, can we hope to provide new insights into the complex way in which ethnicity and culture change affect the individual and the ethnic community.

Appendixes

Psychometric Analysis
of the Data

THE DATA OBTAINED FROM the 381 Phase Two respondents were factor analyzed. In order to factor-analyze the data, items from the questionnaire were pooled as either measuring cultural awareness or ethnic loyalty, according to the premises of the model described in chapter 4. This pooling resulted in 108 items grouped as measuring 18 Cultural Awareness concepts and 77 items grouped as measuring 15 Ethnic Loyalty concepts. These items were then scored in the direction of Mexican cultural awareness and ethnic identity. In this procedure, an item was so coded that a high score reflected awareness or loyalty to the Mexican culture. For example, a "no" response to the question "Do you speak Spanish?" was scored 1, while a "yes" reply was scored 2. For the converse item (that is, "Do you speak English?"), a "yes" was given a score of 1, while a "no" was scored as 2.

After score assignment of the 185 items, a frequency distribution for each item was calculated as well as a correlation matrix for all of the items. On the basis of an examination of the frequency distributions and inter-item correlations, items were eliminated if they met any one of the following criteria:

1. Missing observations totaling more than 25 percent of the sample
2. Extremely skewed or truncated distributions for items with multiple response categories, or highly disproportionate splits for items with dichotomous response categories
3. Low correlations with other items hypothesized to measure the same concept

4. High correlations with other items hypothesized to measure different concepts.

On the basis of this procedure, some items were eliminated or grouped with a different concept. Similarly, some concepts were dropped, others were "split" into two concepts, and still others were revised in terms of item content. The screening and regrouping of items resulted in the elimination of 30 items. Of the remaining 155 items, 90 were grouped into 19 Cultural Awareness concepts, and 65 were grouped into 14 Ethnic Loyalty concepts.

The construction of Homogeneous Item Dimensions (HIDs) was then made according to a procedure which was a slight modification of a strategy used by Comrey (1973). This procedure consisted simply of the addition of scores over items corresponding to each concept, resulting in the construction of 19 Cultural Awareness HIDs and 14 Ethnic Loyalty HIDs. The distribution for each HID was then normalized by using a procedure described by Blom (1958). Normalized HIDs were screened on the basis of distributional properties and visual inspection of all possible pairwise correlations and scattergrams with other HIDs in the same set (Cultural Awareness or Ethnic Loyalty). HIDs that conformed to either of the following criteria were dropped: extremely skewed or truncated distributions, even after the normalizing procedure had been applied; or nonlinear regressions with other HIDs in the same set. These screening procedures of HIDs resulted in the elimination of a total of 7 HIDs, leaving 15 Cultural Awareness HIDs and 11 Ethnic Loyalty HIDs.

Factor analysis was then carried out with the Cultural Awareness and Ethnic Loyalty HIDs that had successfully achieved the criteria of normality and linearity of regression. The procedure followed in the factor analysis of the Cultural Awareness concepts was that of principal factoring with iterations and a computer-assisted "hand-rotation" method (Comrey 1973) to extract factors. Table 13 presents the factor-correlation matrix for the Cultural Awareness concepts.

Inspection of table 13 shows that a reasonable approximation to simple structure was achieved. Only a single variable (parents' cultural inheritance and contact) shows a loading greater than .40 on a second factor. An examination of the intercorrelations demonstrates that the first three factors are moderately intercorrelated, with correlations from 0.20 to 0.30, while Factor IV is orthogonal to all of the other factors.

The factor analysis of the Ethnic Loyalty concepts was also done by using the procedure of principal factoring with iterations, and by using the Direct Oblimin Criterion Method (Harmon 1967) to rotate and extract factors. Again, four factors were obtained from the eleven Ethnic Loyalty concepts. Table 14 presents the factor correlation matrix.

Table 13 Factor Correlation Matrix Resulting from the Factor Analysis of the Fifteen Cultural Awareness Homogenous Item Dimensions

			Factors	
Homogenous Item Dimensions	*I*	*II*	*III*	*IV*
1. R's cultural inheritance and contact	.67	.21	.16	−.08
2. R's language familiarity	.63	.27	.30	−.05
3. R's knowledge of Mexican cultural symbols, historical events, and contemporary personalities	.57	.00	.19	.05
4. Ethnicity of peers during childhood	.52	−.01	.11	.12
5. R's legal first name	.41	.06	.21	.04
6. Spouse's cultural inheritance and contact	.34	.67	−.02	−.09
7. Spouse's ethnic identification	−.02	.67	.15	.11
8. Spouse's language familiarity and preference	.36	.62	.02	−.12
9. Spouse's legal and preferred first name	.29	.53	.15	.03
10. Parent's ethnic identification	−.02	.24	.69	.06
11. Father's legal and preferred first name	.17	.03	.63	.00
12. Parent's language familiarity and preference	.39	.07	.61	.10
13. Parent's cultural heritage and contact	.44	.08	.56	−.07
14. Perceived personal discrimination	−.12	−.05	.07	.63
15. Perceived group discrimination	.21	.00	−.02	.57

Source: Second Mexican American survey. Adapted from Padilla (1980).

Examination of table 14 indicates that all of the concepts load .38 or higher on one of the factors, and that only the first two concepts show loadings greater than .30 on more than one factor. An examination of the intercorrelations between factors demonstrates that the Ethnic Loyalty factors correlate higher with one another than is true with the Cultural Awareness Factors with correlations ranging from 0.15 to 0.46.

The obvious next step was to examine the eight factors of Cultural Awareness and Ethnic Loyalty and to describe the central characteristics of each factor. This was accomplished through an examination of the items that comprised each of the Cultural Awareness or Ethnic Loyalty concepts within each factor. A description of the Cultural Awareness and Ethnic Loyalty factors, along with the vari-

Table 14 Factor Correlation Matrix Resulting from the Factor Analysis of the Eleven Ethnic Loyalty Homogenous Item Dimensions

		Factors		
Homogenous Item Dimensions	*I*	*II*	*III*	*IV*
1. R's language choice in situations dealing with other people	.68	−.08	.23	.37
2. R's language preference in personal situations	.65	.08	.34	.13
3. R's preferred first name and children's first names	.65	.11	−.01	.18
4. Number of children who speak Spanish	.62	.07	.00	.10
5. Perception of Mexican culture	.01	.71	.09	−.08
6. Preference for ethnicity of associates	.04	.54	.00	.20
7. Perception of Mexico and U.S.	.06	.09	.51	.00
8. R's identification with a group name	−.28	−.02	.47	.11
9. Preference for traveling in Mexico	−.09	.10	.38	.16
10. Ethnicity of associates at present	.08	.00	.06	.72
11. Preference for and consumption of Mexican food	.14	.19	.06	.48

Source: Second Mexican American survey. Adapted from Padilla (1980).

ance attributed to each factor, is presented in tables 15 and 16. A list of the specific questions contributing to these eight factors can be found in appendix 2.

It is obvious from table 15 that Respondent's Cultural Heritage (RCH) is the most important factor of the awareness variables reflecting early enculturation and basic knowledge of language and culture. It is also obvious from table 15 that an individual respondent's cultural heritage is distinct from that of parents and/or spouse. This finding is contrary to our assumption that a respondent's level of awareness could be predicted on the basis of their parents' level of awareness. Finally, the orthogonality of Factor IV, Perceived Discrimination, to the cultural heritage factors is clear evidence that Factor IV is not a dimension of Cultural Awareness.

Study of table 16 shows that the factor of Language Preference (LP) accounts for most of the variance (74 percent) on Ethnic Loyalty. It is also interesting to note that LP, like RCH, reflects a language dimension. In fact, language emerges from the analysis as one of the most significant aspects of the process of culture change. Contrary to our initial assumption, however, language familarity and usage is not an independent cultural sphere, but is intimately connected, early in life, with geographical residence in Mexico or in the U.S.

It is also clear from the factor analysis of the Cultural Awareness concepts and the orthogonality of Factor IV that Perceived Discrimination (PD) is not a dimension of Cultural Awareness. Rather than being an aspect of straightforward knowledge, PD is apparently more the result of the respondent's attitudes toward the ethnic minority group and majority group.

The distinction between the Ethnic Loyalty factors of Ethnic Pride and Affiliation (EPA) and Cultural Identification (CI) is noteworthy. Essentially, this means that an individual may identify as American and prefer life in the United States to life in Mexico, and at the same time, have pride in possessing a Mexican heritage and prefer to interact with others of Mexican descent. Of course, the opposite may also be true: a second individual may identity as Mexican and have a negative opinion about the United States, and concurrently display little pride in possessing a Mexican heritage and have no preference for Mexican associates. The distinction between the first and second individuals is generally referred to in the literature as a

Table 15 Description of Factors Emerging from First-Order Factor
Analysis of Cultural Awareness Items

Factor I (71%) Respondent's Cultural Heritage (RCH)

High: R knows Spanish but no English, and uses Spanish media; has Spanish first name; had peers during childhood and/or adolescence who were Mexican; was most likely born in Mexico and immigrated late in life; went to school in Mexico; knows Mexican cultural symbols, historical events, and contemporary personalities; goes to Mexico often.

Low: R knows English but little Spanish, and uses English media; has English first name; had peers during childhood and/or adolescence who were Anglo; was most likely born in U.S. or immigrated early in life; went to school in U.S.; does not know Mexican cultural symbols, historical events, and contemporary personalities; does not go to Mexico often.

Factor II (13%) Spouse's Cultural Heritage and Ethnic Pride (SCH)

High: Spouse knows Spanish but no English; has and prefers Spanish first name; identifies as Mexican; was most likely born in Mexico and immigrated late in life; went to school in U.S.; seldom goes to Mexico.

Low: Spouse knows English but little Spanish; has and prefers English first name; identifies as American; was most likely born in U.S. or immigrated early in life; went to school in Mexico; goes to Mexico often.

Factor III (9%) Parent's Cultural Heritage and Ethnic Pride (PCH)

High: Parents know Spanish but no English; have and prefer Spanish first names; identify as Mexican; were most likely born in Mexico and immigrated late in life.

Low: Parents know English but little Spanish; have and prefer English first names; identify as American; were most likely born in U.S. or immigrated early in life.

Factor IV (7%) Perceived Discrimination (PD)

High: R perceives more group and personal discrimination.

Low: R perceives less group and personal discrimination.

Source: Adapted from Padilla (1980).

Note: The proportion of the variance accounted for by each of the factors is indicated in parenthesis.

bicultural versus a marginal orientation (Dohrenwend and Smith 1962; Ruiz, Casas, and Padilla 1977).

Lastly, it is interesting to find the ethnicity of respondents' associates combined with food consumption in the Ethnic Social Orientation factor (ESO). This should not surprise us, for researchers have often remarked on the relationship between socializing and eating. The relatively strong intercorrelations of ESO with the other three

Table 16   Description of Factors Emerging from First-Order Factor Analysis of Ethnic Loyalty Items

---

Factor I   (74%) Language Preference (LP)

> High: R prefers to use Spanish in personal situations as well as with other people; prefers Spanish first name; has more children with Spanish first name and who speak Spanish.

> Low: R prefers to use English in personal situations as well as with other people; prefers English first name; has few children with Spanish first name and who speak Spanish.

Factor II   (14%) Ethnic Pride and Affiliation (EPA)

> High: R has high regard for Mexican culture and prefers to associate with Mexicans.

> Low: R has low regard for Mexican culture and has no preference to associate with Mexicans.

Factor III   (7%) Cultural Identification (CI)

> High: R identifies as Mexican; prefers Mexico to U.S.; prefers to travel in Mexico.

> Low: R identifies as American; prefers U.S. to Mexico; prefers to travel in U.S.

Factor IV   (6%) Ethnic Social Orientation (ESO)

> High: R associates with Mexicans; prefers and consumes Mexican food.

> Low: R associates with non-Mexicans; does not prefer or consume Mexican food.

Source: Adapted from Padilla (1980).

Note: The proportion of the variance accounted for by each of the factors is indicated in parenthesis.

ethnic loyalty factors (LP, .46; EPA, .28; CI, .36) would also seem to indicate an important interrelationship between self-reported ethnic interaction and preference for language use, ethnic associates, and cultural affiliation. In other words, Mexican people who associate primarily with other Mexicans also commonly prefer to speak Spanish, to associate with people of Mexican descent, and to identify as Mexican. The significance of ethnic social interaction and its implications for ethnicity in general are discussed in detail in chapter 11.

Before going on to discuss our revised model, let us point out that some of the extracted factors of Cultural Awareness and Ethnic Loyalty may be sample-specific and/or questionnaire-specific. Not all respondents, for example, would be married and have the Spouse's Cultural Heritage factor. Nevertheless, it is felt that the hypothesized model presented above conforms reasonably well to the reality of culture change among Mexican Americans. Based on the factor analysis of the data, the next step was to revise our theoretical model of culture change.

Revised Model of Cultural Awareness and Ethnic Loyalty

A stepwise procedure was again used in the revision of the model of Cultural Awareness and Ethnic Loyalty. The first step involved the construction of eight scales corresponding to the four factors each of Cultural Awareness and Ethnic Loyalty. This was accomplished by adding the items from the HIDs which correlated with each of the factors. We will bypass the statistical and psychometric properties of the eight scales, except to state that the scales were highly reliable in terms of internal consistency with four of the scales (RCH, SCH, PCH, and LP), yielding coefficients equal to or greater than .90.

The second step involved a second-order factor analysis employing the eight scales to examine the interdependent structure of Cultural Awareness and Ethnic Loyalty. To accomplish this, each scale was standardized to a mean of 50 and a standard deviation of 10. Furthermore, each scale was normalized by using the Blom procedure. Again, the specific method for factoring the scales was principal-factoring with iterations. This computational procedure resulted in the extraction of two second-order factors. Results for the factor-pattern matrix and the factor-structure matrix are shown in table 17. Factor I accounted for 89 percent of the variance, while Factor II accounted for only 11 percent of the variance. The correlation between the two factors was .37, reflecting a fairly oblique solution.

In our theoretical model, we hypothesized that both Cultural Awareness and Ethnic Loyalty were involved in cultural change. Our model is empirically supported by the results of the second-order factor analysis shown in table 17. Accordingly, by inspection of the scales loading on each factor we labeled Factor I as "Cultural Awareness" and Factor II as "Ethnic Loyalty." Although the two superfactors conform to our initial assumptions, there are some discrepancies from our initial model that should be noted. These are as follows:

1. Language Preference (LP) and Cultural Identification (CI) have high loadings and correlations with Cultural Awareness, and low loadings and correlations with Ethnic Loyalty. Clearly, the language one uses, an identification with people of Mexican descent, and a positive orientation to Mexico are related to background circumstances, and not to current preference.

2. Perceived Discrimination (PD) shows a high loading and correlation with Ethnic Loyalty, but a low loading and cor-

Table 17   Results of the Second-Order Factor Analysis

Scale	Factor Pattern Matrix		Factor Structure Matrix	
	Factor 1	Factor 2	Factor 1	Factor 2
Language Preference	.94	.00	.94	.35
Respondent's Cultural Heritage	.91	−.03	.90	.31
Parents' Cultural Heritage	.82	−.08	.79	.23
Spouse's Cultural Heritage	.75	−.04	.73	.24
Cultural Identification	.64	.06	.66	.30
Ethnic Social Orientation	.55	.22	.63	.43
Ethnic Pride and Affiliation	.14	.54	.33	.59
Perceived Discrimination	−.04	.50	.14	.48

Source: Second Mexican American survey. Adapted from Padilla (1980).

relation with Cultural Awareness. Rather than being primarily associated with cultural background, perceived discrimination is most associated with the *feeling* about one's cultural background. Thus, perceived (not actual) discrimination may really be a manifestation of ethnocentrism, and the development of strong positive feelings about the in-group and negative feelings about the out-group fueled by perceived discriminatory practices of the majority group against Mexican Americans.

3. Ethnic Social Orientation (ESO) exhibits a different pattern from the other scales in that it loads and correlates primarily with Cultural Awareness, but it also shows a relatively high loading with Ethnic Loyalty. The intermediate position of ESO lends confirmation to previous researchers' suggestions that assimilation (here measured by ESO) is a process interrelated with acculturation (measured by CA) and ethnic identification (measured by EL), but it is not clearly a subprocess of either one.

A graphic picture of the two superfactors and the subfactors contributing to each can be seen in figure 1 (chapter 4).

Before concluding this discussion of the composition of CA and EL, some remarks are in order on the relationship between behavior and values and attitudes. As indicated in the review of studies in chapter 4, many investigators have assumed that behavior and values are separate and distinct dimensions (Clark, Kaufman, and Pierce 1976; Shannon and Shannon 1973; Szapocznik et al. 1978). It is clear from our work, however, that no such simple distinction can be made. Self-reported behaviors and attitudes or preferences combine to make up two of the eight factors in the first-order factor analysis (LP and ESO). In the second-order factor analysis, scales including items on attitudes and behaviors contribute to both the Cultural Awareness and Ethnic Loyalty factors, so that neither is solely a measure of behavior or of values. Rather than assume that the distinction between behavior and values is paramount in further research, we suggest the need to better define the specific cultural spheres, such as language preference or ethnic pride, which appear to make up cultural knowledge and ethnic identity.

To summarize the second-order factor-analysis results, Cultural Awareness is the more general component of culture change. Cultural Awareness reflects cultural heritage (of respondent, spouse, and parents), language preference, cultural identification, and ethnic social orientation. Ethnic Loyalty is the more tenuously defined component of culture change, and is derived from items tapping ethnic pride and affiliation, perceived discrimination, and some aspects of ethnic social orientation. Cultural Awareness and Ethnic Loyalty correspond to the concepts of acculturation and ethnic identity, which, as other researchers have proposed, are separate but interrelated processes.

On the basis of the first- and second-order factor analyses described above, our revised model of culture change emerges as multidimensional and hierarchical in nature, and revealing three levels. The lowest level consists of the 26 HIDs listed in tables 13 and 14. The second level consists of the eight dimensions identified in the first-order factor analysis. The third and highest level consists of the two superfactors identified in the second-order factor analysis. The high reliability estimates for the two second-order factors suggest that these factors are quite stable within our sample population. Although our analysis indicates the intercorrelation of CA and EL, a cautionary note is necessary. The correlations between factors are theoretical in nature, and involve estimates of relationships among the latent constructs rather than relationships among observed variables developed to measure these constructs (see Olmedo 1980).

2

Cultural Awareness and Ethnic Loyalty: 136 Items Composing the Eight Scales

SCORING OF RESPONSES for each item is scaled from low to high awareness of or loyalty to Mexican culture and people. Responses are indicated after some questions; where responses are not indicated and a qualitative answer is required, refer to the previous question(s).

I. Language Preference
   A. Respondent's (R's) language preference in personal situations
      1. Do you prefer to speak in Spanish or English? Responses: English; no preference; Spanish.
      2. Do you prefer to read in Spanish or in English?
      3. Do you prefer to write in Spanish or in English?
      4. Do you prefer reading Spanish or English newspapers and magazines?
      5. Do you prefer listening to Spanish or to English radio stations?
      6. Do you prefer watching Spanish or English television stations?
      7. Do you prefer going to Spanish or to English movies?
   B. R's language choice in situations dealing with other people
      1. What language is spoken at your family gatherings, such as at Christmas time? Responses: only English; mostly English, some Spanish; Spanish and English

       equally; mostly Spanish, some English; only Spanish.

2. What language do you use with most of your friends?
3. What language do you use when you are talking about a personal or emotional problem with a relative?
4. What language do you use when you are angry?
5. Do (did) you speak to your father mainly in Spanish or in English? Responses: English; both; Spanish.
6. Do (did) you speak to your mother mainly in Spanish or in English?
7. Do you speak to your spouse mainly in Spanish or in English?
8. How many of your children speak to you mainly in Spanish?
9. How many of your children speak to you mainly in English?
10. Language of questionnaire used? Responses: English, Spanish.
11. Question to be answered by interviewer: Was the interview taken in (1) only English; (2) mostly English, some Spanish; (3) Spanish and English equally; (4) mostly Spanish, some English; (5) only Spanish?

C. Number of children who speak Spanish
    1. How many of your children speak Spanish?

D. R's preferred first name and children's first names
    1. What first name do you prefer to go by? Responses: English spelling; same spelling in English and Spanish; Spanish spelling.
    2. How many of your children's names have Spanish spelling?
    3. How many of your children's names have English spelling?

II. Respondent's Cultural Heritage
   A. R's cultural inheritance and contact
      1. If born in Mexico, at what age did you move permanently to the U.S.?

2. How many years have you lived in the U.S.?
3. If born in the U.S., have you lived in Mexico? Responses: no, yes.
4. Did you attend school in Mexico?
5. How many years did you attend school in Mexico?
6. Did you attend school in the U.S.? Responses: yes, no.
7. How many years did you attend school in the U.S.?
8. Have you ever visited Mexico beyond the border cities (including Ensenada, Tijuana, Mexicali, and others)? Responses: no, yes.
9. How many times have you visited Mexico beyond the border cities in the last five years?

B. R's language familarity
1. Do you speak Spanish? Responses: no, yes.
2. Would you say your ability to speak Spanish is fair, good, or excellent? Responses: fair; good; excellent.
3. Do you carry on conversations in Spanish every day? Responses: no, yes.
4. Did you learn to speak Spanish at home or at school? Responses: school; home and school; home.
5. Can you understand Spanish when it is spoken? Responses: no, yes.
6. Can you read Spanish?
7. Can you write in Spanish?
8. Do you speak English? Responses: yes, no.
9. Would you say your ability to speak English is fair, good, or excellent? Responses: excellent, good, fair.
10. Do you carry on conversations in English every day? Responses: yes, no.
11. Did you learn to speak English at home or at school? Responses: home, home and school, school.
12. Can you understand English when it is spoken? Responses: yes, no.
13. Can you read English?
14. Can you write in English?
15. Do you buy or subscribe to Spanish or English language newspapers or magazines? Responses: English; both; Spanish.

16. Do you listen to Spanish or English language radio stations?
17. Do you watch Spanish or English language television stations?
18. Do you go to Spanish or English language movies?

C. R's knowledge of Mexican cultural symbols, historical events, and contemporary personalities.

1. Who is the current president of Mexico? Responses: incorrect, correct.
2. Who is Pedro Infante (Mexican singer)?
3. Who is José Mojica (Mexican singer)?
4. Who was Diego Rivera (Mexican artist)?
5. Is the following statement true or false: Los Niños Heroes de Chapultepec defended the Mexican flag against American invaders. Responses: false, true.
6. Can you identify this picture (Aztec calendar)? Responses: incorrect, correct.
7. Can you identify this picture (Benito Júarez, former President of Mexico)?

D. Ethnicity of peers during childhood and adolescence

1. Were the children in your grade school mostly of Mexican or Anglo descent? Responses: Anglo or other; both; Mexican.
2. Were your friends in grade school mostly of Mexican or Anglo descent?
3. As a teenager, were your neighborhood friends mostly of Mexican or Anglo descent?

E. R's legal first name

1. What is your first name as it appears on your birth certificate? Responses: English spelling; same spelling in English and Spanish; Spanish spelling.

III. Parents' Cultural Heritage

A. Parents' ethnic identification

1. Given a list of group names, what does (did) your father think of himself as? Responses: American; Spanish American; Latino; American of Mexican descent; Mexican American; Chicano; Mexican or *mexicano*.

2. What does (did) your mother think of herself as?
B. Father's legal and preferred first name
   1. What is your father's first name (as it appears on his birth certificate)?
   2. What first name does your father prefer to go by?
C. Parents' language familiarity and usage
   1. Does (did) your father speak Spanish? Responses: no, yes.
   2. Does (did) your father carry on conversations in Spanish every day?
   3. Does (did) your father speak English? Responses: yes, no.
   4. Does (did) your father carry on conversations in English every day?
   5. Does (did) your father prefer to speak in Spanish or in English? Responses: English, no preference; Spanish.
   6. Does (did) your mother speak Spanish?
   7. Does (did) your mother carry on conversations in Spanish every day?
   8. Does (did) your mother speak English?
   9. Does (did) your mother carry on conversations in English every day?
   10. Does (did) your mother prefer to speak in English or in Spanish?
D. Parents' cultural inheritance and contact
   1. If born in Mexico, at what age did your father move permanently to the U.S.?
   2. If born in Mexico, at what age did your mother move permanently to the U.S.?

IV. Spouse's Cultural Heritage
   A. Spouse's cultural inheritance and contact
      1. If born in Mexico, at what age did your spouse move permanently to the U.S.?
      2. If born in the U.S., has your spouse ever lived in Mexico?
      3. Did your spouse attend school in Mexico?

    4. How many years did your spouse attend school in Mexico?

    5. Did your spouse attend school in the U.S.?

    6. How many years did your spouse attend school in the U.S.?

  B. Spouse's ethnic identification

    1. Given a list of group names, what does your spouse think of himself/herself as?

  C. Spouse's language familarity and preference

    1. Does your spouse speak Spanish?

    2. Would you say your spouse's ability to speak Spanish is fair, good, or excellent?

    3. Does your spouse carry on conversations in Spanish every day?

    4. Does your spouse speak English?

    5. Would you say your spouse's ability to speak English is fair, good, or excellent?

    6. Does your spouse carry on conversations in English every day?

    7. Does your spouse prefer to speak in Spanish or in English?

  D. Spouse's legal and preferred first name

    1. What is your spouse's first name (as it appears on his/her birth certificate)?

    2. What first name does your spouse prefer to go by?

V. Cultural Identification

  A. Perception of Mexico and U.S.

    1. To what extent do you agree or disagree with this statement: A person has a better chance of getting ahead in the U.S. than in Mexico. Responses: strongly agree to strongly disagree.

    2. In Mexico, the people are friendlier than in the United States. Responses: strongly disagree to strongly agree.

    3. There is more discrimination in the U.S. than in Mexico.

    4. I think a child growing up in the U.S. is luckier than a child growing up in Mexico. Responses: strongly agree to strongly disagree.

B. R's identification with a group name
   1. Given a list of group names, what do you think of yourself as, at the present time? Responses: American; Spanish American; Latino; American of Mexican descent; Mexican American; Chicano; Mexican or *mexicano*.
   2. Ten years ago, what did you think of yourself as?
   3. As a child, what did you think of yourself as?
   4. How would you prefer to be know, at the present time, by other people of Mexican descent?
   5. How would you prefer to be known by Anglos?
   6. How would you prefer to be known by Mexican people if you were traveling in Mexico?
C. Preference for traveling in Mexico
   1. If you could take a trip, would you rather travel to Mexico or in the U.S.? Responses: U.S.; no preference; Mexico.

VI. Ethnic Social Orientation
A. Ethnicity of associates at the present time
   1. At the present time, are your friends mostly of Mexican or Anglo descent? Responses: Anglo/other; both; Mexican.
   2. Are your neighbors mostly of Mexican or Anglo descent?
   3. Are the people at the places where you go to have fun and to relax (at parties, dances, picnics) mostly of Mexican or Anglo descent?
   4. What is the name of the church you attend, and where is it located? Responses: Protestant, Catholic non-*barrio*; Catholic *barrio*.
B. Preference for and consumption of Mexican food
   1. Do you usually eat Mexican food at least once a day? Responses: no, yes.
   2. Do you prefer to eat Mexican or American food? Responses: American; no preference; Mexican.
   3. Do you prefer to eat *tortillas* or sliced bread? Responses: bread; no preference; *tortillas*.
   4. Do you prefer using *salsa de chile* or catsup on your food? Responses: catsup; no preference; salsa.

5. Do you usually eat Mexican food (such as *tamales*, *buñuelos*, or *mole*) on holidays? Response: no, yes.
6. Does the person who cooks in your household usually make his/her own *salsa*? Responses: never eat it; no; yes.
7. Does the person who cooks in your household usually make his/her own *tortillas*?
8. Does the person who cooks in your household usually make his/her own *mole*?
9. Does the person who cooks in your household usually make his/her own *tamales*?
10. Does the person who cooks in your household usually make his/her own *menudo*?

VII. Ethnic Pride and Affiliation
  A. Perception of Mexican culture
   1. To what extent do you agree or disagree with this statement: Children of Mexican descent should learn about Mexican history in Americans schools. Responses: strongly disagree to strongly agree.
   2. The best music is Mexican music.
   3. The most delicious food is Mexican food.
  B. Preference for ethnicity of associates
   1. Would you rather eat at a restaurant where most of the people are Mexicans than at a restaurant where most of the people are Anglos? Responses: no, yes.
   2. Would you rather go to a party where most of the people are of Mexican descent?
   3. Would you rather live in a neighborhood where most of the residents are of Mexican descent?
   4. Would you rather have the members of your family marry only people of Mexican descent?
   5. Do you think a person of Mexican descent has fewer marital problems if he/she marries a Mexican rather than an Anglo? Responses: no, yes.

VIII. Perceived Discrimination
  A. Perceived personal discrimination
   1. Have you ever found it difficult to get a job or a

promotion because you are of Mexican descent? Response: no, yes.

2. Have you ever been turned down as a renter or buyer of a place because you are of Mexican descent?
3. Have you ever been turned down for a loan from a bank or a loan service because you are of Mexican descent?
4. Have you ever been treated rudely or been given poor service in a store or restaurant because you are of Mexican descent?
5. Are there any other ways in which you feel you have been discriminated against because you are of Mexican descent?

B. Perceived group discrimination

1. To what extent do you agree or disagree with this statement: Many employers in this town often refuse to hire a person just because that person is of Mexican descent. Responses: strongly disagree to strongly agree.
2. Most teachers in the schools here pay more attention to the Anglo children than to the children of Mexican descent.
3. People who work for public agencies in this town (like welfare, social security, and health clinics) are more concerned about the Anglos than the Mexican Americans.
4. In this town, people of Mexican descent have to work a lot harder to get ahead than Anglos.
5. The police do not respect people of Mexican descent as much as they do Anglos.
6. Most people of Mexican descent are suspected of being illegal aliens by the Immigration and Naturalization Service.

References

Acuña, Rodolfo
  1981 *Occupied America: A History of Chicanos*. New York: Harper and Row.
Allport, Gordon W.
  1954 *The Nature of Prejudice*. Reading, Mass.: Addison-Wesley.
Alvarez, Rodolfo
  1971 "The Unique Psycho-historical Experience of Mexican-American People." *Social Science Quarterly* 52:15–29.
Ambrecht, Biliana C. S., and Harry P. Pachon
  1974 "Ethnic Political Mobilization in a Mexican American Community: An Exploratory Study of East Los Angeles, 1965–1972." *The Western Political Quarterly* 27:500–519.
Barker, George C.
  1947 "Social Functions of Language in a Mexican-American Community." *Acta Americana* 4:189–92.
Barrera, Mario
  1979 *Race and Class in the Southwest: A Theory of Racial Inequality*. Notre Dame, Ind.: University of Notre Dame Press.
Barrera, Mario, Carlos Muñoz, and Charles Ornelas
  1972 "The Barrio as an Internal Colony." In *People and Politics in Urban Society, Urban Affairs Annual Review*, ed. Harlan H. Hahn. Vol. 6, pp. 465–99. Beverly Hills, Calif.: Sage Publications.
Blalock, Jr., Hubert M.
  1967 *Toward a Theory of Minority-Group Relations*. New York: John Wiley and Sons.
Blauner, Robert
  1969 "Internal Colonialism and Ghetto Revolt." *Social Problems* 16:393–408.

Blom, George
>   1958   *Statistical Estimates and Transformed Beta Variables*. New York: John Wiley and Sons.

Broom, Leonard, Bernard J. Siegel, Evon Z. Vogt, James B. Watson, and B. H. G. Barnett
>   1954   "Acculturation: An Exploratory Formulation." *American Anthropologist* 56:973–1000.

Bruner, Edward M.
>   1956   "Primary Group Experience and the Processes of Acculturation." *American Anthropologist* 58:605–23.

Burma, John
>   1954   *Spanish-Speaking Groups in the United States*. Durham, N.C.: Duke University Press.

Camarillo, Albert M.
>   1975   *The Making of a Chicano Community: A History of the Chicanos in Santa Barbara, California, 1850–1930*. Ph.D. diss., University of California, Los Angeles.
>   1979   *Chicanos in a Changing Society: From Mexican Pueblos to American Barrios*. Cambridge, Mass.: Harvard University Press.

Carlos, Manuel L.
>   1972   "Traditional and Modern Forms of Compadrazgo Among Mexicans and Mexican-Americans: A Survey of Continuities and Changes." Paper presented at the Fortieth International Congress of Americanists, Rome, Italy, 3–10 September.

Clark, Margaret
>   1959   *Health in the Mexican-American Culture*. Berkeley: University of California Press.

Clark, Margaret, Sharon Kaufman, and Robert C. Pierce
>   1976   "Explorations of Acculturation: Toward a Model of Ethnic Identity." *Human Organization* 35:231–38.

Cohen, Ronald
>   1978   "Ethnicity: Problem and Focus in Anthropology." In *Annual Review of Anthropology*, eds. B. J. Siegel, A. R. Beals, and S. A. Tyler. Vol. 7, pp. 379–403. Palo Alto, Calif.: Annual Reviews.

Collette, John, and Pat O'Malley
>   1974   "Urban Migration and Selective Acculturation: A Case of the Maori." *Human Organization* 33:147–54.

Comrey, A. L.
>   1973   *A First Course in Factor Analysis*. New York: Academic Press.

Connor, John W.
>   1977   *Tradition and Change in Three Generations of Japanese Americans*. Chicago: Nelson-Hall.

Cross, Malcolm
1968 "Cultural Pluralism and Sociological Theory: A Critique and Reevaluation." *Social and Economic Studies* 17:381–97.

Dashefsky, Arnold, and Howard M. Shapiro
1974 *Ethnic Identification among American Jews: Socialization and Social Structure.* Lexington, Mass.: Lexington Books (D.C. Health).

Despres, Leo A.
1975 "Toward a Theory of Ethnic Phenomena." In *Ethnicity and Resource Competition in Plural Society*, ed. Leo A. Despres, pp. 187–207. The Hague: Mouton Publishers.

Dohrenwend, Bruce, and Robert J. Smith
1962 "Toward a Theory of Acculturation." *Southwestern Journal of Anthropology* 18:30–39.

Dotson, Floyd, and Lillian O. Dotson
1968 *The Indian Minority of Zambia, Rhodesia, and Malawi.* New Haven, Conn.: Yale University Press.

Dworkin, Anthony
1965 "Stereotypes and Self Images Held by Native-Born and Foreign-Born Mexican-Americans." *Sociology and Social Research* 49:214–24.

Eaton, Joseph
1952 "Controlled Acculturation: A Survival Technique of the Hutterites." *American Sociological Review* 17:331–40.

Fanon, Frantz
1968 *The Wretched of the Earth.* New York: Grove Press.

Farris, Buford E., and Norval D. Glenn
1976 "Fatalism and Familism Among Anglos and Mexican Americans in San Antonio." *Sociology and Social Research* 60:393–402.

Fitzpatrick, Joseph P., and Douglas T. Gurak
1979 *Hispanic Intermarriage in New York City: 1975.* Monograph no. 2. Bronx, N.Y.: Fordham University, Hispanic Research Center.

Freeman, Don M.
1969 "A Note on Interviewing Mexican-Americans." *Social Science Quarterly* 49:909–18.

Friedlander, Judith
1975 *Being Indian in Hueyapan: A Study of Forced Identity in Contemporary Mexico.* New York: St. Martin's Press.

Furnivall, J. S.
　　1939　*Netherlands India: A Study of Plural Economy*. Cambridge: Cambridge University Press.
　　1948　*Colonial Policy and Practice: A Comparative Study of Burma and Netherlands India*. London: Cambridge University Press.

Gans, Herbert J.
　　1979　"Symbolic Ethnicity: The Future of Ethnic Groups and Cultures in America." *Ethnic and Racial Studies* 2:1–20.

Garcia, John A.
　　1981　"Self-Identity Among the Mexican-Origin Population." *Social Science Quarterly* 62:88–98.

Garcia, Margarita, and Leonor I. Lega
　　1979　"Development of a Cuban Ethnic Identity Questionnaire." *Hispanic Journal of Behavioral Sciences* 1:247–62.

Geertz, Clifford
　　1963　"The Integrative Revolution: Primordial Sentiments and Civil Politics in the New States." In *Old Societies and New States*, ed. C. Geertz, pp. 105–57. New York: Free Press.

Gilbert, M. Jean
　　1978　"Extended Family Integration Among Second-Generation Mexican Americans." In *Family and Mental Health in the Mexican American Community*, eds. J. M. Casas and S. E. Keefe. Monograph no. 7, pp. 25–48. Los Angeles: Spanish Speaking Mental Health Research Center, University of California, Los Angeles.
　　1980　"Communities within Communities: Social Structural Factors and Variation in Mexican American Communities." *Hispanic Journal of Behavioral Sciences* 2:241–68.

Glazer, Nathan, and Daniel P. Moynihan
　　1963　*Beyond the Melting Pot*. Cambridge, Mass.: Harvard University Press.

Gonzalez, Gilbert G.
　　1974　"A Critique of the Internal Colony Model." *Latin American Perspectives* 1:154–61.

González, Nancie L.
　　1969　*The Spanish-Americans of New Mexico: A Heritage of Pride*. Albuquerque: University of New Mexico Press.

González Casanova, Pablo
　　1965　"Internal Colonialism and National Development." *Studies in Comparative International Development* 1, no. 4:27–37.

Gordon, Milton M.
　　1964　*Assimilation in American Life: The Role of Race, Religion, and National Origins*. New York: Oxford University Press.

Graves, Theodore D.
   1967   "Psychological Acculturation in a Tri-Ethnic Community."
          Southwestern Journal of Anthropology 23:337–50.

Graves, Nancy B., and Theodore D. Graves
   1974   "Adaptive Strategies in Urban Migration." In *Annual Review of
          Anthropology*, eds. B. J. Siegel, A. R. Beals, and S. A. Tyler. Vol.
          3., pp. 117–51. Palo Alto, Calif.: Annual Reviews.

Grebler, Leo, Joan W. Moore, and Ralph C. Guzman
   1970   *The Mexican-American People: The Nation's Second Largest Mi-
          nority.* New York: Free Press.

Greeley, Andrew M.
   1974   *Ethnicity in the United States: A Preliminary Reconnaissance.*
          New York: John Wiley and Sons.

Griffith, James
   1983   "Relationship between Acculturation and Psychological Im-
          pairments in Adult Mexican Americans." *Hispanic Journal of
          Behavioral Sciences* 5, 431–59.

Harman, H. H.
   1967   *Modern Factor Analysis.* Chicago: University of Chicago Press.

Hechter, Michael
   1975   *Internal Colonialism: The Celtic Fringe in British National De-
          velopment, 1936–1966.* Berkeley: University of California
          Press.

Hispanic Almanac. See Hispanic Policy Development Project.

Hispanic Policy Development Project
   1984   *The Hispanic Almanac.* New York: Author.

Humphrey, Norman D.
   1943   "On Assimilation and Acculturation." *Psychiatry* 6:343–45.

Jacobson, Helga E.
   1970   "Urbanization and Family Ties: A Problem in the Analysis of
          Change." *Journal of Asian and African Studies* 5:302–7.

Keefe, Susan Emley
   1974   *Women in Power: Anglo and Mexican American Female Leaders
          in Two Southern California Communities.* Ph.D. diss. University
          of California, Santa Barbara.

   1980   "Personal Communities in the City: Support Networks among
          Mexican Americans and Anglo Americans." *Urban Anthropol-
          ogy* 9:51–74.

   1981   "Folk Medicine among Urban Mexican Americans: Cultural
          Persistence, Change, and Displacement." *Hispanic Journal of
          Behavioral Sciences* 3:41–58.

1982   "Help-Seeking Behavior among Foreign-Born and Native-Born Mexican Americans." *Social Science and Medicine* 16: 1467–72.

1984   "Real and Ideal Extended Familism among Mexican Americans and Anglo Americans: On the Meaning of "Close" Family Ties." *Human Organization* 43:65–70.

1986   "Southern Appalachia: Analytical Models, Social Services, and Native Support Systems." *American Journal of Community Psychology* 14:479–98.

Keyes, Charles F.
1976   "Towards a New Formulation of the Concept of Ethnic Group." *Ethnicity* 3:202–13.

Kitano, Harry H. L.
1976   *Japanese Americans: The Evolution of a Subculture.* Englewood Cliffs, N.J.: Prentice-Hall.

Kluckhohn, Florence R., and Fred Strodtbeck
1961   *Variations in Value Orientations.* New York: Row and Peterson.

Kobrin, Frances E., and Calvin Goldschedier
1978   *The Ethnic Factor in Family Structure and Mobility.* New York: Ballinger Publications.

Kramer, Judith R.
1970   *The American Minority Community.* New York: Thomas Y. Crowell.

Kuper, Leo
1971   "Political Change in Plural Societies: Problems in Racial Pluralism." *International Social Science Journal* 23:594–607.

Kushner, Gilbert
1980   "On Patterson's 'A Critique of The New Ethnicity.'" *American Anthropologist* 82:123–25.

Léons, Madeline B., and William Léons
1977   "The Utility of Pluralism: M. G. Smith and Plural Theory." *American Ethnologist* 4:559–74.

Lewis, Helen Matthews, Linda Johnson, and Donald Askins, eds.
1978   *Colonialism in Modern America: The Appalachian Case.* Boone, N.C.: Appalachian Consortium Press.

Linton, Ralph, ed.
1940   *Acculturation in Seven American Indian Tribes.* New York: Appleton-Century.

Litwak, Eugene
1960   "Geographic Mobility and Family Cohesion." *American Sociological Review* 25:385–94.

Madsen, William
  1964   *The Mexican-Americans of South Texas.* New York: Holt, Rinehart, and Winston.
  1969   "Mexican-Americans and Anglo-Americans: A Comparative Study of Mental Health in Texas." In *Changing Perspectives in Mental Illness*, eds. S. Plog and R. B. Edgerton, pp. 217–41. New York: Holt, Rinehart, and Winston.
Masuda, Minoru, Gary H. Matsumoto, and Gerald M. Meredith
  1970   "Ethnic Identity in Three Generations of Japanese Americans." *The Journal of Social Psychology* 81:199–207.
Matsumoto, Gary H., Gerald M. Meredith, and Minoru Masuda
  1970   "Ethnic Identification: Honolulu and Seattle Japanese-Americans." *Journal of Cross-Cultural Psychology* 1:63–76.
Matthiasson, Carolyn W.
  1968   *The Acculturation of Mexican-Americans in a Midwestern Industrial City.* Ph.D. diss., Cornell University.
McFee, Malcolm
  1968   "The 150% Man: A Product of Blackfeet Acculturation." *American Anthropologist* 70:1096–1103.
McWilliams, Carey
  1946   *Southern California Country: An Island on the Land.* New York: Duell, Sloan, and Pearce.
  1948   *North From Mexico: The Spanish-Speaking People of the United States.* New York: Greenwood Press.
Memmi, Albert
  1965   *The Colonizer and the Colonized.* Boston: Beacon Press.
Mindel, Charles H.
  1980   "Extended Familism among Urban Mexican Americans, Anglos, and Blacks." *Hispanic Journal of Behavioral Sciences* 2:21–34.
Mindel, Charles H., and R. W. Habenstein, eds.
  1976   *Ethnic Families in America: Patterns and Variations.* New York: Elsevier Scientific Publishing Company.
Mittelbach, Frank G., and Joan W. Moore
  1968   "Ethnic Endogamy: The Case of the Mexican Americans." *American Journal of Sociology* 74:50–62.
Moore, Joan W.
  1970   *Mexican Americans.* Englewood Cliffs, N.J.: Prentice-Hall.
  1971   "Mexican Americans and Cities: A Study in Migration and the Use of Formal Resources." *International Migration Review* 5, no. 3:292–308.

Murguía, Edward
   1975   *Assimilation, Colonialism and the Mexican American People.*
          Mexican American Monograph Series no. 1. Austin: Center
          for Mexican American Studies, University of Texas Press at
          Austin.
Nagata, Judith A.
   1974   "What is a Malay? Situational Selection of Ethnic Identity in a
          Plural Society." *American Ethnologist* 1:331–50.
Newman, William M.
   1973   *American Pluralism: A Study of Minority Groups and Social
          Theory.* New York: Harper and Row.
Okamura, Jonathon Y.
   1981   "Situational Ethnicity." *Ethnic and Racial Studies* 4:452–65.
Olmedo, Esteban L.
   1980   "Quantitative Models of Acculturation: An Overview." In *Ac-
          culturation: Theory, Models and Some New Findings*, ed. Amado
          M. Padilla, pp. 27–45. Boulder, Colo.: Westview Press, AAAS
          Selected Symposium.
Olmedo, Esteban L., Joe L. Martinez, Jr., and Sergio R. Martinez.
   1978   "Measure of Acculturation for Chicano Adolescents." *Psycho-
          logical Reports* 42:159–70.
Ornelas, Charles, and Michael Gonzalez
   1971   Review of *The Mexican American People: The Nation's Second
          Largest Minority. El Grito* 4, no 4:12–20.
Ortiz, Vilma, and Carlos H. Arce
   1984   "Language Orientation and Mental Health Status among Per-
          sons of Mexican Descent." *Hispanic Journal of Behavioral Sci-
          ences* 6:127–43.
Padilla, Amado M.
   1980   "The Role of Cultural Awareness and Ethnic Loyalty." In
          Acculturation: Theory, Models and Some New Findings, ed.
          Amado M. Padilla, pp. 47–84. Boulder, Colo.: Westview
          Press.
Park, Robert E., Ernest W. Burgess, and Roderick D. MacKenzie
   1925   *The City.* Chicago: University of Chicago Press.
Patterson, G. James
   1979   "A Critique of 'The New Ethnicity.'" *American Anthropologist*
          81:103–5.
Peters, Robert
   1976   "An Unobstrusive Measure of Acculturation." In *Urbanism,
          Urbanization, and Change: Comparative Perspectives*, 2d ed., ed.
          P. Meadows and E. H. Mizruchi, pp. 470–77. Reading,
          Mass.: Addison-Wesley.

Pierce, Robert C., Margaret Clark, and Sharon Kaufman
1978   "Generation and Ethnic Identity: A Typlogical Analysis." *International Journal of Aging and Human Development* 9, no. 1:19–29.
Pierce, Robert C., Margaret Clark, and Christie W. Kiefer
1972   "A 'Bootstrap' Scaling Technique." *Human Organization* 31:403–10.
Poggie, Jr., John J.
1973   *Between Two Cultures: The Life of an American-Mexican.* Tucson: University of Arizona Press.
Ramirez, Oscar
1980   *Extended Family Phenomena and Mental Health among Urban Mexican Americans.* Monograph no. 1. Reston, Va: Latino Institute.
Redfield, Robert, Ralph Linton, and Melville J. Herskovits
1936   "Memorandum for the Study of Acculturation." *American Anthropologist* 38:149–52.
Reminick, Ronald A.
1983   *Theory of Ethnicity: An Anthropologist's Perspective.* Lanham, Md: University Press of America.
Rose, Peter Isaac
1964   *They and We: Racial and Ethnic Relations in the United States.* New York: Random House.
Rosen, Bernard C., and Manoel T. Berlinck
1968   "Modernization and Family Structure in the Region of São Paulo, Brazil." *America Latina* 11, no. 3:75–96.
Rubel, Arthur J.
1966   *Across the Tracks: Mexican-Americans in a Texas City.* Austin: University of Texas Press.
Ruiz, Rene A., J. Manuel Casas, and Amado M. Padilla
1977   "Culturally Relevant Behavioristic Counseling." Occasional Paper no. 5. Los Angeles: Spanish Speaking Mental Health Research Center, University of California, Los Angeles.
Salgado de Snyder, Nelly, and Amado M. Padilla
1982   "Cultural and Ethnic Maintenance of Interethnically Married Mexican Americans." *Human Organization* 41:359–62.
Salgado de Snyder, Nelly, Cynthia M. Lopez, and Amado M. Padilla
1982   "Ethnic Identity and Cultural Awareness among the Offspring of Mexican Interethnic Marriages." *Journal of Early Adolescence* 2:277–82.
Samora, Julian, and William N. Deane
1956   "Language Usage as a Possible Index of Acculturation." *Sociology and Social Research* 40:307–11.

Shannon, Lyle, and Madeline Shannon
1973   *Minority Migrants in the Urban Community: Mexican-American and Negro Adjustment to Industrial Society.* Beverly Hills: Sage Publications.
Simirenko, Alex
1964   *Pilgrims, Colonists, and Frontiersmen.* New York: Free Press of Glencoe.
Smith, M. G.
1960   "Social and Cultural Pluralism." *Annals of the New York Academy of Sciences* 83:763–85.
1969   "Some Developments in the Analytic Framework of Pluralism." In *Pluralism in Africa,* ed. Leo Kuper and M. G. Smith, pp. 415–58. Berkeley: University of California Press.
Spicer, Edward H.
1980   *The Yaquis: A Cultural History.* Tucson: University of Arizona Press.
Spindler, George D.
1955   *Sociocultural and Psychological Processes in Menomini Acculturation.* Berkeley: University of California Press, University of California publications in Culture and Society, Vol. 5.
Stavenhagen, Rodolfo
1965   "Classes, Colonialism, and Acculturation." *Studies in Comparative International Development* 1, no. 6:53–77.
Stephan, Walter G., and John C. Bringham
1985   "Intergroup Contact: Introduction." *Journal of Social Issues* 41, no. 3:1–8.
Stonequist, Everett V.
1937   *The Marginal Man: A Study in Personality and Culture Conflict.* New York: Charles Scribner's Sons.
Sussman, Marvin B.
1959   "The Isolated Nuclear Family: Fact or Fiction." *Social Problems* 6:333–40.
Sussman, Marvin B., and Lee Burchinal
1962   "Kin Family Networks: Unheralded Structure in Current Conceptualizations of Family Functioning." *Marriage and Family Living* 24:231–40.
Suttles, Gerald D.
1968   *The Social Order of the Slum: Ethnicity and Territory in the Inner City.* Chicago: University of Chicago Press.
Szapocznik, José, Mercedes Arca Scopetta, William Kurtines and María de Los Angeles Aranalde

1978   "Theory and Measurement of Acculturation." *Interamerican Journal of Psychology* 12:113–30.

Teske, Jr., Raymond H. C., and Bardin H. Nelson

1973   "Two Scales for the Measurement of Mexican-American Identity." *International Review of Modern Sociology* 3:192–203.

1974   "Acculturation and Assimilation: A Clarification." *American Ethnologist* 1:351–67.

1976   "An Analysis of Differential Assimilation Rates among Middle-Class Mexican Americans." *The Sociological Quarterly* 17:218–235.

Tharp, Roland G., Arnold Meadow, Susan G. Lennhoff, and Donna Satterfield

1968   "Changes in Marriage Roles Accompanying the Acculturation of the Mexican-American Wife." *Journal of Marriage and the Family* 30:404–12.

Valentine, Charles A.

1975   "Voluntary Ethnicity and Social Change." *Journal of Ethnic Studies* 3, no. 1:1–27.

Wallace, A. F. C.

1956   "Revitalization Movements." *American Anthropologist* 58: 264–81.

Walls, David

1978   "Internal Colony or Internal Periphery? A Critique of Current Models and an Alternative Formulation." In *Colonialism in Modern American: The Appalachian Case*, ed. Helen Lewis, Linda Johnson, and Donald Askins, pp. 319–49. Boone, N.C.: Appalachian Consortium Press.

Warner, W. Lloyd, and Leo Srole

1945   *The Social Systems of American Ethnic Groups*. New Haven: Yale University Press.

Watson, James L., ed.

1977   *Between Two Cultures: Migrants and Minorities in Britain*. Oxford: Basil Blackwell.

Weaver, Jerry L.

1973   "Health Care Costs as a Political Issue: Comparative Responses of Chicanos and Anglos." *Social Science Quarterly* 53:846–54.

Williams, Jr., Robin M.

1975   "Race and Ethnic Relations." In *Annual Review of Sociology*, ed. Alex Inkeles. Vol. 1, pp. 125–64. Palo Alto, Calif.: Annual Reviews.

Wirth, Louis
    1938   "Urbanism as a Way of Life." *American Journal of Sociology* 44:1–24.
Yancey, William L., Eugene P. Erickson, and Richard N. Juliani
    1976   "Emergent Ethnicity: A Review and Reformulation." *American Sociological Review* 41:391–403.

Index

acculturation: assimilation and, 15–23, 157–59, 175; measures of, 2, 41–45, 119–27; model for, 46–53; pluralism and, 6–9; typology for, 53–60, 97. *See also* Cultural Awareness

Acculturative Balance Scale (ABS), 45

Acuña, Rodolfo, 20, 159

age, 57, 122, 123, 125, 127, 134, 135, 143. *See also* generation

Algeria, 20

Allport, Gordon W., 193

Alvarez, Rodolfo, 20

Ambrecht, Biliana C. S., and Harry P. Pachon, 18, 159

American Anthropologist, 42

Anglo Americans, 5, 130, 133, 168–69

anthropologists, 3–4

Appalachians, 20

Aranalde, María de Los Angeles. *See* Szapocznik, José

Arca Scopetta, Mercedes. *See* Szapocznik, José

Arce, Carlos H. *See* Ortiz, Vilma

Askins, Donald. *See* Lewis, Helen Matthews

assimilation: acculturation and, 15–23, 157–59, 175; as distinct process, 6–8, 50, 208; measures of, 2, 119–27. *See also* Ethnic Social Orientation

attitude and acculturation, 45

Barker, George C., 18

Barnett, B. H. G. *See* Broom, Leonard

Barrera, Mario, 20; with C. Muñoz and C. Ornelas, 21

barrios, 4, 8–10, 18, 21, 28, 29, 57–58. *See also* neighborhood

behavior, 43–45, 208

Berlinck, Manoel T. *See* Rosen, Bernard C.

biculturalism, 16, 18, 96, 194, 205

Blacks, 20, 131

Blalock, Hubert M., Jr., 175

Blauner, Robert, 20

Blom, George, 200, 206

boundaries, 158, 171–76

Brigham, John C. *See* Stephan, Walter G.

Broom, Leonard, 15

Bruner, Edward M., 16

Burchinal, Lee. *See* Sussman, Marvin B.

Burgess, Ernest W. *See* Park, Robert E.

Burma, John, 23

California, 3, 25, 135, 144

Californios, 177–82

Camacho, Margaret, 60, 111–16, 152

Camarillo, Albert M., 176, 182

Carlos, Manuel L., 130

Casas, J. Manuel. *See* Ruiz, Rene A.

Chicanos, 5, 20, 123, 125, 159, 165, 194–95; respondents as, 87, 89, 95–96, 101, 105, 113

D

D